D1551425

TEACHERS' WORK
Individuals, Colleagues, and Contexts

Edited by

Judith Warren Little
University of California, Berkeley

Milbrey Wallin McLaughlin
Stanford University

Teachers College, Columbia University
New York and London

Published by Teachers College Press, 1234 Amsterdam Avenue, New York, N.Y. 10027

Teachers' work : individuals, colleagues, and contexts / edited by
    Judith Warren Little, Milbrey Wallin McLaughlin.
        p.   cm. — (Professional development and practice series)
    Includes bibliographical references and index.
        ISBN 0-8077-3229-X (alk. paper). — ISBN 0-8077-3228-1 (pbk. :
    alk. paper)
    1. Teachers.   2. Self-culture.   I. Little, Judith Warren.
    II. McLaughlin, Milbrey Wallin.   III. Series.
    LB1775.C85 1993
    371.1—dc20
                                                            92-34794

ISBN 0-8077-3229-X
ISBN 0-8077-3228-1 (pbk)

Printed on acid-free paper
Manufactured in the United States of America
99 98 97 96 95 94 93   8 7 6 5 4 3 2 1

Contents

Foreword

This volume is part of the Professional Development and Practice series, which seeks to present books whose insights are drawn from contemporary work on the transformation of schools, the reinvention of teaching, and the rethinking of teacher education. *Teachers' Work: Individuals, Colleagues, and Contexts* examines teachers' work in relation to a central tension of their lives in schools: teachers as individual "artisans" who are members of a professional community. Within the current context of school reform, although policy initiatives encourage teachers to participate more in their own growth and change, they also encourage greater control over teachers' practices. This book is powerful and significant in that it involves us as partners in attempts to deal with these contradictions.

At this time of continuing pressure to restructure schools, there is unprecedented agreement on the part of policymakers, reformers, and school people alike that the teacher/student relationship is at the heart of any authentic school change. There is agreement, too, about the necessities for greater colleagueship among teachers, for development of a community of learners, and for establishment of concurrent standards at the district, state, and national levels. Although we have gone a long way toward identifying our collective concerns about the importance of better schools for all students, we have fallen far short of understanding how to bring such schools to life, what that means for the role of the teacher and the school community in general, and the specifics of what that looks like in different communities.

Teachers' Work: Individuals, Colleagues, and Contexts takes on particular significance as it delves deeply into two central issues of school and classroom life: the tension between teachers' individual and collective autonomy, and the growing movement to understand the meaning of professional community and its connection to a changed concept of student learning. The press for teachers to work together as colleagues is strong, but so also is the desire or perhaps necessity for teachers to feel that they have the freedom and autonomy as individuals to construct classrooms that make sense to them and their students. Are individual autonomy and collective autonomy in conflict? What conditions allow for and support both views of what it means to be a teacher and a colleague? How much colleagueship can or should an individual be expected to participate in? What constrains or encourages colleagueship and community?

We have a tendency in educational reform circles to latch onto a single idea or concept and reify it so that it appears to be *the* answer to all our troubles. So it has been with the concept of collegiality. No one will argue the need for teacher isolation to be broken. However, how, under what conditions, with what supports, and for what purposes can teachers be colleagues? Difficult questions such as these are illuminated by the authors in their convincing descriptions of teachers, their students, the subjects they teach, and the varied communities to which they belong.

The concept of community itself is analyzed, critiqued, and developed. Challenging a monolithic notion of community, the authors show the variety of forms that community takes (for example, departments, subject matter collaboratives, and magnet schools) and how community differs from school to school, responding to the many local conditions that shape and create opportunities for development and participation by and with teachers.

The contexts within which teachers work (made up of students, subject matter, departments, districts, and a variety of communities) are not seen as a kind of matrushka doll, a rigid wooden structure with all pieces fitting smoothly together. Instead, these contexts are seen as a dynamic interaction of constituent parts with powerful effects on the nature of their participants and on how teaching and learning are carried on. This becomes the power of the book: It teaches us to embrace and struggle with the contradictions of the individual needs and the collective needs of teachers, while making us aware of the varied possibilities for engagement in professional communities that exist inside and outside the school.

Ann Lieberman
Series Editor

Judith Warren Little
University of California, Berkeley

Milbrey Wallin McLaughlin
Stanford University

Introduction

Perspectives on Cultures and Contexts of Teaching

This book embraces a central theoretical and practical problem: to chart the multiple and complex dimensions of teachers' cultures and contexts and to do so in a manner that realistically anticipates their consequences for teaching and schooling. The papers are part of a cumulative literature that relates issues of teachers' individual or collective autonomy to the public or institutional requirements of schools. They are also part of a policy context in which teachers encounter both widened professional opportunities and expanded control over their work.

The book has its origins in an escalating interest in the conditions and circumstances of teachers' work. In the studies that inform these papers, we found ourselves grappling in unexpected ways with the tensions among teachers' independent pursuits or perspectives, their institutional workplaces, and their participation in a wider professional community. These emergent tensions between choice and constraint, between individual initiative and institutional imperative, link papers that are otherwise varied in their theoretical origins and empirical bases.

For the past decade, we have witnessed a virtual campaign to break the bounds of privacy in teaching. It is a campaign waged less often by teachers themselves than by those who would reform their work and workplaces. On the basis of small-scale case studies of collaborative schools, advocates of reform have trumpeted the anticipated benefits of increased collaboration among teachers. However, these same case studies detail the ways in which the social organization of schools makes genuine interdependence among teachers rare. Reform initiatives have pressed teachers toward collaboration and collegiality with a fervor that far outstrips our present understanding of the conditions, character, and consequences of such relationships. As the number and types of experiments in collaboration have grown, so, too, have the opportunities to expand our understanding of their possibilities and limitations.

Initial enthusiasm about the benefits of collegiality has been followed by increasing skepticism and by a closer look at the conditions, substance, and consequences of teachers' professional relations. This second look began with heightened scrutiny of teachers' collegiality. Little (1987) argued that much of what passed for collegiality did not add up to much, and she later observed that constructs of collegiality found in the U.S. literature have tended to be "conceptually amorphous and ideologically sanguine" (1990, p. 509; 1992). Hargreaves and Dawe (1990) coined the term "contrived collegiality" to describe occasions on which teachers were invited to collaborate on agendas devised by administrators and policymakers. Indeed, most of the enthusiasm and much of the criticism have centered on project-based collaborations and other structured occasions of joint work, whether initiated and controlled by teachers (for example, some teacher networks) or by the institutions that employ them (for example, many curriculum development projects). The dynamic interplay of individual and collectivity is arguably different in the communities that arise from teachers' proximity and common circumstance, those that develop out of teachers' shared perspectives and mutual interests, and those that are imposed on teachers by others.

RESTORING INDIVIDUALITY AND INDEPENDENCE

Inevitably, perhaps, our reexamination of collegiality also leads us to take a fresh look at its counterpart: the expression of individuality and the norm of privacy. Converging portraits of the prevailing privacy in teaching, highlighted by Lortie's *Schoolteacher* (1975), stressed the negative aspects of the isolation of teachers in "egg-crate" schools. In Lortie's analysis, the isolation of teaching reinforces a culture of "presentism, individualism, and conservatism." Numerous reform efforts have been dedicated in part to altering the individualistic dispositions of teaching. But recent critics have taken the advocates of reform to task for their failure to recognize other functional aspects of teacher isolation (Flinders, 1988; Hargreaves,

1989). Their analyses are in some respects reminiscent of claims regarding the deeply embedded individualism of American culture (for example, Bellah, Madsden, Sullivan, Swidler, & Tipton, 1985)—and, some might reasonably argue, of Western societies more generally.

In sum, we believe that a large measure of the apparent disagreement over the limitations of privacy and the value of collegiality can be attributed to the theoretical flaccidity of the central concepts and to a failure to differentiate among various forms and occasions of teachers' workplace interactions. To date, the literature has achieved only a modest level of conceptual discrimination. Both privacy and collegiality have been framed in global, undifferentiated, and largely dichotomous terms. When we rely on categorical distinctions between a norm of privacy and a norm of collegiality, for example, we fail to distinguish between strong and weak forms of teacher interactions or to explore the character and consequences of individual practice. Discussions of collegiality often appear to assume that privacy signals the absence of collegiality rather than a relatively elaborate set of situated expectations for interaction and interpretations that define collegiality of a particular stripe. Consider, for example, that the norm of privacy is, itself, a form of collegial relation, with its own forms of mutual obligation and its own criteria for assigning respect (or contempt).

RECONCEPTUALIZING COMMUNITY AND COLLEGIALITY

A more robust theoretical conception of teachers' professional lives requires more systematic attention to the ordinary pattern of life in schools and the ordinary configurations of independence and collegueship among teachers. To specify the meaning of teachers' cultures, we argue, requires close attention to the contexts in which they are formed, sustained, and transformed over time. We thereby orient ourselves to situated constructions of independence and colleagueship to challenge a number of assumptions in prevailing theory and policy.

LOCATIONS AND OCCASIONS OF COMMUNITY

The characteristic concentration on school-level collegiality obscures the multiplicity of salient reference groups both within the school and in the larger occupation. Teachers associate with colleagues in many settings or circumstances: in their department, groupings associated with instructional or cocurricular assignments, the school, district-level activities, and teachers' organizations. Teachers' affiliations with one another may be circumstantial, a by-product of a common teaching assignment; they may be induced, a result of mandated committee responsibilities, special assignments, or special projects; or they may be elective, an attachment to teachers' organizations, informally organized special-interest groups, and friendship nets. Each of these occasions and locations of teacher interaction provides a microcontext for collegial relations that may operate by quite different rules, focus on different issues, and carry different significance for teachers' lives and careers.

Whole-school studies have tended to overemphasize the school as a site for professional community and to define community as originating in school-level goal consensus (for example, Rosenholtz, 1989). Within the school environment—in even the most collaborative of schools—teachers can and do embrace multiple views (for example, Nias, Southworth, & Yeomans, 1989). They can and do align themselves with one another in multiple and sometimes shifting configurations. And out-of-school collegial groups can modify the significance of school-level groups or collegial subunits and provide yet another standard of professionalism or colleagueship. Strong subject area networks, for example, may provide the collegial context most salient to some secondary school teachers. In one mathematics network, teachers' active engagement in the construction of new practices and their involvement in the broader professional community of mathematics educators are highly valued and supported (Lichtenstein, McLaughlin, & Knudsen, 1991; Little & McLaughlin, 1991). Such energetic participation earns teachers "good colleague" status in the network but sometimes brings disapproval in their schools or departments. Teachers faced with a conflict between external and internal reference groups tended to develop and insulate strong ties to the extra-school math network and to hold only weak ties to their workplace collegial context. Thus, because teachers typically hold multiple memberships in collegial groups, a teacher may be a "good" and "bad" colleague simultaneously, depending on the group norms by which that value is assigned (for example, when teachers find themselves caught between the policy stance of a union and the situational dynamics by which agreements and loyalties are forged within a particular school).

The occasion, location, and boundaries of collegial interaction cannot be taken for granted. Yet few studies take account of all of the ways in which groups are constituted or of the manner in which "group-ness" or "we-ness" provides a template for interaction and thus an important lens through which to view a school's culture or cultures. Subgroup analyses may reveal not only differences in perspective and practices but also different points of institutional leverage for productive change in educational policies and practices (Scott, 1989). Who are the culture bearers who most visibly communicate broad norms of practice? To what extent are the norms, values, and expectations of a school's various subgroups congruent or at odds? Answers to these questions trace maps of power and influence within the school setting and provide a reference for the evaluation of collegial behavior within that context.

THE PUBLIC GOOD AND THE GOOD COLLEAGUE

Recent policy initiatives and the studies of collaborative cultures by which they are sometimes justified (including some of our own) have tended to assume that collegiality constitutes a public good and that more of it is better. Under this assumption, teachers working together will work in the best interests of children. Yet collegial interactions or notions of a good colleague in some settings may conceivably diverge from accepted notions of what is good for children, what is good practice, or what is good for the education enterprise more generally. Nearly a decade ago, Hammersley (1984) and Woods (1984) described staff room interactions that demonstrated a high level of mutual support among teachers but subverted the conceptions of good practice or professionalism held by society at large. In these staff rooms, teachers employed the resources of humor or information exchange to enhance their own sense of identity at the expense of students. In Bruckerhoff's (1991) more recent analysis of two faculty cliques in a high school social studies department, both the Academics and the Coaches reinforced collegial norms that, although different from one another, are equally troublesome when set against a standard of student benefit. In these two groups, norms of appropriate collegial behavior and judgments about good colleagues supported the expenditure of minimal teacher energy on teaching and on students. These instances underscore the limitations of theoretical and empirical work devoted primarily to collegial forms and processes that give comparatively superficial attention to the content expressed: the beliefs that teachers hold singly and collectively about children and learning and the professional expertise that teachers admire (or do not admire) in their own and others' teaching.

THE SHAPE OF PROFESSIONAL COMMUNITY

Until recently, constructs and measures of teachers' professional relations have remained relatively global or flat (for one example of an effort to differentiate the concept in scale measures, see Smylie, 1988). Underlying the papers in this volume—particularly those in the section entitled Community in Context—are three largely unexplored dimensions of teacher-to-teacher interactions.

The first we term *intensity,* expressed as the distinction between strong and weak ties among teachers with respect to professional practice and commitment. Compared with other sources of identity and community, do fellow teachers matter? On the one hand, intensity reflects the respective pulls of individual judgment and preference versus institutional or collective obligation as teachers establish a justification for their professional practice. The strong professional ties—those with multiple demonstrable links to classroom choices and to the meanings that individuals attach to being a teacher—are exemplified by the "collaborative cultures" that Nias, Southworth, and Campbell (1989) have described. Strong ties, Huberman and Hargreaves would argue—and we would concur—are rare.

A second dimension of culture or community can be expressed as *inclusivity* of teachers' collegial groups. This attribute highlights the membership boundaries of teachers' groups and underscores the importance of multiple reference groups, an aspect of school life that tends to be obscured by a focus on the school as a unit and by efforts to link norms of collegiality to goal consensus. As recent work on the nature and significance of subunits in organizations would suggest (Scott, 1989), the various parsing of the school organization creates substantively different microclimates with substantively different micropolitics and notions of collegiality (Ball, 1987; Hoyle, 1988). Thus, we explore the boundaries of community by examining the dynamics of occupational versus organizational affiliations and the dynamics of multiple subgroups within schools.

The third dimension, expressed as *orientation,* combines aspects of teachers' value dispositions and depth of expertise. What beliefs are there about children, teaching, and learning that engender a "consciousness of kind" (Gusfield, 1975) among teachers? What views are held in common, whether explicitly acknowledged or tacitly held? What is the common or disparate rhetoric that unfolds in the staff room, hallways, offices, and meeting rooms? Embedded in this dimension are the criteria by which teachers judge one another and the concepts of colleagueship by which teachers may judge more or less congruently the accepted notions of a good colleague.

CONVERSATIONS AND COMMITMENTS

Thus, concepts of the independent artisan and the good colleague are local, particular, and complex constructions. They are derived from shared circumstances and local values and are intertwined in ways we are only beginning to grasp. Global or situationally indiscriminate "shoulds" and "oughts" about colleagueship have little substantive significance in teachers' lives and little to offer policymakers. The papers in this volume underscore the problems of aggregating to the school level to analyze the consequences of workplace factors for teachers' performance and commitment, and also challenge monolithic notions of community as the basis of strategies for school reform. Contextualized understanding of teachers' independent practice, their collegial relations, and the contexts in which both take shape is more than theoretically interesting; it has direct and important implications for reform policies. What are the consequences of particular professional communities with respect to teachers' capacity and inclination for innovation in teaching? Are unions, in fact, a conservative force with respect to scrutiny of teaching practice? What about subject departments? Are informal teacher collaborations necessarily a force for innovation? That is, why and under what conditions would teachers or others with a fundamental interest in their work want to penetrate or preserve the independence of the classroom? Promote or suppress the formation of a professional community?

Our main contribution, as we see it, is to help define (that is, complicate!) the character of professional identity and community and to trace their biographical, organizational, and occupational roots. Our analyses of teachers' worlds is shaped, too, by a concern for the integrity of the broader educational enterprise and for the vitality of schools as places in which children and adults work and learn.

These papers are the result of a conversation shaped by our intellectual curiosities and our professional commitments. They began formally with a series of symposia at the annual meetings of the American Educational Research Association from 1989 to 1991 and continued more informally as a kind of floating seminar that has spanned several years, many thousands of miles, and the varying contexts of schooling in Europe and North America. This book, we hope, will widen and deepen that conversation.

REFERENCES

Ball, S. J. (1987). *The micro-politics of the school: Towards a theory of school organization*. London: Methuen.

Bellah, R. N., Madsden, R., Sullivan, W. M., Swidler, A., & Tipton, S. M. (1985). *Habits of the heart: Individualism and commitment in American life*. Berkeley: University of California Press.

Bruckerhoff, C. (1991). *Between classes: Faculty life at Truman High*. New York: Teachers College Press.

Flinders, D. J. (1988). Teacher isolation and the new reform. *Journal of Curriculum and Supervision, 4*, 17–29.

Gusfield, J. (1975). *Community: A critical response.* Oxford: Basil Blackwell.

Hammersly, M. (1984). Staffroom news. In A. Hargreaves & P. Woods (Eds.), *Classrooms and staffrooms: The sociology of teachers and teaching* (pp. 203–214). Milton Keynes: Open University Press.

Hargreaves, A. (1989). *Elementary teachers' use of preparation time* (Project report, transfer grant 51/1070). Toronto: Ontario Institute for Studies in Education.

Hargreaves, A., & Dawe, R. (1990). Paths of professional development: Contrived collegiality, collaborative culture, and the case of peer coaching. *Teaching and Teacher Education, 6,* 227–241.

Hoyle, E. (1988). Micropolitics of educational organizations. In A. Westoby (Ed.), *Culture and power in educational organizations* (pp.255–269). Milton Keynes: Open University Press.

Lichtenstein, G., McLaughlin, M., & Knudsen, J. (1991). *Teacher empowerment and professional knowledge.* Stanford, CA: Center for Research on the Context of Secondary School Teaching, Stanford University.

Little, J. W. (1987). Teachers as colleagues. In V. Richardson-Koehler (Ed.), *Educators' handbook: A research perspective* (pp. 491–518). New York: Longman.

Little, J. W. (1990). The persistence of privacy: autonomy and initiative in teachers' professional relations. *Teachers College Record, 91,* 509–536.

Little, J. W. (1992). Opening the black box of professional community. In A. Lieberman (Ed.), *The changing context of teaching* (pp. 157–178). Chicago: University of Chicago Press.

Little, J. W., & McLaughlin, M. W. (1991). *Urban mathematics collaboratives: As the teachers tell it.* Stanford, CA: Center for Research on the Context of Secondary School Teaching, Stanford University.

Lortie, D. (1975). *Schoolteacher.* Chicago: University of Chicago Press.

Nias, J., Southworth, G., & Yeomans, R. (1989). *Staff relationships in the primary school: A study of organizational cultures.* London: Cassell.

Rosenholtz, S. (1989). *Teachers' workplace.* New York: Longman.

Scott, W. R. (1989). *Work units in organizations: Ransacking the literature.* Stanford, CA: Center for Research on the Context of Secondary Teaching, Stanford University.

Smylie, M. (1988). The enhancement function of staff development: Organizational and psychological antecedents to individual teacher change. *American Educational Research Journal, 25,* 1–30.

Woods, P. (1984). The meaning of staffroom humour. In A. Hargreaves & P. Woods (Eds.), *Classrooms and staffrooms: The sociology of teachers and teaching* (pp. 190–202). Milton Keynes: Open University Press.

Part I

INDIVIDUALITY AND COMMUNITY

The two papers in this section challenge conventional wisdom about the nature of individualism and collegiality among teachers. Huberman argues that the model of the teacher as "independent artisan" more accurately and persuasively fits the prevailing social organization of schools than do competing models derived from communitarian, effective workplace, or effective schools literatures. Hargreaves distinguishes between forms of *individualism* that weaken social unity and compromise the public good and patterns of *individuality* that supply initiative, creativity, and principled dissent.

In an important sense, these two papers question the pursuit of collegiality as a remedy for the isolation of the classroom. Discourse framed by an emphasis on teachers' *privacy* tends to underscore various deleterious conditions of independent classroom practice: teachers' apparent freedom from scrutiny, their isolation from sources of expertise or companionship, and their prerogative to remain aloof from wider organizational concerns. Casting the discussion in terms of teachers' relative *independence* and *individuality*, Huberman and Hargreaves illuminate other aspects of individual practice: teachers' latitude to forge intensely personal relations with students, engage in creative classroom practice (or at the least respond to the immediacies of classroom life), and pursue individually compelling avenues of intellectual growth.

Michael Huberman

Harvard University and
Northeast Laboratory for
School Improvement

The Model of the Independent Artisan in Teachers' Professional Relations

The vision of the schoolhouse as a bonded community of adults and children is very much among us. On the face of it, it is an unlikely vision to transport into real life. Think of it: a sort of vastly extended family comprising at least a few hundred people, most of them unrelated to one another, all the children put together simply by virtue of living in the same neighborhood, and most of the adults coming together more by the vagaries of their career paths and the arbitrary assignments of the central office than by affiliation or community of purpose. More like a ship of fools, actually, than a gathering of kindred souls.

If such an exalted vision persists, then, it must correspond to some fundamental need. From the perspective of teachers, the lure of a community of peers is probably related to the sense of isolation and of creeping infantilism in the classroom, to the support sorely needed in times of real difficulty, to the availability of other minds in moments of uncertainty, and to the pleasures of working for at least part of the time with fellow adults on projects of common and abiding interest. From the perspective of school-level or district administrators, the temporary or long-standing missions of the school are better met when the practices, judgments, and engagements of the staff are pooled and articulated. From an administrative view, the more fragmented the working arrangements, the less the possibility of enacting a common set of objectives that can be translated into binding and interdependent classroom practices—where the contingencies of one classroom actually impinge on another.

Working together to accomplish the chief missions of the school is a desirable, even irresistible, objective. So desirable that we have to ask ourselves why so little of it appears to be going on at present and, when it has gone on, why it seems so difficult to sustain. Longitudinal studies of school leadership or of school-based innovation suggest that task-related collegiality—as distinct from contacts with no bearing on classroom practices per se—is much more evanescent, volatile, and brittle than initial observations had suggested. There are couples and cliques, sudden and unexpected allegiances among former adversaries, arrivals and departures that change the social alchemy overnight, flare-ups that give way to emotional reconciliations, hundreds of unintended slights that are never pardoned, and hundreds of small kindnesses that are appreciated far beyond their immediate import. We often appear to be in a soap opera or in an interpersonally dense, combustible social hothouse in which staff can use and abuse one another with few real consequences for their core instructional tasks inside the classroom. In fact, it may well be that in the current organization of schooling, functional interdependencies among staff are not strong enough to weather the multitude of small crises and conflicts but are not weak enough to allow each actor to get on with his or her work without having to accommodate constantly to the demands of others.

INTRODUCTION

CONSTRAINTS TO COLLEGIALITY

If collective collaboration at the building level or the department level is difficult to create and sustain, we have to ask why. Do the constraints lie chiefly in the vagueness and polymorphism of the school's mission, to which an entire staff can subscribe while carrying on radically divergent classroom practices? Are the constraints bound up with the social organization of work: functionally independent units created simply by dividing the number of pupils by the number of adults at successive ages or levels of progression? Is the actual process of instruction a barrier? That is, is the resistance to team teaching or to tighter coupling between one grade level and the next justified by the fact that, in the long run, solitary practice and loose connections between practitioners provide better instructional conditions than any alternative arrangements we can dream up when faced with a large number of children and a limited number of adults?

Finally, are there constraints to collaboration in the very nature of the profession and in the kind of people who self-select to it? How much can administrators demand of a professional staff that claims some of the same rights—functional autonomy, loose supervision, and little codification of what constitutes acceptable practice—as doctors, lawyers, and architects? And how seriously should we take studies of elementary school teachers' career motives that highlight their possessive longings for "my own children . . . my own classroom . . . my own materials"?

Looking closely at these constraints makes sense if we are interested in creating alternative arrangements for instructional work. It is important to understand why those constraints are there, what purpose they now serve both for staff and pupils, and how they operate when we try to make changes in the context of work—how resilient or malleable, in fact, they are to change. We also need to be hardheaded about the relative costs and benefits of other working arrangements. Collegiality is not a fully legitimate end in itself unless it can be shown to affect, directly or indirectly, the nature or the degree of pupil development. And tighter coupling of practices within a classroom or across classrooms takes away an important degree of instructional freedom. By the same token, intensive collaboration—planning, exchanging materials, and regulating pupil performance—does not automatically translate into observable changes in classroom practice and may, if pushed too hard, actually eat into time for ongoing instructional work in class.

Finally, the lure of a common mission enacted by a family of like-minded adults—of professional work planned, observed, and carried out in concert—can be a hazardous one. To begin with, it is strongly normative; that is, it allows some people to interpret the professional practice of others in moral terms rather than in technical terms. Second, it may not square with the actual conditions, limitations, and perversities of school life. As a result, by obliging people to subscribe to commitments they may not have or may feel unable to meet under normal working conditions, we run the risk of creating more defensiveness and vulnerability among staff, all in perpetuating most of the same instructional practices.

Scope of the Paper

In the remainder of this paper, I shall continue to play the devil's advocate to the collegiality thesis, first by making a countervailing case for an image of the teacher as independent artisan. This image, I believe, corresponds to what we find empirically when we observe ongoing instructional practices and listen to the rationale that teachers make for them. The artisan model is thus a response to and a determinant of the ecology of classroom teaching. In addition, the validity of such a model is buttressed by the most recent research in teaching, in particular by work on teacher planning, on expertise in teaching, and on the improvisational quality of interactive instruction.

In succeeding sections, I will take up aspects of the artisan model that are reinforced by the organization of school life, by the ways in which teachers construe their roles and careers, and by the spontaneous practices on the part of teachers to improve their craft. The paper will then turn to an image of the schoolhouse as a community of artisans, to the interplay between community and individuality, and to the ways in which this community is likely to respond when stronger interdependencies are created between units. Finally, there will be an attempt to define a workable balance between individual needs and collective responsibilities, one that transcends the artisan model but falls well short of either the communitarian or the more managerial models now circulating in the educational research community.

THE TEACHER AS AN INDEPENDENT ARTISAN

TEACHING AS BRICOLAGE

Let us imagine, for a moment, the classroom teacher as a tinkerer or an instructional handyman, a do-it-yourself craftsperson who can put to use a host of materials lying around at various stages of a construction or repair job. Unlike, say, an engineer, a teacher works seldom with predesigned materials or tools. Nor does a teacher start with a blueprint, but rather reaches for some scrap or surplus material from previous jobs as a project takes shape. These materials meet the particular need that emerges at a specific point and are fashioned to fit this particular purpose. Gradually, of course, the teacher "craftsperson" accumulates a workshop full of materials most likely to be needed at some still-unknown moment for the kinds of things he or she builds or fixes. In *Working Knowledge*, Harper (1987) provides some wonderful, lovingly detailed examples of a virtuoso car mechanic who buys virtually no spare parts but instead turns an old boiler into a car radiator and scrap metal into engine fittings. Finally, as our tinkerer accomplishes a succession of different tasks with ever-varying combinations of the materials at hand or materials made to fit the purposes of each job, he or she develops an increasingly differentiated and integrated set of procedures, representations, and algorithms for reading the next task to be accomplished and for knowing which materials will be required at the outset.

The image of the tinkerer, or bricoleur, is derived from Lévi Strauss's (1962) work on primitive thinking and has more recently been used as a metaphor for the teaching process (Hatton, 1989; Huberman, 1988; Perrenoud, 1983; Yinger, 1987). It envisions the teacher as creating or repairing learning activities of different kinds with a distinctive style or signature. He or she adapts on the spot the instructional materials that have been bought, given, or scavenged, as a function of the time of day, the degree of pupil attentiveness, the peculiar skill deficiency emerging in the course of the activity, the little unexpected breakthrough on a grammatical rule, and the apparent illogic to the children of mathematical bases other than 10. In doing this, the teacher relies heavily on concrete bits of practice that have proved successful in the past but that must be reconfigured as a function of the specific situation in the classroom, in order to make them work.

What we have here is not a teacher who formulates in advance a codified lesson plan containing a series of sequenced, timed routines that are run through serially—for example, presentation of a scripted math lesson for 10 minutes, followed by the working of a few problems at the board by three or four children, then 20 minutes of individual work in the exercise book, and then a 5-minute oral quiz to test levels of understanding and mastery. Rather, the teacher has a general goal for the time period, usually expressed less in terms of what is to be achieved by pupils than in terms of activities that can be undertaken in the time allotted. The core materials for these activity formats are prepared and ready at hand, and the teacher begins the sequence as planned. As soon as he or she sees, however, that several children are squirming in their seats or wrinkling their brows in apparent confusion or that the two problems worked at the board entail faulty algorithms, the remainder of the sequence is cast aside, and our teacher begins improvising with a series of ad hoc responses to the new situation. The teacher puts up, say, two problems that test mastery of the operations prerequisite to those introduced earlier, works them through with the class, and then digs some remedial exercises out of the closet and has the whole class work on them as he or she circulates among the pupils. As the teacher monitors work on the exercises, he or she decides to divide the class into four groups and invents a slightly more difficult problem for each group. Each pupil in the group is to see the solution independently and then compare and justify his or her solution with the others. While this is going on, the teacher gets out the materials for the work on reading comprehension to follow or, if a secondary-school teacher, moves quickly from group to group to make certain that the task is accomplished before the period is over.

In this example, the unraveling of the math lesson is a continuously reinvented process, with dozens of decision points at which the teacher moves on to the next activity format, which has only just emerged as a likely follow-on exercise, or switches to another exercise as a result of the drift of pupils' oral responses, the level of pupils' task engagement, the time remaining until recess or the end of the period, or, more likely, all these factors. The continuous readjustment results from what Lévi Strauss (1962) has called, felicitously, "engaging in a dialogue with the situation" as that situation unfolds. To tinker well here seems to depend on how quickly and accurately the teacher can read the situation—can call up from a store of similar situations a range of likely responses, can choose a procedure quickly, can find or cobble together the materials needed to engage the pupils, and can move the class smoothly into the new task environment—all without breaking the flow of the lesson.

Before moving on, a few remarks are warranted. The first is that the teacher in our illustration could have gone ahead with the original plan: the lesson, blackboard work, individual exercises, and an oral quiz. Many—possibly most—teachers do just that, especially at the secondary level, with its tight 45- to 50-minute lesson cycle. The material would then have been "covered," and the math program would have "advanced." In terms of pupils' levels of representation and mastery of the material, however, it's a fair bet that the initial format would have been inappropriate for 45 percent to 60 percent of the class and that these pupils' difficulties would have increased when slightly more demanding material was presented the following day or week. In other words, the kind of interactive, responsive, and dynamic mode of instructional management implicit in the tinkerer model is likely to be more motivating and meaningful to a greater number of pupils and, in terms of their representation of or proficiency with the task, more efficient than a highly scripted instructional sequence. Apart from the obviousness of this point, some modest empirical work lends support to it (Yinger, 1986).

The second remark is that unlike the procedures used in more stable or predictable fields of application, such as engineering, medicine, or architecture, the tinkerer model assumes that there is no set of nomothetic knowledge—theories, concepts, and principles—that is valid across all instructional situations from which a specific sequence of actions can be derived to resolve the instructional problem at hand. In other words, to return to our illustration, there is no prescriptive theory of mathematics learning that could have dictated in advance the appropriate activity or response formats for this set of pupils at this point in their progression. In fact, it is precisely the craftsmanship or artistry of the tinkerer in this situation that compensates for the inadequacies in the knowledge base (Gage, 1985). Teaching, like other highly complex, unstable, and furiously interactive tasks, poses what Churchman (1971) calls "wicked problems," problems whose solutions are not inherent in the problem space itself and thus which need to be progressively transformed into simpler problems for which the solutions at hand are likely to be appropriate.

Now for a third remark: If the set of responses to the task environment are not governed by any pedagogical theory, they are then inherently pragmatic—they constitute a stock of possible responses to problems as they arise—and are thereby idiosyncratic. They make up a sort of individually contrived pedagogical biography. Moreover, as much of the teacher's response set has become automatic—"When fidgeting gets to level Z, I call on three of the slower pupils to test general levels of understanding"—a good deal of this biography is no longer available to consciousness. The teacher can no longer explain the logic of the three or four action sequences that strike an observer. She just does it; the sequence is a cognitive chunk that triggers automatically a series of chained responses when several, often subtle, indices appear in the behavior of the class.

This has two important consequences. First, it makes technical communication between teachers a very difficult exercise because the repertoire under discussion is a wholly personal invention and because so much of it has been automatized. The information is unique and, in important ways, inarticulate. This may be why, to an observer, the level of discussion among teachers—even among those teaching the same subject matter at the same academic level—seems often appallingly molar, undifferentiated, unicausal, and conducted more in a narrative mode than in a descriptive or clinical idiom. And this from teachers whose observed performance in class often borders on the virtuoso!

One finds, of course, the same phenomenon among superior artists, athletes, craftspeople, mechanics, and even surgeons: levels of automaticity that serve the important purpose of freeing cognitive space for more complex operations but that can also reduce articulate awareness and explication of one's behavior to mush. We excuse it less among teachers, perhaps, because they are in the business of making knowledge meaningful to others and of diagnosing how well their pupils can express their understanding and skills. But there is no reason why the diagnosis of children's learning processes should transfer to a differentiated, explicit awareness on the part of their teacher of how instructionally to manage that process in real time. The teacher has reached the point of doing far more and far better than he or she can ever tell. And the telling does not in and of itself lead that teacher—or others—to do any better, at least not under the present conditions of schooling.

The second consequence: If the development of an instructional repertoire is idiosyncratic, if each teacher crafts the task environment as a function of a stored set of action schemata extended and honed through thousands of small ad hoc experiments, it is hard to imagine two such people equally responsible for the same pupils at the same time. The response set of one person would collide, early on, with that of the second, whose reading of the situation and whose rapid, on-line responses would necessarily be different—unless, of course, the instructional sequences were highly scripted. The more interactive and responsive the instructional setting, the less likely it can be managed simultaneously by more than one adult of the same status. Otherwise, we will have collisions. And these collisions relate only to the more technical aspects of classroom life. To add the affective aspects (types of children to whom one relates especially well or poorly), the ideological aspects (beliefs in the appropriate thresholds of directiveness, tenderness, challenge, and individual and group centeredness), the aesthetic aspects (decorations, plants, and arrangement of desks and activity centers), and so on, is to envision dozens of such potential collisions and to understand why team teaching has been so difficult to generalize or sustain. The same would hold, presumably, with two weavers on the same loom, two sculptors on the same block of marble, two lead trumpeters in an improvisational jazz band.

So, there probably are some rapidly reached limits to instructional collaboration between teachers in real time unless tasks or pupils are partitioned or unless there is a mutually ratified status hierarchy between collaborating teachers. This jibes with Lortie's (1975, p. 193) findings that even among the 25 percent of the secondary-level teacher sample who reported "much contact," most of this contact had to do with joint planning of classes, joint review of pupils' work, or switching of classes for special purposes. Even in these instances, there was a sort of pairing arrangement between two teachers who selected one another informally and on the basis of friendship. In other words, pairing was not determined by the rational division of labor within the school but was mediated by preexisting interpersonal ties. Note also that even in these cases, none of the respondents taught the same students at the same time. "Cooperation could be extensive outside the classroom, but teachers preferred to keep the boundaries intact when they actually worked with students" (p. 193).

What this means is that unless we can construe other arrangements for interactive instruction, the classroom is likely to remain the most meaningful locus of action for both teachers and pupils—"the cathected forum," as Lortie (1975) calls it—but will not be the locus of collaboration among staff. Moreover, collaborative preparation and monitoring and debriefing of classroom activity will necessarily be perceived not only as a less modal task but also as a provisional, mutually nonbinding one—one that can always be suspended legitimately by contingencies within the classroom, which only the classroom teacher concerned can see and interpret: "No sense trying that writing unit in my third grade class for now; the kids are still in the reading workbooks, and it's hard to keep them on task even for that. You others go ahead; maybe I can catch up later in the month." So, arrangements outside the classroom may set the frame for the next day or week or month but, like the activity formats for the math lesson described earlier, they will be subject to all manner of legitimate redefinition as the instruction unfolds, at least in the eyes of the teacher concerned. To press the point, to plan collaboratively in far greater detail or in anticipation of explicit and deliverable outcomes is to trespass against some of the most sacrosanct norms of professional autonomy in classroom instruction as it now stands and, at the same time, is to reduce the degree of freedom required for the multitude of context-sensitive, continuously evolving, interactive responses that many teachers call on in order to run stimulating, instructionally effective classrooms.

SOME EMPIRICAL EVIDENCE

The artisan model gets some support from recent empirical work on teaching. This research takes three forms: work on teacher planning, work on teacher expertise, and work on improvisation in teaching. The basic gist of this work is that we need to let go of the image of the clinical diagnostician enacting a tightly planned and sequenced series of interventions to attain specific cognitive outcomes in class. This does not, however, entail our running in the opposite direction, embracing all instructional work as commedia dell'arte. And it sets up the following paradox: As we become increasingly aware that tighter articulations are needed between classrooms to ensure that pupils compile the requisite and prerequisite skills for mastery at each successive level, we also realize that within each classroom the degree of freedom in instructional planning should be as great as possible. We appear to need simultaneously institution-level tightness and large realms of instructional looseness in the classroom.

The initial work on teacher planning emphasized the importance of careful, goal-focused modes of instructional activity. Globally, teachers set objectives for a given lesson or sequence of lessons, considered the obvious set of givens (for example, pupil characteristics and type and availability of materials), and then planned the sequence of operations necessary to attain those objectives. That sequence of tasks came to be known as instructional tasks. In their initial forms, directive instruction and mastery learning resembled this image fairly closely. The basic script called for a testing of prerequisite skills or knowledge, an instructional sequence taking into account the class profile, another diagnostic exercise to test emerging levels of mastery, remedial loops for pupils unable to meet interim objectives, another instructional cycle, and then a summative test. The lesson-level script was often a miniature of the larger frame, much as in the example of the highly scripted math lesson described earlier.

Even researchers who had been weaned on research in instructional systems management, clinical diagnosis, probabilistic modes of decision making, and so on, began to see the limits of this approach when applied to the classroom setting (Shavelson & Stern, 1981). Unlike weapons systems, patients with relatively classic symptoms, or administrators in hierarchical organizations, the classroom had an ecology that was apparently more complex, more unpredictable, more dynamic, and less manageable, and that bedeviled any linear linkage between instructional treatments and observed outcomes. The literature then moved closer to the image of the teacher as decision maker in a universe of bounded rationality—that is, one in which teachers behaved reasonably in making judgments and decisions in a complex, dynamic, more uncertain stimulus environment.

Empirically, studies began to indicate that objectives for a lesson or sequence were not the functional unit of teacher planning (Borko & Niles, 1987; Clark & Yinger, 1979). Rather, teachers in the lower grades planned in terms of activities and supporting materials, identifying the outcomes they were seeking in the actual course of instructional interactions. In actually executing the lesson, primary in teachers' minds was the task of keeping the lesson flowing and of capitalizing on one of the several opportunities that might emerge to introduce, reinforce, or transfer a core skill or content area. This was not the case, of course, for teachers who relied heavily on workbooks keyed to teachers' manuals, although these teachers, too, were far less concerned with achieving instructional objectives than with covering a predetermined amount of material in a given time period. This same logic—cover a given amount of content with predetermined activity formats (a short lecture, then exercises at the board, and then individual work coupled with homework assignments)—characterized many secondary-level teachers. But here again, there was a tendency to move back and forth between preplanned routines and situationally adjusted responses in the course of a lesson as new information became available.

Some of this empirical work has suggested that overplanning can be problematic. For example, Peterson, Marx, and Clark (1978) clearly associated highly scripted instructional planning and execution with more rigid patterns of behavior in class, ones that were appropriate for some of the lower-order tasks (systematic practice or review of homework) but that got in the way of more complex tasks (discussions or clarification of pupils' ideas or procedural errors). And some have made an outright case for the instructional power of improvisation (Yinger, 1986, 1987, 1988). In Yinger's example of a math teacher, Mr. Knight simply puts a homework problem up on the board and begins to work it through with students. Depending on the questions or responses, he transforms the problem or the answer or takes an erroneous answer and works it out, backpedaling when the result is incorrect, inserting a few examples that show the faulty algorithm underlying the error made by the pupil—all while keeping the lesson flowing, calling on several pupils, and interjecting moments of humor (for example, by making deliberate errors himself or by creating problems that are insoluble) into an otherwise task-centered math lesson.

For Yinger, what is going on here is a "conversation of practice," a form of thinking in action that is heuristic rather than deliberative, more an ongoing improvisation than the implementation of a lesson plan with a set of goals and ordered actions for teaching a particular topic. The lesson itself is a frame with some socially scripted "subroutines" (taking out homework, selecting or generating a problem, working a problem at the board, calling a pupil to the board, and soliciting responses) and with a pace dictated by the apparent progression in pupils' understanding of the mechanics of a task or of the underlying rules for accomplishing it.

Beyond that, Yinger's description is consonant with others provided earlier in the paper. Much as in the jazz band or in commedia dell'arte, the succession of instructional acts is dictated by the drift of events after the initial stimulus situation. The teacher does some sophisticated planning in the very midst of the uncertainty he or she has willingly introduced, but that planning does not usually extend beyond the very next segment and relies on a storehouse of situationally grounded patterns: on patterned memories of similar situations encountered earlier, each having led to a distinct response that might or might not be forthcoming from this class at this point in the lesson. The teacher matches these situations quickly, usually with no conscious deliberation, and decides on a move that apparently fits, but is ready to change the course of events if they should prove unworkable.

Yinger also hints at a point worth making at this juncture: Mr. Knight appears to be having a rousing good time in his math class, as, by the way, do his pupils. In other words, by deliberately creating situations of uncertainty, Mr. Knight fashions some instructional challenges for himself and thereby stretches his instructional repertoire. Or, to return to the previous section, Mr. Knight appears to engage in the intrinsic pleasures of his artisanry, reaching left and right for little bits of practice that may construct or remedy the instructional task at hand, delighting in the unexpected shape his lesson is taking, and trying out a different combination of materials he has used previously. To the extent that constriction of the task environment and redundancy of the tasks themselves can take a terrible toll over time on classroom teaching (Huberman, 1989; Huberman, Grounauer, & Marti, 1989), Mr. Knight's solution is an appealing one. He creates uncertainty, diversity, and challenge in the place that matters the most to him and where he spends most of his time. When we make a case for the importance of intrinsically interesting learning tasks for children, we might spend a moment, too, on the value of intrinsically interesting instructional situations for classroom teachers. It may even be the case that the two are related in important ways.

Mr. Knight illustrates one aspect of recent work on teacher expertise—work that contrasts novices with experienced teachers or ordinary teachers with others identified by peers or by supervisors as exceptional. As Clark (1988) puts it, "expertise in teaching is less a matter of knowing all the answers than a matter of making the most of the unexpected" (p. 10). But other analysts (Leinhardt & Greeno, 1986) have insisted that making the most of the unexpected relies on well-grooved techniques of visual scanning of the class and well-scripted routines once the situation has been assessed. These are not irreconcilable viewpoints. Both assume a rapid and accurate pattern recognition capacity accumulated over hundreds of hours of experience that tell the teacher what to expect or how to exploit the emerging instructional situation, along with an array of routines or instructional acts that follow through on the assessment just made and that can be set in gear quickly and smoothly (Berliner, 1986; Berliner & Carter, 1986). In an ingenious empirical study of physical education teachers, for example, Housner and Griffey (1985) showed that experienced teachers were far better able than novices to anticipate situations that were likely to be encountered and to generate appropriate contingency plans. In fact, about 20 percent of all instructional strategy decisions of the experienced teachers had to do with adaptations in case the planned lesson did not work out. In reviewing this and other work, Berliner (1986) makes the important point that experts appear to "look inside" student work to pull out what is important in lesson planning or to read pupils' responses in class at a less superficial, more diagnostic level than novices do. In other words, relative experts are not simply better at doing the same things as others do; they also do things differently (Bereiter & Scardamalia, 1986).

THE INSTITUTIONAL CULTIVATION OF ARTISANRY

I have been gradually building a case for the legitimacy of the artisan model of teaching, one that is highly individualistic and context-sensitive and that, as a result, implies the idiosyncratic accumulation of a requisite knowledge base and skill repertoire rather than the application of a more "principled" knowledge base to a formatted sequence of instructional tasks. Crudely put, these are teachers who work alone, learn alone, and derive their most important professional satisfactions alone—or, rather, from interactions with pupils instead of with peers. And I have insinuated, more invidiously, that instructional constraints imposed by others—for example, in the form of objectives to be met at specified points in time or of coordination of curriculum sequences between grade levels—can get in the way of instructionally responsive modes of classroom work.

I will also argue shortly that when artisans do seek out peers in relation to their craft, they will be more interested in fellow artisans who are slightly farther along than they themselves are (for example, fellow ninth grade math teachers with promising materials in plane geometry or fellow second grade teachers experimenting with activity corners). Unless one teaches in a very large school, these people will tend to be in other buildings. And they will have potentially more to offer, instructionally speaking, than people in the same building who teach other levels or other subject matters or, even if they are fellow ninth grade math teachers, who are no farther along instructionally or who march to a different pedagogical drummer.

So, the spontaneous professional pull is not toward increased interaction of a substantive nature with peers or with administrators in the same institution. If, as a teacher, one turns to these people, it is usually because one needs them to provide the conditions that allow one to get on with core tasks, as one chooses to define and execute these tasks within the limits of the prescribed curriculum. Or one needs to turn to them because they are getting in the way of classroom work.

Institutionally speaking, what is it that allows one to reason and to function in this way? How, beyond one's own preferences, does one legitimate one's behavior and, in concert with others, maintain it? This section reviews some factors in the social organization of work in the schoolhouse that appear to reinforce the pull toward professional privacy. Although some of these factors have been touched on, they need to be put in better conceptual order.

THE STRUCTURAL INDEPENDENCE OF THE CLASSROOM

At the core of the problem is the structural issue of low interdependency between successive levels of influence and, at each level, between units. This means simply that contingencies at the district level are, in most cases, functionally "unhooked" from those in effect at the school level, which in turn are "decoupled" from the contingencies of the classroom. On an organizational chart, all three units are closely and rationally linked, but if a single issue (directive, initiative, or internal analysis) is followed from its origin in the district office down to the school building and then into the classroom, there is an observable succession of transformations, each reflecting the wide amount of latitude granted or taken at each step. Empirical studies of the "school improvement" process (Berman & McLaughlin, 1978; Crandall et al., 1982; Huberman & Miles, 1984) have charted such mutations in following the career of district-level innovations that were variously implemented in local schools. Even in programs in which operational success depended explicitly on strong coordination between levels, there is evidence that each functional unit—the district office, the school building, or the classroom—simply appropriates the program at its level of operations and then buffers it from external intervention (for example, the California Early Childhood Education Program, as studied by Deal & Celotti, 1987).

On a day-to-day basis, functional interconnections are tighter for managerial issues (for example, administrative, personnel, and budgetary issues) than for technical ones (for example, curriculum, instructional, and evaluation issues). In the latter cases, it is true enough that instructional activities in one schoolhouse have virtually no bearing on activities in another building and that, within a given schoolhouse, each classroom is functionally independent. When a population of school-age children is partitioned rationally into smaller, physically proximate school buildings and then each building is partitioned into age-graded, physically separate classrooms of 15 to 25 pupils at successive levels of academic complexity, functional separation is what we get. No unit is then operationally dependent on another to get its core tasks accomplished. The logical inference at the classroom level is then that to accomplish these tasks successfully yet to do it virtually alone requires a maximal amount of autonomy (Rosenholtz, 1985).

In other words, unless some of the structural features that determine the division of labor within the school are altered, patterns of behavior are likely to persist. As a result, if carried on in the conventional division of labor within the school, common goal setting, coordinated planning, rational apportionment of instructional units, design and exchange of materials, and the like may not translate into any subsequent instructional changes at the classroom level. Recall, for example, the ambitious I/D/E/A study (Goodlad, 1983; Heckman, 1987). Although the "renewing" schools (characterized by competent and forceful principals, staff cohesiveness, mutual assistance, and collaborative planning and goal setting) were measurably different from the "taking-care-of-business" schools, there were very few measurable differences between the two sets of schools at the classroom level. Similarly, teachers in the renewing schools did not attend closely to what colleagues actually did in their classrooms, nor was much time devoted to discussion of specific problems encountered at the classroom level beyond the ritual, cathartic exchange of "war stories."

It is clear, then, that we cannot assume that collaborative activity outside the classroom will translate automatically into instructional changes inside the classroom, even when such changes are apparently agreed on or are derived logically from school-level interactions. Forceful monitoring of the degree of follow-through, for example, on the part of principals or department heads may create as many problems as it resolves (more on this later). However, the pitfalls of magical thinking or hyperrationalism are also there: that is, the assumption that intensive, interpersonally rewarding, goal-directed interactions outside the classroom will carry over to day-to-day instructional management in class.

In part—but only in part—the problem is that such within-building activity does not in itself provide any participating teacher with a greater repertoire of instructional skills. Plans and discussions, as we saw earlier, may provide useful frames, but the classroom is better managed with heuristics. Also, the (unlikely) logic here seems to be that instructional changes within the classroom can be mastered simply by their being construed collectively and then by adaptive coping on the part of each teacher, leavened by peer nurturance. If the innovation literature teaches us just one thing, it is that practice change is an uneven, uncertain affair that seldom transcends trivial levels when teachers are left by themselves.

Collaborative goal setting and planning, in fact, can eat up the time that teachers need to get on top of the new math modules or reading enrichment activities that are to be introduced in order to meet the newly formulated set of schoolwide goals (Hyde & Sandell, 1984). Also, school time allotted for collaborative planning or consulting is time spent away from one's class, which, in the elementary school at least, takes its toll rapidly. Nor does this activity usually stipulate with any precision what needs to be done at the classroom level to follow through on these plans or to attain those goals. What it does, to be sure, is create new dilemmas.

THE IMMEDIACY AND SPECIFICITY OF CLASSROOM LIFE

More likely, however, there are factors at work in the context of conventional classroom life that impede the fluid transfer of public arrangements to private enactments. Analysts of the classroom ecology (Barker & Gump, 1964; Doyle, 1978; Hatton, 1987) have covered this terrain well.

The basic premise here is that classroom settings can be analyzed by identifying the structure of opportunities that they make available, along with the kinds of situational constraints that they impose (cf. Huberman, 1983). For example, several within-building factors impinge on classroom life. To review some of these briefly: Classrooms are affected, for example, by input instability and the indeterminacy of outcomes. There are imposed changes in instructional materials. There are yearly cohort changes, each with its own personality and each with a different response to the same instructional treatment. Even within a given cohort, responses can vary from one moment of the year to the next, as shown by the chronic weakness of stability coefficients in classroom observation studies. At the elementary school level, teachers are also frequently subject to grade-level shifts from one year to the next, and teachers introduce instructional changes voluntarily, less with the aim of increasing pupil performance than of bringing some variety and spice to their work. All this means that planned activity cannot be carried on over an extended period and that the effects of instructional treatments cannot be clearly gauged; thus, the link between instruction and outcome remains insecure. As this link is no better ensured in the scientific research base—there are not enough strong generalizations to override apparently minor variations in pupils, teachers, or instructional situations (Snow, 1974)—most outcomes remain stubbornly indeterminate. Small wonder, then, that the core of teachers' "naive" theories has to do with principles derived from observations of their own—and virtually no one else's—experience in the classroom.

By the same token, pinning down the extent and source of achievement gains, for example, is not helped by working alone in a complex stimulus environment with an annually changing group of 25 children or, in secondary schools, with 150 pupils for 50-minute segments. Chronic busyness in isolation allows little chance to monitor accurately and correct one's behavior. In a classic study (1968) and reanalysis (1977), Jackson documented the "existential vividness" of the classroom: the great number and rapid pace of events; the multiplicity of seat-of-the-pants decisions; and the necessarily reactive nature of much instruction, whereby teachers are bombarded with complex, often conflicting demands and spend much of the day in partial control of pupil behavior. The classroom is not a propitious environment, Jackson noted, for cool and circumspect reasoning. Rather, with the classroom's inherent complexity, the simultaneity of tasks to be addressed in it, and its apparent unpredictability (the unresponsive pupil who suddenly comes to life or the spectacular experiment that wows the first class of eighth graders and bombs with the next), classroom events gradually appear to be beyond comprehension. As a consequence, judgments regarding the appropriate actions to be preferred at any given moment in class are never more certain than, to use Dewey's (1929) felicitous phrase, a "precarious probability."

More important, perhaps, for our purposes here is the fact that such a heavy diet of immediacy and concreteness affects the way individuals process information and attend to data furnished by others. In cognitive terms, information that is obtained firsthand through multisensory modes is more likely to influence one's judgments and inferences than is information obtained verbally or in writing. We store, remember, and retrieve data first from our own experience and then from secondhand sources. If, as in teaching, incoming information is likely to be tested against cumulative personal experience rather than against probative or evidential criteria, and if individuals are disproportionately influenced by vivid and concrete input from other individuals in settings perceived as isomorphic to one's own, it becomes very difficult to exchange information of a technical nature. Information exchanges are likely to be atheoretical and even nonreflective—exchanges of narratives rather than of programmatic messages.

A convincing argument for or against an instructional treatment, thus, is foremost a story told by a fellow teacher about the use of that treatment in a specific situation encountered in class. That is probably how he or she will justify an argument, in any event. It is a story to which one, as a colleague, may resonate or not, as a function of the anchors in one's own classroom experience. To the extent that one does resonate, one may well decide that one can work with this person, but one will continually test the phenomenological intersections between them as they progress, and those tests will become progressively more stringent. The more tacit the knowledge they exchange, the better the exchanges. The more their exchanges appear to an outsider to be more like communions than communications, the more likely they will appreciate them and, from there, be able to influence one another's practice. Fundamentally, teachers are trying to reach beyond their instructional solitudes. And just as fundamentally, teachers will collaborate not because they agree on instructional priorities for the school, nor because a rational study of a colleague's second grade program and one's own third grade program calls for a redistribution of coverage between them, nor because mastery test levels in geometry need to be raised. These are programmatic agreements, which appeal to the disembodied gods to whom a principal or department head seems to pray. Rather, teachers will use these objectives as the occasion, even the pretext, for collaboration because teachers appear to have similar ways of making sense of their experience.

It is a short step from here to the artisan or artistic orientation outlined earlier in this paper. There may well be conceptually informed ways of ordering classroom instruction, but they are not directly translatable into teacher-usable form. As a result, experienced practitioners cannot transfer a valid body of practice-relevant knowledge to novices but can provide only highly general theory and brief, structured apprenticeships.

These apprenticeships are usually initially inadequate for successful role performance. In effect, unlike other professionals, novice teachers are confronted with the same complexities and dilemmas as fully experienced teachers, so much so that novices play a large role in training themselves through what has come to be called sink-or-swim socialization. Such training—progressively less stressful sequences of trials, errors, and new trials—is enacted alone and leads necessarily to a highly individualistic, experiential conception of one's work.

Finally, the process of gradually evolving one's own instructional style, along with the belief that most classroom contingencies are neither replicable nor always predictable, leads invariably to a sort of tool centeredness. If there is no replicable, transferable technology of instruction and if the stimulus environment is forever shifting as a function of the interactions between teacher and pupils, it is more important to have tools that deal with the largest number of contingencies, ones that allow for variations and for irregular and unexpected sequences of action. Somewhat like a squirrel, then, the elementary teacher gradually stores a chemistry kit here, a vocabulary game there, and a series of math drills elsewhere, and then picks and chooses bits from each, compiling the lesson or activity that the emerging level of attention or skill deficiency or the end of the term calls for.

We are back in the realm of bricolage. More to the point, however, such tool centeredness implies two things. First, the most likely source of new tools is fellow teachers at the same grade level or with the same subject matter as oneself. If they are close at hand—in the same building—so much the better, unless, for other reasons, they are competitors for scarce resources or higher status. In other words, if one's first priority in dealing with one's classroom is to expand and diversify one's instructional repertoire—and I am arguing that it is—one's strongest incentive for collaboration within the building will be the exchange of instructional materials and formats between peers in settings similar to one's own (Zahorik, 1987). Other forms of collaboration will become secondary and more abstract, as a direct function of how much they take one's eye off the classroom. As long as one's prime concern is how to introduce a new physics unit next week, institutional concerns are lower priorities. One gets to them when one's own house is in order or when one sees that they can help get that house in order—later. Perhaps never.

Second, one is likely to find more and better resources outside one's building than within it. As a craftsperson, one is especially on the lookout for peers slightly ahead who have experimented a bit with the materials that one has just discovered or who have activities under way in their classes that one is interested in trying out. To some extent, then, the calls made on one's time and energy from within the school building will compete with the interest in enriching one's own instructional repertoire, on which professional proficiency ultimately depends.

EGALITARIAN TRADITIONS AND CLASSROOM AUTONOMY

Nor is the recourse to colleagues for help in one's own building a straight-forward operation. Here the literature on social assistance, both in generic situations (DePaulo & Fisher, 1980; Rosen, Mickler, & Collins, 1987) and in school settings (Glidewell, Tucker, Todt, & Cox, 1983), is instructive. Whereas it is legitimate for novices to openly request assistance from more experienced peers, such requests among peers in the school building can be and often are construed as admissions of incompetence on the part of the seeker. One of the conclusions drawn by Little (1990) in her later work was that "teachers with many years' experience, armed with well-formulated and well-grounded views on effective teaching, nonetheless refrain from advocating specific approaches even to beginning teachers" (p. 516).

Similarly, unsolicited offers of advice or technical assistance are widely interpreted as an expression of arrogance or as a play for higher status. This is one of the reasons why staff members who are given consultant status within their own school buildings are on such dangerous ground and usually make do with largely peripheral or decorative tasks—ones that involve no intrusion into the classrooms of their peers and that render services with no demands explicit for reciprocity. Such peer consultants, along with master teachers, typically have much larger followings in other school buildings than their own, but there, too, their advice is nonbinding.

In addition, the empirical work on help also suggests that when colleagues offer unsolicited advice that is then spurned, the resulting resentment takes its toll insidiously on the interpersonal climate. As Mauss (1967) showed so brilliantly in *The Gift*, the refusal of gifts invariably creates tension between the parties involved; there is no clean way out. In schools, we would expect the refusal of offered help or advice not to be discussed thereafter but also not to be forgotten. When the next crisis looms and emotions run high, it may well emerge in the context of a discussion in which logically it has no place but in which emotionally it has been screaming for months to be expressed.

The implication here is clear: Professional egalitarianism runs deep in school buildings, and noninterference with the core work of others constitutes a sign of professional respect. It may be one of the reasons why the conversation in the teachers' lounge steers clear of instructional topics: to avoid the attribution of relative competence among members (Bishop, 1977). Although the stories told in the lounge or even in staff meetings may well have especially sad or happy endings and may in fact be covert cries for help, they respect some important ground rules: Triumphalism is bad form, a story of failed intervention should summon up a reciprocal story of failure on the part of one of the listeners, and advice can be nested in a story that responds to the original one only if it underlines the peculiarity of the conditions or the context from which the advice originated ("No, my pupils responded well to those lab materials, but only if I had them work in very small groups. And I could never have done that with the kids I have in the last afternoon period.").

As Little (1990) has pointed out, at the heart of such norms lies the acknowledgment and tolerance of individual preferences and styles. To be sure, if there is no authoritative theory of instruction, if each teacher must derive alone a custom-fitted repertoire of instructional skills and resources, if outcomes are attributed more to the unstable alchemy between the idiosyncracies of each practitioner and the traits of each cohort of pupils, this is a sensible norm, just as the cellular division of work is then a sensible working arrangement. To each artisan a separate workshop, with some common lighting and plumbing.

The problem, of course, is that a wide degree of professional latitude is a two-edged sword. Who takes responsibility for abuse and incompetence? Who looks at the sum of the parts from the perspective of the pupils passing from one class to the next or from this building to the next? Who represents the legitimate interests of the civic and economic sectors, which will face the consequences of the variable levels of social attitudes and cognitive skills exercised in the schools? To assume that the norms and arrangements of professional autonomy will operate spontaneously to achieve the major missions of the institution is another of the many magical assumptions prevalent in contemporary educational thought. Normative permissiveness, in which task definition and execution are left to the discretion of the individual, is gratifying to the aggregate of members but does not necessarily serve the purposes of the collectivity.

ALTERNATIVE IMAGES OF THE SCHOOL
AS A COLLECTIVITY

Up to now, I have made the case for liberalism and autonomy in the workplace, both on their own merits and because they are the mainstream perspectives from which other arrangements are necessarily construed. Let us now look at some of these other arrangements. They are assembled arbitrarily in three families: a communitarian image of the school, the effective workplace perspective, and the effective schools perspective.

COMMUNITARIAN IMAGES

Let us take as an example the recent work of Nias and her associates (Nias, 1989; Nias, Southworth, & Yeomans, 1989). From my reading, their work makes two important assumptions. The first is that teachers suffer from what Hargreaves (1989) calls the "fragmented individualism" in which each is obliged to work—working alone in the densely populated jungle of the classroom. The underlying malady is what Durkheim called "anomie," the lack of meaningful contact with others over long periods of time. The second assumption is that schools have a series of missions or objectives around which there is consensus and which can form the basis for collaborative interactions among staff. Both premises, I think, are reasonably founded, but far more so at the elementary school level than elsewhere.

We need no new evidence for the first assumption. The trade-off for professional privacy is clearly the acuteness of the sense of isolation: isolation in an infantilized environment, in which teachers can roam no further, intellectually speaking, than the brightest of their pupils. Our own recent work on teachers' career trajectories (Huberman, 1989) brings many of these points home. Isolation feeds the continuous insecurity about one's pedagogical capacity because one's work is wrought alone, never subjected to outside scrutiny, and deflated by fantastic images of better teachers lurking in other classrooms or other schools. Isolation in infant settings or adolescent settings breeds infantile behavior in adult settings outside the school. Isolation intensifies the pain of temporary setbacks or breakdowns, even when institutional conditions have clearly contributed to the problem. Yet isolation is also what teachers are after from the moment of getting tenure, both at the primary level ("Finally, my kids, my classroom, my wall decorations, and my seating plan") and at the secondary level ("No one telling me anymore how to teach or what to teach; I just tell them to get out of my classroom and let me do my work").

In fact, it may be that the apparently gratuitous, unfocused conversations in the staff room, together with the meandering exchanges in formal meetings are due, in large part, to the isolation of professional practice. They are, of course, antidotes to loneliness, but they are, above all, instances of pure sociability, of interactions as ends in themselves. These archetypal stories, typically of angelic and demonic pupils and of magical and awful moments during lessons, do serve a larger purpose in that they acknowledge in public that teachers are all fallible in the classroom and, more important, that teachers are all members of the same guild.

This brings us to the second dimension of the communitarian image of the school: what Nias (1989) called "a culture of collaboration." She makes a compelling case for the social construction of collective norms, which, "by ensuring a sense of mutual security and encouraging interpersonal and interprofessional openness" (p. 2), facilitates collaborative work. One illustration is the school assembly, in which collective beliefs and key missions of the school are expressed through symbols, rituals, and ceremonies: giving out swimming certificates, giving gifts and thanks to people who are leaving, welcoming new members, singing together, and giving a performance for the school.

It is not at all clear, however, how the practice of these ceremonies leads, as Nias (1989) insinuates it does, to "learning from one another's practice." She makes the point at several junctures that teachers are careful not to suggest openly that others might profit from their example and that, aside from these moments of collective exchange, teachers in the building "felt together but worked apart." She also steps gingerly around the issue of head teachers' influence. In these six exemplary schools, teachers "gave a serious hearing" to the modifications in curriculum or in classroom practice that were suggested by heads, who "had the right to articulate the kind of school they wanted." Although she offers little supporting evidence, Nias says most teachers "were disposed to accept their [heads'] influence. . . . Head teachers could, and did, influence practice by hints, suggestions, oblique comments and praise" (p. 3).

Few thorough changes in classroom practice are brought about through hints, suggestions, and oblique comments. Rather, the very obliqueness on the part of administrators can only strengthen the norm of inviolability of the classroom. Also, the norms and symbols expressed in assemblies are far easier to sustain at the elementary school level, where the mandate for socialization is more univocal and more binding on both children and adults. Normatively speaking, for example, high schools are more centrifugal places. There may even be something sexist here—I am trying to say this carefully—something resolutely feminine in the notion that the missions of institutions are dependent foremost on the quality of the relationships (the "mutual security and openness") among their members. Finally, studies of exemplary schools suffer chronically from halo effects and involuntary collusion, whereby informants help the researchers to focus most on the exemplary features of the setting, leaving the more unsavory aspects in the shadows. What happens, for example, to teachers who choose not to participate actively in assemblies? What deeper-running controversies, conflicts, or incompatibilities are simply papered over with ceremonies designed to preserve a collective sense of decorum for children and observers?

Nonetheless, Nias and her associates are on to something important. Collective experiences of rejoicing, grief, and fellowship, along with ritual expressions of the school's mission, are, without a doubt, important preconditions for collaborative work of a more technical nature. They create friendship, tolerance, and solidarity, and in so doing, they clearly make it easier to intrude on each other's instructional practices in the name of a larger purpose. Without such a foundation, in fact, more rational or technical collaboration (integrating segments of the curriculum, reviewing lesson plans, or analyzing test results) may break down quickly. Alternatively, such collaboration may amount to a sophisticated shell game, with no bearing on what each teacher does ultimately in his or her classroom.

Hargreaves (1989) has expanded incisively on the work of Nias and her associates. For Hargreaves, it is the form of the school culture—its patterns of relationship and its modes of association between members—that drives the content of collaboration. He agrees that collaborative teacher cultures operate almost imperceptibly in the minutiae of school life:

> in the small gestures, jokes and glances that signal sympathy and understanding; in kind words and personal interest shown in corridors or outside classroom doors; in birthdays, treat days and other little ceremonies; in the acceptance and intermixture of personal lives with professional ones; in overt praise, recognition and gratitude; and in sharing and discussion of ideas and resources. (p. 14)

Such cultures, Hargreaves argues, do not arise by "a kind of emotional spontaneous combustion. They have to be created and sustained. Like good marriages, they have to be worked at" (p. 14). He also argues that in such a social climate, experiences of failure and uncertainty on the part of staff members can be expressed openly with a view toward getting help.

As Hargreaves points out, virtually all these exchanges are informal; they are not derived, for example, from an assessment of the school's objectives, nor from a master plan to tighten vertical linkages between grade levels. What Hargreaves is suggesting is that any such "productive" discussions or operational plans will ultimately abort if the requisite social climate is not undergirding them or, alternatively, if the density and cohesion of social relationships are not prime components of the planning and execution process itself. Planning jointly, reviewing lesson plans, setting objectives for the year, implementing a new geography module, using consultants, and the like cannot be mandated into existence by administrators in a hurry to rationalize instruction in the school building—by administrators "looking for swift implementation expedients," as Hargreaves puts it (p. 24). Managerial efficiency calls for rapid, task-centered planning and execution, whereas the kinds of collaborative cultures depicted by Nias and Hargreaves grow more like plants; rushing their growth is tantamount to pulling them up. If the culture is there, planning and execution can be rapid and efficient. If not, we will have essentially an exercise in rhetoric, followed probably by a clumsy, ephemeral, vain attempt on the part of building administrators to force the issue.

EFFECTIVE WORKPLACES

Presumably, if the social environments described earlier grow slowly but steadily, they attain some degree of stability. If we came back in 5 years, we should see few untoward changes, even with a change in headmaster. What to make, then, of the literature reviewed by Little (1987) that suggests that "collegial relations and structures have proved relatively fragile. . . . Relationships, habits and structures that have taken years to build may unravel in a matter of weeks" (p. 507). In this connection, Little mentions the "fairly constant refrain" in the empirical literature and in the field that "cooperative work among teachers is scarce, fruitless, or hard to maintain" (p. 507).

   If we take the perspective of Hargreaves and Nias, the explanation would probably be that these instances of collaborative planning and execution were not grafted onto a preexisting web of dense social interactions among staff but were, rather, enacted on more managerial grounds. As such, these instances would then prove to be ephemeral or superficial. They would dissolve when administrators left the scene, when the first ornery problems were encountered, when staff came to make judgmental comments on one another's practice, or when teams began planning or teaching together and realized that there were real incompatibilities in ideology or instructional style. In more collaborative cultures, presumably, it is easier to weather these storms and to know in advance who should definitely not be working with whom. I say "presumably" in the first instance simply because the data required to answer this question are lacking and thus other explanations are plausible. For example, the mobility of teachers and administrators is far greater in schools in the United States, from which Little's data are reported, than in schools in the United Kingdom, where Nias and her colleagues are working. Cultural differences may also be in play here; Nias' accounts of school assemblies come across as fairly exotic to, say, the French or Swiss observer. Above all, however, one should also consider the leap from what Little calls casual camaraderie of the staff room to negotiations that bear directly on classroom work. Citing Zahorik (1987), she notes that even enduring friendships may suffer strain "when teachers attempt to carry fundamentally social relations into the classroom" (p. 6). Closer to the classroom, Little notes elsewhere, is "closer to the bone. . . . The prospects for conflict are high" (p. 505). In Nias' data, we are not close to the bone; there is very little on the line in terms of professional self-esteem or in terms of external demands to modify ongoing instructional practices that teachers would not have spontaneously changed.

This leaves us in the uncomfortable position of lacking hard, consistent data to show that instances of collaborative planning, review, and construction of didactic units or team teaching result in durable, meaningful, and measurable changes in classroom-level instruction. Little herself (1987) admits that the data base is slim. She relies heavily on the work of Cohen, Deal, Meyer, and Scott (1979) and Cohen (1981), where the evidence is somewhat equivocal and findings are often of a more cognitive nature (for example, changes through collaborative exchanges in teachers' "reflective decision-making") than of an instructional nature (for example, changes in instructional skills or repertoires). Nor do these data address the durability of such findings.

Some of the data that Rosenholtz (1987) and Little (1990) mention relate to research that may be more compelling: research on the implementation of innovations. Here, "harder" data indicate that significant classroom-level changes in practice can and do result from attempts to introduce new programs, projects, or organizational arrangements. However, a few quick comments are warranted here. First, the evidence showing that such practice changes are consolidated and maintained over time is less robust; backsliding and freezing new practices at weak levels of implementation are all too frequent (Huberman & Miles, 1984). Next, consolidated changes in instructional repertoires often seem to depend on high levels of administrative pressure and support, both of which are hard to sustain over time. Essentially, administrators oblige teachers to go cold turkey with prior instructional practices and to implement the new practices virtually in their entirety from the start. Administrators then pump in large amounts of assistance while modifying organizational procedures as required to facilitate implementation. Both sides perceive this situation as transitory ("until things settle down") and as intolerable over the long haul.

By the same token, peer advice and technical assistance, along with assistance from external consultants, are normatively legitimate in situations of generalized experimentation. As everyone is confronted with novelty and complexity, lateral assistance can be construed as mutual problem-solving in the face of uncertainty (Cohen, 1981; DePaulo & Fisher, 1980), with no implication of status discrepancy between the helpers and the helped. In other words, innovations are temporary systems, and in temporary systems, norms and procedural rules can be suspended for the time needed to reestablish them in, at best, a slightly different form.

What is intriguing in Little's earlier work (1982) is that such norms of experimentation and collegiality appear to carry over to everyday practice in the "relatively successful" schools studied. Presumably, we are not in feverish periods of innovation here, and we find teachers valuing norms of collegiality and continuous improvement and pursuing a wide range of interactions (precise talk about instruction, structured observations, and shared planning or preparation). "Teachers teach each other the practice of teaching" (p. 331). Principals announce and describe expectations reinforcing those norms; model or enact desired behaviors; and sanction technical exchanges and experimentation through released time, evaluation of teacher performance, public praise for collegial or experimental efforts, and tolerant absorption of temporary failures, and so on.

This is precisely what we find in empirical studies of schoolwide innovations—innovations being implemented, one should remember, in typical, garden-variety schools—and it does, in these cases, translate into observable practice changes at the classroom level and from there into measurable changes in pupil attitudes or performance. These innovations, however, constitute a 2- to 3-year cycle and recur infrequently in the career of a teacher (Huberman, 1988, 1989).

To imagine the conditions allowing for continuous implementation of these practices, as in the effective workplace literature, is to make a long conceptual stretch. Very few educational workplaces look like this or are likely to in the short term. Too much of this research is, in effect, being conducted with outlier sampling—that is, with contrasting cases at the extremes of a distribution—although the overwhelming majority of cases are lumped in the middle. When these collaborative workplaces constitute, say, 15 percent of a state-level population of schools and when at least 90 percent of these still qualify 5 to 10 years after their initial selection, we can talk business. By the same token, we have no observational data to trace this "decision culture" down to the classroom level. And there are indications that despite the gently transitive nature of the language, these principals are tough, intrusive customers who are bound to get at least a minority of teachers' backs up and thereby create more conflict than we see in the data base provided us. When principals reinforce certain instructional practices at the expense of others, for example, they are basically making a power play; there can be no unequivocal evidence to show that these practices are uniformly superior to those that the recalcitrant teachers are now using, and there is some likelihood that they would work less well in classrooms where teachers perceive them as pedagogically uncongenial. Even if there was strong evidence for the merits of a particular approach, most administrators would not be perceived as credible advocates because they are neither instructional specialists nor more experienced peers who are themselves confronting the changes in the classroom environments that they are advocating. Administrators who no longer teach or who teach token hours or token subject matters are not fellow artisans but, rather, are patrons of another occupational species, with a different reward system and, above all, a different barometer of organizational quality and efficiency.

EFFECTIVE SCHOOLS

The muscular nature of the principal's role is more pronounced still in the effective schools literature. From the original work of Edmonds (1979) and Rutter (1983), extended by empirical studies in the past decade, we have come to know the hallmarks of these schools: strong administrative leadership, high expectations for children's achievement, an orderly atmosphere conducive to learning, an emphasis on skill acquisition, and frequent monitoring of pupil progress. In this literature, administrators in effective schools devote more time to coordination and control of instruction, observe teachers' work closely, and discuss instructional problems more frequently with their staff.

From analyses of pupil achievement scores, there is little doubt that this constellation of factors translates first into instructional changes at the classroom level and then into pupils' academic task engagement and productivity. So, this is a strong prima facie case of school-level coordination resulting in classroom-level change. And it is an example of how greater task interdependence—specific objectives set for the school, tighter coordination between consecutive segments of the curriculum, and frequent monitoring of individual classroom effects to assess schoolwide performance—constrains individual practices in ways that are apparently beneficial for the system's ultimate "clients"—the pupils—rather than for solely the functionaries and professionals who service those clients. This is, in many ways, the antithesis of the independent artisan model, and it does appear at first blush to deliver important instructional outcomes.

However, it raises as many questions as it answers. Some of those questions have already been raised (Cuban, 1984). For example, we seem to be talking primarily about urban schools serving low-income or minority children, be they in England or in the United States. In middle-class schools, principals tread far more lightly, professional autonomy in the classroom remains high, and standardized achievement scores are not the Holy Grail. For another thing, we are once again acting under the singularly American delusion that there must be a single best formula for effectiveness, much as we did in the heyday of teacher effectiveness research. Even the meta-analyses of effective schools research show widely varying configurations of school-level factors that result in achievement gains. Myriad formulas result in such effects—there are myriad ways to be "effective"—and we would be fools to restrict the range of possibilities. It is as if, at some point, we simplemindedly translated the statistical logic governing these results into a prescriptive logic for producing and managing them in specific contexts, whereas the two logics have no necessary relationship. If one uses the logic of regression, discrimination, and determination, by which we distinguish high-performing schools from low-performing schools, and then assembles the factors independently, accounting for variance between the two sets of schools, one would very likely find no single school in either set that corresponds to the constellation constituting the coefficient of determination (R2). Or maybe one or two. And if we then were to spend some time in each of those two schools, we would see in a flash that they bear, in fact, little resemblance to one another and that many of the factors are products of the particular context in which they live rather than traits that are in any way exportable. For example, "strong emphasis on skill acquisition" may result from irresistible (and temporary) political pressures in one school and, in another, from an especially influential teacher-training program with a strong behaviorist orientation.

In other words, the factor may be there all right, but it can't be lifted out and put somewhere else. Strong leadership in one effective school may translate directly into administrative thuggery in another because of personality differences between the two administrators or professional norms within the building.

Obviously, the administrators in the effective workplace literature and even the effective schools literature are cunning, charismatic, and probably manipulative characters with what appears to be a benevolent authoritarian streak. As none of those assumptions are met by the 22 secondary-school principals with whom I now work in Geneva, I can only imagine with fear and trembling what would happen if they decided to turn into "strong leaders" who "observe and monitor closely the classroom work of teachers in the school." Some, I suspect, would quickly become pariahs in their own buildings, objects of pity and derision. Others would be good-naturedly humored by their staff, who would consent to frequent, animated collaborative discussions followed by the setting of objectives and the drafting of some systematic plans for meeting them, and would then wash their hands and retire to the privacy of their classrooms to get on with their own self-governed instructional activities. And other principals—most, one suspects—would quickly learn that it was not in their best interests to engage in close observation and monitoring of classroom instruction (Shapiro & Crowson, 1985). As Boyd and Hartman (1989) have argued persuasively, public school principals depend heavily on the cooperation of teachers to get their core administrative, custodial, and political tasks accomplished. Such cooperation is endangered by close supervision. Teachers have a thousand subtle means of retaliation (for example, forgetting requests, overloading administrators with trivial demands, working to rule, slacking off on monitoring in the corridors, and feeding parental grievances). And teachers know that the punishment and reward system of administrators, as fixed in the central office, depends first on the semblance of maintaining control, harmony, and parental inactivity, with instructional effectiveness as a secondary or longer-term goal.

An artisan image of teaching supports two more serious critiques of the effective schools literature. The first is this: The effective schools literature—and possibly the effective workplace literature as well—associates instructional goal setting and coordination at the building level with instructionally directive practices in the classroom. It is no accident that the effective schools studies report a strong reliance on "direct instruction" (Hallinger & Murphy, 1986). In other words, an administrative system of managing schoolwide practice is translated into a behaviorist approach to classroom instruction, whose validity is, to put it charitably, uncertain. There is here a curious, Alice-in-Wonderland connection being made between managerial ergonomics and neobehaviorist models of learning.

It is easy enough to see where the connection is made. When specific objectives are fixed at the department level or the school level, they can be tested at the classroom level through any variety of standardized or criterion ("mastery") achievement batteries. The teacher can then pretest the pupils, key his or her initial instruction to areas of weakness, retest the pupils periodically, and work individually and collectively on remedial exercises before the final testing is done. In the same way, curricular sequences can be partialed out systematically both within a given discipline and between classes to be sure that pupils will move coherently from one level of difficulty or complexity to the next.

The remainder falls neatly into place. Discussions among staff of test results and curriculum segments can then be highly technical, principals and staff can closely monitor pupils' progress, emphasis can be properly placed on levels of skill acquisition, and administrators can then exert leadership in a mode of work in which they feel right at home: They can set and monitor progress in the achievement of instructional objectives. They can oversee the administration and analysis of achievement tests. They can rationalize the division of labor among staff. They can help to plan and coordinate instructional sequences over grade levels. They are often quite good at all these things. Better still, administrators may feel, with all these test results, that they can administer this enterprise in the course of all these collective meetings and still have their hand right on the pulse of activity in the classroom.

Unfortunately, this is in many ways a house of cards. Instruction closely tied to mastery tests invariably works best at the lowest cognitive level (recognition, factual knowledge, and simple algorithms), which is where most instruction will then be keyed. It will suffice to change slightly the formulation of problems confronted in tests to depress the results (weak levels of transfer). Higher-achieving pupils may well tune out early in the cycle. After a relatively short time, most teachers will find that a strong diet of this essentially remedial work is deadening, even demeaning. In effect, they, too, will be working at the lowest level of their professional repertoires. Also, given the tighter sequencing of the curriculum and the necessity of covering it to bring pupils to the next level of mastery commensurate with grade-level objectives, teachers will find themselves pulled inexorably along a track with little latitude to slow down, deviate, dig deeper, and give expression to what they view as their own distinctive instructional voice. They will find that, all too often, there is a discrepancy between their professional judgment about what they need to be attending to instructionally at a particular moment and what they find themselves obliged to do as a function of constraints that have been externally imposed or even consensually agreed on.

More seriously, a heavily behaviorist approach can often be, in cognitive terms, literally mindless and meaningless. That is, pupils may score well on tests with superficial or fully distorted representations of the underlying concepts or operations. With no understanding of the ways in which pupils actually process or construe a historical text or a division problem, teachers may well be reinforcing misrepresentations in the name of correcting errors or skill deficiencies that appear on mastery tests. The only sensible way to counter this problem is to slow down, multiply the number of interactive exchanges, start with a pupil's logic and deconstruct it carefully, vary instructional formats and materials as a function of emerging levels of understanding and interest, do something else for a few days to promote latency, move up and down the cognitive ladder from simple recognition to more complex and varied applications, and, perhaps most important, sustain one's own level of interest and engagement in the process so that pupils will maintain theirs.

In short, the teacher will have to improvise, as a function of the constellation of pupils, the didactic materials at hand, the vicissitudes of the moment, and the richness inherent in his or her own diagnostic and instructional repertoire. Some of this improvisation, it is important to say, may well be of a neobehaviorist nature, as the need arises for systematic practice, for decomposition of a skill into subcomponents, or for testing of prerequisite levels of understanding and mastery. However, these are parts of a larger, more ecumenical, more situationally shaped instructional frame. And with this frame, the reader will notice that we are once again in the realm of bricolage.

By taking all these detours, of course, our teacher may fall behind or fall out of step with others who precede or follow him or her and with the sequence of instructional objectives planned in common. This, of course, will turn up in test results to his or her disadvantage, and he or she will have to defend him- or herself. This, in turn, could presumably lead to "technical discussions" or perhaps to "mutual observations" or "assistance" designed to help our teacher get back on track. The principal would then follow up with observations followed by a focused debriefing. . . .

This scenario has been made deliberately provocative, to the point of caricature, to signal a problem. Conceptually, there is no necessary reason why agreement among school staff on a set of academic objectives, giving rise to intensive interaction of a technical nature and to greater task coordination to achieve those objectives, should necessarily mutate into more instructionally constrained work for each teacher inside the classroom or should necessarily lead to neobehaviorist approaches to learning. Empirically, however, at least in the U.S. context, this is what seems to happen if events follow their natural course. Managerial rationality turns into instructional Taylorism. It is as if administrators—along with subcommunities of researchers—have trouble holding in their heads simultaneously the constructs of central coordination and individual autonomy, whereas successful private-sector managers of the Peters and Waterman school (1982) appear to thrive in their organizations on that very combination.

Now for a second and shorter critical remark. In her cogent defense of the effective schools literature, Rosenholtz (1985) argues that such schools are characterized by more systematic, targeted exchanges among teachers about instructional practices and how to improve them. This leads to a greater consensus on school goals and thereby "increases the likelihood that student achievement will be viewed as a highly salient aspect of school life" (p. 366). At the same time, such "frequent, task-focused interactions" enhance social cohesiveness and, from there, facilitate the "collaborative arrangements" needed to achieve those goals. The principal oversees this process of "rational planning and action" and mobilizes teachers "against the single common enemy: low student achievement" (p. 381). This argument is buttressed by the logic inherent in Bandura's recent work on "outcome efficacy" and "self-efficacy" as applied to teaching (Ashton & Webb, 1986): that the experience of obtaining higher levels of achievement provides teachers with the psychic rewards necessary for them to focus their energies singly and collectively on achieving these goals.

I would like to suggest respectfully that the incentives and satisfactions of teachers, as played out in the universe of classroom instruction, are more complicated than that. Taking the long view from a 30-year career in the classroom, the single common enemy is more probably the number of apathetic or disruptive cohorts of pupils to be faced each day or each year. In the secondary school, with three such groups in a seven-period day, the year is a shambles, psychically speaking. With three such groups in yearly succession in the elementary school, most teachers will take a leave of absence or transfer. Inversely, three years of lively, responsive, even demanding cohorts may well charge teachers' psychic batteries for a decade, essentially because these cohorts bring out the best in most teachers, push them to their limits, inject novelty and adventure into the most banal lesson or exercise, and drive teachers to the hills in search of new instructional resources to keep these kids turned on. In the long haul, it is above all the diversity, stimulation, and pleasure that teachers can suck out of the potentially redundant, constrained, interpersonally depleting universe of the classroom that will determine how much energy they can put back into it. And I would claim further that this is, in fact, where they summon the requisite energy to work purposefully on increasing levels of pupil achievement.

This means that raising achievement levels is one source of perceived professional commitment and self-efficacy, but not necessarily the primary source. I would contend, in fact, that most teachers would derive more professional satisfaction from resuscitating three sullen, low-performing pupils on the brink of dropping out than from raising class-level achievement tests by half a standard deviation in 6 months. Bringing back three such pupils is a far more stringent and sophisticated test of professional capacity. Also, it provides a more tangible, possibly durable reward; it amounts, after all, to a small miracle rather than to the accomplishment of a valued institutional outcome. It is also probably a more legitimate source of craft pride—of respect and admiration from members of one's guild—than would be a high mean performance on a state-level achievement test for a previously low-performing class. Most peers would assume that they, too, could do as well if only through the kind of doggedness and systematic review that many come to associate gradually more with drudgery than with virtuosity.

More generally, associating teaching effectiveness with gains in pupil achievement levels, as Rosenholtz (1985) essentially does, is an extremely restrictive way of defining either the social mandate of the school or the professional capacity of the teaching staff. Here, once again, we are trying to refloat the demonstrably bankrupt tradition of process-product studies of teacher effectiveness, this time by aggregating the unit of analysis from the classroom level to the institutional level. Assessments of individual development or learning have been simplemindedly and inappropriately converted to residualized gains on achievement tests and then aggregated into a sort of ersatz productivity index for the school as a whole.

Not that achievement levels are unimportant; cognitive outcomes are what schools are best equipped to provide and what they are expected to deliver on. However, equating cognition with achievement scores is like equating a gourmet meal with caloric intake or a Fabergé egg with an egg. Also, once we reach that point, 80 percent of teachers' skills become superfluous. For example, given the state of the art, we may just about be at the stage where strong achievement levels on machine-scored batteries can be turned out as well by computer-assisted instruction as by interactive instruction in the classroom, which is, of course, far more labor intensive and unkempt. Aside from the simpleminded, surreal quality of this logic, when taken to its extreme, this kind of thinking is intrinsically, revealingly anti-intellectual and will in a relatively short time corrode an educational enterprise from the inside out. It also collides head-on with the ideology of teacher professionalism that is put forward in much of the writing in the effective workplace literature.

In their literature review of the "cultures of teaching," Feiman-Nemser and Floden (1986) include some data that speak on this register, but do it evenhandedly. After citing some work that suggests that teachers do not select learning activities because they lead to valued outcomes but because teachers value such activities in and of themselves, the authors conclude:

> Some teachers prefer activities designed to foster achievement; others, activities designed to be nurturant. Some teachers get rewards from conducting carefully planned lessons; others get satisfaction from creating a classroom environment where students have opportunities to follow their own interests. (p. 511)

Fair enough. As long as we bear in mind that many teachers love—or at least tolerate—their work precisely because it leaves space for activities with no immediate didactic payoff. Acting out legends, singing in class, conducting an apparently aimless physics experiment suggested by pupils, reading parts from a play—all may produce no more than an exciting period or a pleasurable day for the class. For many teachers, this is a highly valid indicator of productivity; they suspect, perhaps with good reason, that the reactions of amused curiosity or real engagement will pay off further down the line, without knowing exactly where and how. They may well boost achievement scores, provide a respite from an unrelenting string of remedial exercises in workbooks, or reveal to pupils the relationship between skill mastery and intellectual culture. Whatever the effects, they will be nonlinear ones, just as cognitive growth is unequivocally nonlinear. For the teachers themselves, this may also be the best way to transcend a piecework approach to their craft or to make colleagues understand what they are about, instructionally speaking, and thereby the best way to embark on a collaborative interaction of real substance.

CONCLUSION

Public schools with at least a dozen classes remain, I think, mongrel assemblies of adults and children, ones that represent different constituencies within the educational and lay communities. To some extent, then, the loose coupling between classes, the deliberately ambiguous goals of the institution, and the refusal to seek out a common instructional technology to achieve those goals constitute an adaptive arrangement. They keep the peace and let everyone get on with their work with a maximum of professional autonomy and a modicum of coordination. In the classroom, in particular, they allow teachers a wide degree of freedom to minister to classes and pupils of different levels, capacities, and moods. We should be very careful when we presume to mess with this system, especially when we do so in the name of managerial rationalism.

In particular, we should not forget that this loosely coordinated, professionally individualistic system has its own rationality and that it is oiled with thousands of implicit bargains and mutual accommodations to reduce frictions in the machinery. It is a far more complex, coherent, and resilient ecosystem than most observers realize, and it has an awesome capacity to wait out and wear out reformers who would introduce a different division of labor. Finally, it respects the more contradictory, tragicomic, and slightly sordid aspects of social life in schools, all while allowing these more subterranean aspects to be covered decorously by the more purposeful, reasonable, and ennobling features of school life—those that the workplace literature and the effective schools literature are banking on exclusively.

This does not mean, of course, that we should leave this subterranean system alone. It has become all too clear that the individual comforts and needs of school people, teachers, administrators, and all the supporting cast have too often taken precedence over the social responsibilities of the institution. Few schools are organized around the concept of managing the academic careers of their pupils, in coherent and nurturant ways, as these pupils traverse the successive units of the institution. Rather, each teacher manages his or her pupils, year, and curriculum and studiously avoids his or her neighbor, and each administrator keeps the ship afloat, with as few waves as possible.

Clearly, the effective workplace movement and the effective schools movement recenter staff energies on the primary mission of the school, all in breaking through the isolation of its adult members. But neither current has proved to date that it can significantly improve instructional activity in the classroom and can deliver a variety of significant outcomes in cognitive or conative terms. Neither has looked carefully, either, at the potentially perverse second-order effects of norms and practices that ask more of many people than they are willing or able to give. And both currents appear to contain fundamental flaws: the effective workplace literature in its somewhat all-consuming discussion culture and its curious indifference to the instructional capacities actually needed to follow through in the classroom, and the effective schools literature in its manic rationalism and its tendency to restrict the pedagogical range to mechanistic and associationist approaches to learning and instruction.

What I have suggested in this paper is that we might do better not by setting specific schoolwide objectives and then rationalizing the tasks and functions to be accomplished by school staff, but by grafting such deliberative work on the ways in which teachers spontaneously construe their work and relate to their peers. We might do better, in short, by swimming with the tide instead of swimming against it. We would get further, and we would have fewer institutional perversions.

For example, I submit that the logic of using the school building as the unit of analysis and intervention is goofy when we are talking about at least 25 or 30 teachers and support staff and 500 pupils. Why the school? How far can first grade teachers go with sixth grade teachers? How much collaboration can we expect between 8th grade physics teachers, 11th grade English teachers, and physical education instructors? Why are we putting these people together to draft objectives, plan curricula, and monitor one another's test results when their actual instructional contexts are so different? How did we ever think we could bank on a workable collaboration between teachers who have despised one another for years? Why must we become, at virtually all costs, a socially cohesive community when so few of the requisite conditions for becoming so are met?

From the artisan's logic, I might look instead to the department or to the grade level as the unit of collaborative planning and execution in a secondary school. This is where people have concrete things to tell one another and concrete instructional help to provide one another; this is where the contexts of instruction actually overlap. In the primary school, one would probably first study existing friendship patterns and pedagogical styles and then try to extend them slightly in constituting working groups that span two or three grade levels. In general, one would salt away half the released time or consultant help to allow teachers to look outside the school for peers or experts who could actually help them to implement the instructional changes agreed on during staff meetings. Above all, one would set a clear line of demarcation between collaborative planning at the grade level or at the department level and instructional activity in the classroom by preserving or even extending individual degrees of freedom allotted to teachers.

And from an artisan's logic, applied this time to the district level, one might not even bank on individual schools as a unit of analysis but on subgroups of teachers from different schools. Here again, these are people who can have specific, mutually useful instructional business to transact with one another, both because they teach the same subject matter or the same age groups or work in the same kinds of neighborhoods and because they are intrinsically interested in the tools that others have come up with in settings like their own. Moreover, these people would be more likely to remain in professional contact, as nodes in an artisan's professional network, long after everyone has forgotten the existence of these task groups.

More to the point, however, is that what these teachers can plan, exchange, and construct together can be translated directly into the classroom, discussed concretely, and revised periodically through technical exchanges. Some people would need to be in such groups from each building—people who represented a minimum of intrabuilding coherence and continuity in each school (secondary teachers with the same seventh graders, primary teachers of successive grade levels, and secondary teachers of the same subject matters taught in consecutive years). In other words, although the logic of independent artisanry would be respected, such groups would oblige teachers to take into account the progression of pupils' academic careers within their schools.

This is obviously a messier, more fragmented, and far more incremental scenario than those described in the literature. But it may well square better with the dynamic ecology of life in the schoolhouse and in the classroom, whereas the communitarian, workplace, and effective schools scenarios are more institutionally and instructionally naive. They are generous and rationally elegant, but they may not be sufficiently street smart or school smart. They may not carve up schools or school people at their functional joints in the ways in which these variables actually configure and play out empirically in the setting. Nor do they look at these teachers and these schools over time, as a function of the individual and institutional cycles that characterize life in this profession. As a result, they may seduce us into consuming untold resources and energies to create and artfully maintain a few such environments, which are then paraded in front of mostly disbelieving principals and superintendents.

Beyond this, however, I am suggesting that we can get on the road to the same place in a different way but via a less orderly, more fragmented, and more pedestrian route. Many administrators will find it managerially uncongenial and will see right off that this route creates more work, more anarchy, and less direct influence for them. Social architects in the research community will complain that where we could have built a shiny new city, we are settling for a few extensions and a lot of small clubhouses dumped into the same grubby villages. Both critiques are legitimate ones. Empirically speaking, however, I think they are pretty much beside the point. Starting with the premise of the teacher as an independent artisan collaborating selectively within the local and expanded community of his or her peers, we can build some scenarios for school improvement that may not come apart quite so readily in our hands.

REFERENCES

Ashton, P., & Webb, R. (1986). *Making a difference: Teachers' sense of efficacy and school achievement.* New York: Longman.

Barker, R., & Gump, P. (1964). *Big school, little school.* Stanford, CA: Stanford University Press.

Bereiter, C., & Scardamalia, M. (1986). Educational relevance of the study of expertise. *Interchange, 17*(2), 10–19.

Berliner, D. (1986). In pursuit of the expert pedagogue. *Educational Researcher, 15*(7), 5–13.

Berliner, D., & Carter, K. (1986). *Differences in processing classroom information by expert and novice teachers.* Paper presented at a meeting of the International Study Association on Teacher Thinking, Leuven, Belgium.

Berman, P., & McLaughlin, M. (1974–1978). *Federal programs supporting educational change.* Santa Monica, CA: Rand Corporation.

Bishop, J. (1977). Organizational influences on the work orientations of elementary teachers. *Sociology of Work and Occupation, 4,* 171–208.

Borko, H., & Niles, J. (1987). Descriptions of teacher planning: Ideas for teachers and researchers. In V. Richardson-Koehler (Ed.), *Educators' handbook: A research perspective* (pp. 67–83). New York: Longman.

Boyd, W., & Hartman, W. (1989). The politics of educational productivity. In D. Monk & J. Underwood (Eds.), *Micro-level school finance* (pp. 271–308). Cambridge, MA: Ballinger.

Churchman, C. W. (1971). *The design of inquiring systems.* New York: Basic Books.

Clark, C. (1988). Asking the right questions about teacher preparation. *Educational Researcher, 17,* 5–12.

Clark, C., & Peterson, P. (1986). Teachers' thought processes. In M. Wittrock (Ed.), *Handbook of research on teaching* (3rd ed., pp. 255–296). New York: MacMillan.

Clark, C., & Yinger, R. (1979). *Three studies of teacher planning* (Research Series No. 55). East Lansing, MI: Michigan State University, Institute for Research on Teaching.

Cohen, E. (1981). Sociology looks at team teaching. *Research in Sociology of Education and Socialization, 2,* 163–193.

Cohen, E., Deal, T., Meyer, J., & Scott, W. R. (1979). Technology and teaming in the elementary school. *Sociology of Education, 52,* 20–33.

Crandall, D., Bauchner, J., Cox, P., Eiseman, J., Havelock, R., Huberman, M., Loucks, S., Miles, M., Schmidt, W., Shive, G., Taylor, J., & Thompson, C. (1982). *People, policies and practices: Examining the chain of school improvement* (Vols. 1–10). Andover, MA: The Network.

Cuban, L. (1984). Transforming the frog into a prince: Effective schools research, policy and practice at the district level. *Harvard Educational Review, 54,* 129–151.

Deal, T., & Celotti (1987). How much influence do (and can) educational administrators have on classrooms? In R. Carlson & E. Ducharme (Eds.), *School improvement: Theory and practice* (pp. 205–216). Baltimore: University Press.

DePaulo, B., & Fisher, J. (1980). The costs of asking for help. *Basic and Applied Social Psychology, 1,* 23–25.

Dewey, J. (1929). *The quest for certainty.* New York: Minton, Balch.

Doyle, W. (1978). Paradigms for research on teacher effectiveness. In L. Shulman (Ed.), *Review of research in education* (Vol. 5) (pp. 163–190). Itasca, IL: Peacock.

Durkhein, E. (1951 [1897]). *Suicide: A study in sociology.* Tr. by J.A. Spaulding and G. Simpson. New York: Free Press.

Edmonds, R. (1979). Some schools work and more can. *Social Policy, 9,* 28–32.

Feiman-Nemser, S., & Floden, R. (1986). The cultures of teaching. In M. Wittrock (Ed.), *Handbook of research on teaching* (3rd ed., pp. 505–526). New York: Macmillan.

Gage, N. (1985). *Hard gains in the soft sciences.* Bloomington, IN: Center of Evaluation, Development and Research.

Glidewell, J. C., Tucker, S., Todt, M., & Cox, S. (1983). Professional support systems: The teaching profession. In A. Nadler, J. Fisher, & B. DePaulo (Eds.), *New directions in helping* (pp. 189–212). New York: Academic Press.

Goodlad, J. (1983). *A place called school.* New York: McGraw-Hill.

Hallinger, P., & Murphy, J. (1986). The social contexts of effective schools. *American Journal of Education, 94,* 328–355.

Hargreaves, A. (1989). *Contrived collegiality and the culture of teaching.* Paper presented at a meeting of the Canadian Society for Studies in Education Conference, Laval, Quebec, Canada.

Harper, D. (1987). *Working knowledge.* Chicago: University of Chicago Press.

Hatton, E. (1987). Determinants of teacher work: Some causal complications. *Teaching and Teacher Education, 3,* 55–60.

Hatton, E. (1989). Lévi-Strauss' bricolage and theorizing teachers' work. *Anthropology and Education Quarterly, 20(2),* 74–86.

Heckman, P. (1987). Understanding school culture. In J. Goodlad (Ed.), *The ecology of school renewal* (pp. 63–78). Chicago: National Society for the Study of Education.

Housner, L., & Griffey, D. (1985). Teacher cognition: Differences in planning and interactive decision making between experienced and inexperienced teachers. *Research Quarterly for Exercise and Sport, 56*, 45–53.

Huberman, M. (1983). Recipes for busy kitchens. *Knowledge, 4*, 478–510.

Huberman, M. (1988). *Teacher professionalism and workplace conditions.* Paper presented at the Holmes Group Conference on Conceptions of Teachers' Work and the Organization of Schools. East Lansing, MI: Michigan State University, College of Education.

Huberman, M. (1989). The professional life cycle of teachers. *Teachers College Record, 91*, 31–58.

Huberman, M., Grounauer, M.-M., & Marti, J. (1989). *La vie des enseignants.* Neuchâtel/Paris: Delachaux et Niestle. English version, *The Lives of Teachers. London:* Cassells (in press).

Huberman, M., & Miles, M. (1984). *Innovation up close.* New York: Plenum.

Hyde, N., & Sandall, C. (1984). *The impact of the Priority Schools Programme in 15 primary schools.* Perth, Australia: Research Branch, Educational Department of Western Australia.

Jackson, P. (1968). *Life in classrooms.* New York: Holt, Rinehart & Winston.

Jackson, P. (1977). The way teachers think. In J. Glidewell (Ed.), *The social context of learning and development* (pp. 19–50). New York: Gardner Press.

Leinhardt, G., & Greeno, J. (1986). The cognitive skill of teaching. *Journal of Educational Psychology, 78*(2), 75–95.

Lévi-Strauss, C. (1962). *La pensée sauvage.* Paris: Plon.

Little, J. W. (1982). Norms of collegiality and experimentation: Workplace conditions of school success. *American Educational Research Journal, 19*, 325–340.

Little, J. W. (1987). Teachers as colleagues. In V. Richardson-Koehler (Ed.), *Educators' handbook: A research perspective* (pp. 491–518). New York: Longman.

Little, J. W. (1990). The persistence of privacy: Autonomy and initiative in teachers' professional relations. *Teachers College Record, 91*, 509–536.

Lortie, D. (1975). *Schoolteacher.* Chicago: University of Chicago Press.

Mauss, M. (1967). *The gift: Forms and functions of exchange in archaic societies.* New York: Norton. (Original version: Mauss, M. [1923]). Essai sur le don: Formes et raison de l'échange dans les sociétés archaïques. *L'année sociologique, 1*, 30–186.)

Nias, J. (1989). *Meeting together: The symbolic and pedagogic importance of school assemblies in a collaborative culture.* Paper presented at annual meeting of the American Educational Research Association, San Francisco, California.

Nias, J., Southworth, G., & Yeomans, R. (1989). *Primary school staff relationships: A study of organizational cultures.* London: Cassell.

Perrenoud, P. (1983). La pratique pedagogique entre l'improvisation reglée et le bricolage. *Education et recherche, 5*, 198–222.

Peters, T., & Waterman, R. (1982). *In search of excellence: Lessons from America's best-run companies.* New York: Harper & Row.

Peterson, P., Marx, R., & Clark, C. (1978). Teacher planning, teacher behavior, and student achievement. *American Educational Research Journal, 15,* 417–432.

Rosen, S., Mickler, S., & Collins, J. (1987). Reactions of would-be helpers whose offer of help is spurned. *Journal of Personality and Social Psychology, 53,* 288–297.

Rosenholtz, S. (1985). Effective schools: Interpreting the evidence. *American Journal of Education, 93,* 352–388.

Rosenholtz, S. (1987). Education reform strategies: Will they increase teacher commitment? *American Journal of Education, 95,* 534–562.

Rutter, M. (1983). School effects on pupil progress: Research findings and policy implications. In L. Shulman and G. Sykes (Eds.), *Handbook of Teaching and Policy,* pp. 3–41. New York: Longman.

Shapiro, J., & Crowson, R. (1985). *Rational choice theory and administrative decision making.* Paper presented at meeting of the American Educational Research Association, Chicago, Illinois.

Shavelson, R., & Stern, P. (1981). Research on teachers' pedagogical thoughts, judgments, decisions and behavior. *Review of Educational Research, 51,* 455–498.

Snow, R. (1974). Representative and quasi-representative designs for research on teaching. *Review of Educational Research, 44,* 263–291.

Yinger, R. (1986). Examining thought in action. *Teaching and Teacher Education, 2,* 263–282.

Yinger, R. (1987). *By the seat of your pants: An inquiry into improvisation and teaching.* Paper presented at meeting of the American Educational Research Association, Washington, D.C.

Yinger, R. (1988). *The conversation of teaching: Patterns of explanation in mathematics lessons.* Paper presented at meeting of the International Study Association on Teacher Thinking, Nottingham, England.

Zahorik, J. (1987). Teachers' collegial interaction: An exploratory study. *Elementary School Journal, 87,* 385–396.

2

Andy Hargreaves

Centre for Leadership Development,
Ontario Institute for Studies in Education

Individualism and Individuality: Reinterpreting the Teacher Culture

A school should have a mission or a sense of mission. Such is the increasingly accepted wisdom of reformers in the fields of educational leadership, school effectiveness, school improvement, and staff development (Mortimore, Sammons, Stoll, Lewis, & Ecob, 1988; Purkey & Smith, 1983). Missions mitigate the uncertainties of teaching by forging common beliefs and purposes among the teaching community (Rosenholtz, 1988). Through building common goals along with a shared expectation that they can be met, missions also strengthen teachers' sense of efficacy and their belief that they can improve the achievement of all their students irrespective of background (Ashton & Webb, 1986). Missions build motivation, and missions bestow meaning. Particularly for those who have participated in their development, missions mean a lot.

THE HERESY OF INDIVIDUALISM

Developing a sense of mission builds loyalty, commitment, and confidence in a school community. It is a powerful spur to improvement. But if mis-

Reprinted with permission from *International Journal of Educational Research,* Vol. 19, #3, Andy Hargreaves, Individualism and Individuality: Reinterpreting the Teacher Culture, January, 1993, Pergamon Press, Ltd., Headington Hill Hall, Oxford, OX3 OBW, United Kingdom.

sions develop loyalty among the faithful and confidence among the committed, they also create heresy among those who question, those who differ, and those who doubt. The narrower and more fervent the mission, the greater and more widespread the heresy. For the missionary, heresies are beyond the walls of wisdom, the boundaries of belief. Heresies are not to be debated. They are to be derogated or dismissed. To deem an idea heretical is thereby to dismiss it without counsel or consideration. The social construction of heresy is in this sense a powerful ideological force. It suppresses the proper discussion of choices and alternatives by patronizingly disregarding their seriousness or by undermining the personal credibility of those who advance them. Heretics are not merely dissenting or disagreeable, then. They are personally flawed. Weakness, madness, or badness—these are the hallmarks of the heretic, the qualities that mark him or her out from the rest.

In his extensive and intriguing discussion of heresy as a social phenomenon, Szaz (1976) argues that heresy "has to do with not believing what everyone else believes or what one ought to believe; with proclaiming disbelief when the right thing to do is to proffer belief or at least remain silent" (p. 1). Heresy will be present, says Szaz, "so long as there is tension between the individual and the group" (p. 10). Individuals must think for themselves. That is what makes them individuals. Yet the group wants its members to echo its beliefs. This is what Szaz calls the constant structure of heresy.

Heresy is a commonly understood accompaniment to religious beliefs and doctrines. But it can also be associated with scientific and technological ideals or political and cultural belief systems, too. To proclaim that the virgin birth is not a literal truth but a literalized metaphor is a heresy in the Christian tradition. To assert that the West has much to learn from the East (and not merely vice versa) or that progress is not always good: these are heresies of Western democracies. Educational systems and those who work within them or on behalf of them also have their heresies. That schools might best be run without the office of principalship, that schools should be primarily responsible for the development of their own curricula, that many children with special needs are better off *not* being integrated into regular classrooms—these are heresies of modern educational thought. Within modern educational systems, heresies such as these are unspeakable. To utter them is not merely to disagree, but to be wicked or weak. Heresies lie beyond the bounds of reason.

All these heresies are what might be called substantive heresies, or heresies of content. They are heresies that question or threaten particular parts of the belief system, particular doctrines that the faithful hold dear. But beneath these heresies are even deeper, more profound heresies.

These, I want to call generic heresies, or heresies of form. Generic heresies challenge the central purpose of the mission itself and the principles on which it is founded.

In the fields of school improvement, staff development, and educational change, a fundamental generic heresy is the heresy of individualism. Teacher individualism, teacher isolation, teacher privatism—the qualities and characteristics that fall under these closely associated labels have come to be widely perceived as significant threats or barriers to professional development, the implementation of change, and the development of shared educational goals.

Terms like *collegiality* and *individualism* are actually quite vague and imprecise, open to a range of meanings and interpretations. Of collegiality, Little (1990) has remarked that the term is "conceptually amorphous and ideologically sanguine" (p. 509). Much the same can be said of individualism. Such terms are in many respects used and understood less as accurate descriptions of types of practice, policy, or even aspiration. Rather, the terms are mostly symbolic—motivating rhetorics in a mythical discourse of change and improvement. Here, collaboration and collegiality have become powerful images of preferred aspiration; isolation and individualism have become equally powerful images of professional aversion. Individualism, isolation, and privatism have therefore become preoccupations of and key targets for the educational reform movement. Their eradication, like the eradication of all heresy, has become a high priority.

This paper analyzes the phenomenon of individualism as a generic heresy of educational change. It begins by critically reviewing existing research and other literature on teacher individualism, isolation, and privatism and identifies what are claimed to be their constituent features and patterns of causation. Findings that emerged from a qualitative study of elementary school teachers' perceptions and uses of scheduled preparation time are then counterposed with this existing knowledge base. One of the special capacities of qualitative research is its capacity to make as well as take problems (Seeley, 1967): to be open, sensitive, and responsive to problems and issues in the field as they are defined by the participants, not as they are presumed to be by policymakers and reformers. Some of the findings from the qualitative research reported in this paper reveal teacher-based explanations for individualistic preferences in the use of preparation time that provide interesting and surprising points of contrast with the existing literature. Together, the critical review of the literature and the findings of the qualitative study lead to a reinterpretation and reconstruction of the concept of teacher individualism and its implications for improvement and change, which are less consistently negative than other writers have led us to believe.

PERSPECTIVES ON INDIVIDUALISM

The continuing and pervasive presence of isolation, individualism, and privatism within the culture of teaching is not a matter of serious doubt or disagreement among writers on the subject (Zahorik, 1987; Zielinski & Hoy, 1983). Although pockets of collaborative and collegial practice among teachers are acknowledged, these are widely understood to be exceptions to the general rule, requiring special conditions for development and persistence (Little, 1984; Nias, Southworth, & Yeomans, 1989). Despite numerous efforts at improvement and reform, individualism stubbornly prevails within the teacher culture. Why?

INDIVIDUALISM AS A PSYCHOLOGICAL DEFICIT

Within the research literature, two kinds of explanation are commonly advanced as determinants of individualism. In the first, more traditional interpretation, individualism is associated with diffidence, defensiveness, anxiety, flaws, and failures in teachers that are partly natural and partly a result of the uncertainties of their work.

Lortie (1975), the first to discuss the phenomenon of teacher individualism in any systematic way, associated it with qualities of uncertainty and anxiety, which led teachers to rely on orthodox doctrines and their own past experience as students when forming their styles and strategies of teaching. "Uncertainty," observed Lortie, "is the lot of those who teach" (p. 133), for the goals of teaching are diffuse and the feedback on success in achieving them is unreliable. The majority of teachers whom Lortie interviewed did not just happen to be isolated from one another by the architecture of the school; they actively preferred isolation. They argued that if they were allocated more time, they would spend it in their own classrooms, not with colleagues.

In England, in a series of essays on the occupational culture of teaching, D. Hargreaves reiterated Lortie's (1975) judgment that teacher individualism "is not cocky and self-assured, but hesitant and uneasy" (p. 210). Although seeking to distance himself a little from Lortie's depiction of teacher individualism, by describing it as a caricature, D. Hargreaves' depiction is nonetheless extensive and otherwise unhedged (1982) and elsewhere not qualified as a caricature at all (1980b). In D. Hargreaves' (1980a) characterization of teacher individualism, the metaphorical language of deficiency and pathology is rife. "The cult of individualism," he claims, "has *deeply infected* the occupational culture of teachers" (p. 194). Teachers, says D. Hargreaves, guard their autonomy "jealously" (p. 206). They do not like being observed, still less being evaluated, because they suffer competence anxiety and are fearful of the criticism that may accompany evaluation. Defenses of isolation and independence of a more dignified and virtuous nature are dismissed as mere rationalizations. "Autonomy," claims D. Hargreaves (1982), "is the polite word used to mask teachers' evaluative apprehension and to serve as the rationale for excluding observers" (p. 206).

Much more recently, in her study of 78 elementary schools in Tennessee, Rosenholtz (1988) identified 15 schools that she called *isolated* and 50 that she called *moderately isolated* in character. Schools were characterized as isolated or moderately isolated in terms of the frequency of stated helping behaviors. Isolated schools were those in which frequency variables averaged approximately a standard deviation below sample means. Fifty-five teachers were then randomly selected from a subsample of these isolated and moderately isolated schools and were interviewed. In this, one of the most comprehensive studies of teachers' collegial relations yet undertaken, Rosenholtz makes some useful, insightful, and well-grounded observations on teachers' statements about their behavior in isolated settings. She finds that help giving is infrequent, that (as in Lortie's 1975 study) it rarely extends beyond sharing existing materials and ideas, that planning and problem solving with colleagues scarcely happen at all, and that isolated teachers prefer to keep discipline problems to themselves.

All this is helpful, informative, and well substantiated. However, when outlining some of the psychological associations and implications of these data, Rosenholtz shifts deceptively beyond them. For instance, one of the key themes in the social organization of teaching that Rosenholtz associates with teacher isolation is what, following Lortie, she calls teacher uncertainty (see also Jackson, 1986). However, the isolated teachers whom Rosenholtz interviewed do not actually *say* they feel uncertain. Rosenholtz, rather, imputes the construct of *uncertainty* to describe the social organization of the teachers' group and of the teaching culture as a whole in isolated settings (p. 4). Here, she uses *uncertainty* to describe a lack of clear agreement, common definition, or collective confidence about effective and desirable teaching methods. In this, there is no problem of interpretation. It is perfectly proper to develop and use concepts in this way to articulate, at one remove, the relationships between the more directly visible elements of a social structure or organizational culture. But the status of the construct as a construct of social organization should be stated unambiguously.

Rosenholtz, however, shifts almost imperceptibly from this use of uncertainty as a property of *social organization* to its use as a *psychological quality* of teachers themselves when teachers are claimed to *feel* certain or uncertain (p. 209). In this way, a perfectly legitimate use of uncertainty to describe the loose articulation of goals and purposes in the social organization of isolated settings becomes subtly transformed into a defective psychological quality, with strong insinuations of individual deficit and personal disorganization. In places, these subtle imputations of psychological shortcomings expand into wider swathes of sweeping hyperbole, as for instance in the following passage:

> Like the oyster that neutralizes an irritating grain of sand by coating it with layers of pearl, isolated teachers seem to coat their irritating self-doubts and inadequacies with comforting layers of self-deception. (p. 52)

There is little or no direct evidence of these less-than-flattering psychological qualities in isolated teachers in Rosenholtz's data. The warrant for Rosenholtz's interpretation of teacher meaning as mere self-deception, over the teachers' own meaning, is not to be found directly in the data. Nor are the psychological attributes of hesitancy and uneasiness to be found directly in Lortie's data either. Ashton and Webb (1986), in an extensive study of the relationship between teachers' sense of efficacy and their working conditions, also use a little interpretive license to describe the way in which "on the psychological level, insularity functions to protect the professional image of individual teachers by placing a buffer between them and the *criticism they fear* they might receive if others saw them at work" (p. 47, my emphasis). Here, Ashton and Webb's allegations of feared criticism are not directly observed but are functionally imputed. Last, D. Hargreaves' (1982) caricature of teacher individualism rests on no firsthand data, but on his application of findings drawn mainly from U.S. research—particularly Lortie's—to the English context. In all cases, relatively sound and well-established findings and interpretations concerning the *workplace conditions* of teacher isolation and individualism shift deceptively into attributions of rather unflattering psychological characteristics to teachers within those workplaces.

It is through such shifts in and extensions of conceptual usage within much of the literature on teacher individualism that problems of the workplace get transposed into problems of the teacher. Some of this author's own characterizations of teacher individualism in earlier writings, it should be noted, are not entirely immune from this sort of critique, either (A. Hargreaves, 1988, 1990).

Translating the meaning of individualism, isolation, and privatism from a property of workplace cultures and structures to a psychological characteristic of teachers themselves has special significance when it occurs in the context of interventions designed to develop collective working relationships between teachers and their colleagues. Such translations of meaning in the context of change and improvement can lead to teacher resistance being interpreted as a problem of the teacher, not of the system. The teacher can all too easily become the scapegoat of unfulfilled change. Joyce, Murphy, Showers, and Murphy (1989) fall into just this trap in their account of a schoolwide effort, in which they were involved, to develop closer collaborative working relations among teachers. Commenting on the substantial presence of anxiety among teachers involved in the project, they assert their belief that "anxiety is a natural syndrome that arises from two sources [including] fear of exposure and incompetence in the more public teaching environment" (p. 14). The roots of anxiety here are located not in workplace conditions or even in any rational objection to what the teachers are being asked to collaborate *about,* but in the teachers themselves—in their own naturally vulnerable skills and qualities.

None of this is to say that teachers cannot ever be blamed for their preference to remain in splendid isolation. It is possible that the kinds of personalities attracted to teaching feel more comfortable in the company of children than in the company of adults. Such heresies, too, must be entertained. It is also possible that it *is* primarily diffidence, defensiveness, and fear of observation and evaluation that drive most teachers into the imagined security of their classrooms. All these things are possible. But they are not proven. Their presence in the data of the studies reviewed here is not strong. They do not inhere in the data but have mainly been grafted onto the data. In short, it seems that the privileged interpretation of teacher individualism as embodying a cluster of implied psychological deficits has little or no warrant. Other possible explanations merit equally serious consideration.

INDIVIDUALISM AS A WORKPLACE CONDITION

Revised interpretations of teacher individualism adopt a different tack. They view teacher individualism less as a personal shortcoming than as a rational economizing of effort and ordering of priorities in a highly pressed and constrained working environment. At the simple and most obvious level, teacher individualism is seen as arising from the physical facts of isolation, embedded in the traditional architecture of schools and in their cellular patterns of organization into separate classrooms. These physical facts of isolation form a second important strand of Lortie's (1975) explanation of individualism, for instance.

However, the workplace determinants of individualism extend far beyond the facts of physical isolation as such. Flinders (1988) helpfully distinguishes between three different perspectives on teacher isolation: isolation as a *psychological state;* isolation as an *ecological condition* under which teachers work (in the sense of physical isolation); and his own alternative, isolation as an *adaptive strategy* to conserve scarce occupational resources. For Flinders, "isolation is an adaptive strategy because it protects the time and energy required to meet immediate instructional demands" (p. 25). Isolation is something that is self-imposed and actively worked for. It fends off the digressions and diversions involved in working with colleagues, to give focus to instruction with and for one's own students. This need for time to support instruction is felt to be particularly urgent given the open-ended, endless nature of teaching and the constraints of large classes, assessment demands, and the like. Isolation in this view, then, is a sensible adaptive strategy to the work environment of teaching. Flinders argues that the rooting of isolation in workplace conditions such as these explains why attempts to eliminate teacher isolation by removing physical barriers (for example, by taking down walls) or by developing psychological skills and qualities suited to collaborative work are not usually successful. They are directed at the wrong causes.

McTaggart (1989) outlines a further set of working conditions that explains the persistence of what he calls privatism even in a specially supported aesthetic education initiative ostensibly devised to promote collaboration among teachers. The disincentives to collaborate in this project, McTaggart observes, were rooted in a system dominated by principles of bureaucratic rationality, which stifled teacher initiative and gave teachers little to collaborate about. Systems of accountability and evaluation at the district level placed basics at the center of teachers' priorities, thrusting aesthetics to the periphery. Curricula and textbooks were standardized at the district level, too—once changes were made, they then became binding. Teacher participation in curriculum development therefore became circumscribed, controlled, and coopted. Reflecting on Fullan's (1982) injunctions to "crack the walls of privatism" in teaching, McTaggart concludes from his study, "It was not the walls of privatism that needed cracking in this school district, but the social milieu and conditions of work which so effectively undermined the confidence and devalued the knowledge, wisdom and credibility of its best teachers" (p. 360).

In these revised interpretations of individualism, the culture of teaching is rooted more realistically in the continuing work context of the job. Individualism is a consequence of complex organizational conditions and constraints, and it is these that need to be attended to if individualism is to be removed. It is interesting that the assumption that individualism and isolation are ultimately harmful and in need of elimination still remains beyond question even here. It is not at all a matter of doubt.

Clearly, although there are important differences between the traditional interpretation and the revised interpretation of individualism, there are also some unexpected similarities. In both interpretations, individualism is primarily a shortcoming, not a strength; a problem, not a possibility; something to be removed rather than something to be respected. The heresy of individualism remains largely intact.

The remainder of this paper will draw on a recent qualitative study of elementary teachers' uses of scheduled preparation time to identify and explore some alternative portrayals and explanations of teacher individualism. In these data-driven interpretations of individualism, we will find positive elements as well as negative elements, things to cherish as well as things to chide. Individualism will be reinterpreted and reconstructed, and through that reconstruction, at least some aspects of teacher individualism will no longer be automatically dismissed as heresy but considered as matters of defensible choice. This reconstruction, we shall find, achieves more than a balance of the ethical books. Through this reconstruction, we might also begin to understand what would otherwise be a seemingly peculiar and perverse finding in the preparation time study: that an important number of elementary school teachers may not really want additional preparation time at all and may not want the supposed benefits for which their federation representatives have been bargaining so hard.

A CASE STUDY

The proposal for the study reported here was constructed with almost mathematical elegance and simplicity. (The full study is reported in A. Hargreaves & Wignall, 1989.) It focused on what for most school systems was a particularly unusual innovation: the recent introduction of guaranteed preparation time within the school day of at least 100 to 120 minutes per week for each elementary school teacher. This newly provided time had potentially significant implications for what was then understood as the culture of individualism among teachers and its persistence. One of the most consistently mentioned obstacles to the elimination of individualism and the development of more collaborative working relations among teachers has been a shortage of time for teachers to meet, plan, share, help, and discuss within the regular school day (Campbell, 1985; Fullan, 1982). A study of the uses and interpretations of teacher preparation time thereby provided a *critical case* of intriguing theoretical possibilities. Would scheduled preparation time bring about fundamental change in the teacher culture, inclining teachers more toward developing collaborative relations with their colleagues? Or would it be *absorbed* by the existing culture of teaching and be used to support and extend teachers' present purposes and practices for individual classroom-centered work, such as marking, photocopying, and the like?

The social world of education is more complicated and less predictable than the symbolic world of mathematics. It is therefore not surprising that the study's findings were less neat and less elegant than its questions. Individualism and collegiality, it was discovered, were considerably more complex phenomena than we and many other writers had imagined.

The discovery of complexity was made possible by the study's qualitative and exploratory nature. Its purpose was not to establish patterns and distributions of preparation time use across large numbers of schools and school systems. To do that with any reasonable degree of validity would have required us to already have a sense of the questions that were important and relevant to ask teachers and principals across a large sample—questions that spoke accurately and meaningfully to their existing experiences, problems, and understandings. When the project was conceived, knowledge of such experiences, problems, and understandings was weak. The key research purpose was therefore to undertake an exploratory investigation of the meanings that teachers and principals attached to preparation time and to other noncontact time, and their interpretations of its use. Here, the project looked not only at specific issues concerning actual, proposed, and preferred uses of preparation time but also at wider patterns of working as a teacher and the ways in which those patterns related to teachers' lives more generally.

The chosen methodological approach consequently centered on semistructured interviews with principals and teachers across a range of school settings. We asked about specific and preferred uses of preparation time. We asked about the usual patterns to the teachers' working day inside and outside school, on weekdays and weekends, and during term time and vacation time. We asked about professional development and experiences of working with colleagues. Lest references to general patterns lead to unintended distortions or selective perceptions on the teachers' part, we also asked specific questions about how teachers had used their last three preparation time periods.

All interviews took place in private surroundings—often the principal's office or a resource room—and were taped (with the interviewees' consent) and then transcribed, generating almost 1,000 pages of typescript for analysis. The transcripts were analyzed by reading and rereading them to establish close familiarity with the data. We listed emergent themes in the text and then modified and reclassified these as a result of active searches for confirming and disconfirming evidence in the data. This led to important refinements—for instance, the specification of different forms of collaborative culture among teachers and distinctions between individualism and individuality. Summary reports of each interview were then written according to these themes, which led to further modification and development of original categories. As a result of this process, data could be searched and analyzed by theme across interviewees or by interviewees across themes (both within and across schools).

The study was conducted in a range of school sites across two school boards in southern Ontario, Canada. In each board, the principal, a fourth grade teacher, and a second grade teacher were interviewed in each of six schools. Within French immersion schools, where immersion and nonimmersion teachers shared responsibility for a class, both teachers were interviewed; thus, in two of the schools, four teachers were interviewed instead of two.[1] No teacher or principal refused to participate or declined to be taped. The overall data therefore consisted of interviews with 12 principals and 28 teachers across two school boards. In the first board, board administrators whom we contacted regarded preparation time as an uncontentious issue among its teachers and stated that informal preparation time had been provided for a number of years. In this board, where no special initiatives appeared to be taken regarding the use of noncontact time, we hoped to get an indication of the relationship of preparation time to the individualistic culture of teaching under relatively ordinary circumstances.

The data discussed here are from the second board, in which six sample schools were involved in a 3-year initiative to develop cooperative planning among school staff. Judging from the wider literature on teachers' working relations, this group of schools was certainly not typical but in many respects constituted a limiting case in which collaborative relationships between teachers and their colleagues might most be expected and in which the nature and extent of those relationships under circumstances of administrative support and encouragement would be of special interest. The aspects of individualism discussed here are therefore not claimed to be *typical*, but are those that are less expected and less well understood.

THREE DETERMINANTS OF INDIVIDUALISM

Despite its many possible meanings, teacher individualism, we have seen, has taken on increasingly negative connotations over the years. Individualism has come to be associated with bad and weak practice, with teacher deficiencies, and with things that need to be changed. Yet in practice, individualism has other meanings and connotations that are not nearly so negative in character. Flinders (1988), for instance, in his analysis of the closely related concept of teacher isolation, notes that "what one . . . group of teachers regards as isolation, others may see in terms of individual autonomy and professional support" (p. 21). Even Lortie (1975), from whom much of the critical writing about teacher individualism springs, pointed to positive aspects of the phenomenon as well as negative aspects. In particular, he drew attention to what he called the *psychic rewards* of elementary school teaching: to the joys and satisfactions that intensive, sustained, and caring relationships with children bring to the classroom teacher. Not even for Lortie was individualism all bad. With the long philosophical and political tradition underpinning the concept of individualism, things could scarcely be otherwise. Indeed, reviewing the concept of individualism within social and political philosophy, Lukes (1973) has identified no less than 11 meanings of the term, including those associated with human dignity, autonomy, privacy, self-development, possessive individualism, economic individualism, religious individualism, and ethical individualism.

Clearly, when we speak of individualism, we are speaking not of a singular thing but of a complex social and cultural phenomenon with many meanings—not all of them necessarily negative. If we are to develop a sophisticated rather than a stereotyped understanding of how teachers work with their colleagues and of the benefits and drawbacks of these different ways of working, it is important, both conceptually and empirically, that we unpack this concept of teacher individualism more carefully and reconstruct it in professionally helpful ways. It is time we approached individualism in a spirit of understanding, not one of persecution.

Three broad determinants of individualism that were identified in the main study have close but not exact parallels with Flinders' (1988) typology of teacher isolation. These determinants of individualism I call *constrained* individualism, *strategic* individualism, and *elective* individualism. I will review the first two determinants of individualism in brief and then concentrate the analysis in more detail on the third:

1. *Constrained individualism* occurs when teachers teach, plan, and generally work alone because of administrative or other situational constraints that present significant barriers or discouragements to their doing otherwise. In this study, these constraints included noninvolving styles of administration; egg-crate structures of school architecture; a scarcity and low quality of available space in which adults can work together; a shortage of the supply of teachers; overcrowding, with its attendant proliferation of segregated portable classrooms; and difficulties of scheduling teachers to plan together due to timetabling complexities in large schools, the unavailability of released partners in small ones, and the complications brought about by split-grade classes in all of them.

2. *Strategic individualism* refers to the ways in which teachers actively construct and create individualistic patterns of working as a response to the daily contingencies of their work environment. The impressive dedication of teachers to their work, the diffuse goals of the job, and the mounting external pressures and expectations for accountability and for modified programming in relation to the growing number of special education students in ordinary classes—these things together tended to make teachers in the study highly classroom centered in their pursuit of the impossibly high standards and endless work schedules that they set for themselves and that others set for them. Individualism here was a calculated concentration of effort. It was strategic. In this context, preparation time was a scarce resource that could not be wasted on relaxation but, in most cases, it was felt, needed to be spent on the many little things that made up the endless list of teachers' jobs. The same strategic principle governed preferences for preparation time cover—these being exercised in favor of segregated, self-contained specialisms like music and art, which would require no further planning with the covering teacher.

3. *Elective individualism* refers to the principled choice to work alone all or some of the time and sometimes even when there are opportunities and encouragement to work collaboratively with colleagues. Elective individualism describes a preferred way of being, a preferred way of working rather than merely a constrained or strategic response to occupational demands and contingencies. It is a form of individualism that is experienced less as a response to forces of circumstance or less as a strategic calculation of efficient investment of time and energy than as a preferred form of professional action for all or part of one's work. Of course, in practice, voluntary choice and institutional constraint are not as easily segregated as this. Choices themselves are often the result of history, biography, and professional socialization. But whatever its ultimate origins, at any one point of action, elective individualism describes patterns of working that are preferred on pedagogical and personal grounds more than on grounds of obligation, lack of opportunity, or efficient expenditure of effort.

In our data, elective individualism comprised a number of closely interrelated themes—some of which might be viewed as positive and some of which might be viewed as negative within the traditional literature on teacher individualism. I will review just three of these themes now and will then assess their unexpected implications for preparation time policy. The three aspects of elective individualism on which I shall focus are those concerned with personal care, individuality, and solitude.

INDIVIDUALISM AND PERSONAL CARE

The greatest satisfactions of elementary school teaching are, as a rule, found not in pay, prestige, or promotion but in what Lortie (1975) called the *psychic rewards* of teaching. By this, he meant the joys and satisfactions of caring for and working with young people—of being in their company. The teachers we interviewed talked a lot about the pleasures of being with the kids. In one or two cases, they preferred to take their recesses and lunches in the classroom with the kids rather than in the staff room. They spoke of the immense pleasure of hearing a child read his or her first word or first sentence. One teacher commented that when children cheered on being given a new project, "that was its own reward." Several were eager to say, at the end of the interview, that although they had been critical of certain ways in which preparation time was allocated or used, they did not want me to think they disliked teaching. Teaching gave them immense satisfaction, they said. For some, it was "a wonderful job." "I think I'm paid too much sometimes!" Even when bureaucratic pressures and constraints seemed overbearing, it was the kids and being with them that kept some of these teachers going. A number questioned the value of meetings, required cooperative planning, and other administrative initiatives insofar as they took them away from their kids.

These psychic rewards of teaching are important. Their significance should not be minimized. They are central to sustaining teachers' sense of self and their sense of value and worth in their work. In many ways, what the primacy of these rewards points to is the centrality among elementary teachers of what Gilligan (1982) calls an *ethic of care*. In this ethic, actions are motivated by concerns for care, nurturance of others, and connectedness to others. It is an ethic that is extremely common among but not exclusive to women, says Gilligan. Women, of course, make up the vast proportion of elementary school teachers. It is in many respects their commitment to the ethic of care that brings them to elementary school teaching in the first place.

In many respects, administrative justifications to collaborate with colleagues often appear to be presented less in terms of an ethic of care than in terms of a contrary *ethic of responsibility* (Gilligan, 1982). Professional obligations are emphasized. Improvements to planning and instruction are stressed. In the face of such demands, what looks like a retreat to insecure individualism may actually be a conservation of care.

Classroom care is often surrounded by other sentiments and orientations, however, which make its presence less obvious and its impact more complex. In particular, care is commonly bound up with other orientations toward ownership and control. Ownership entails more than care, nurturance, and connectedness in the relationships that teachers develop with their classes. It suggests that teachers have prime, perhaps even sole, responsibility for their classes and that students somehow belong to their teachers, like possessions. As one principal observed, "Teachers are a very possessive lot." When portable classrooms isolated teachers from their colleagues, for instance, this tended to make the teachers within them overly possessive and protective about "their own" children. One such teacher said:

> Part of it, being in portables, is you never have team teaching. Even the fact that—this is what I find is the isolation—if I have to go to the washroom, I can't even leave my portable—where, in the school, you can knock on the teacher's door and say "Keep an eye on my class." But you get very mothering. I think even more so out there because they're your family and you have this little house. I don't find people, I don't look at them as being intruders, but there just doesn't seem to be the flow. Nobody comes. Nobody goes. So you become your own little body of people.

On the one hand, ownership can mark a taking on of onerous responsibility. On the other, it can acquire characteristics of possessiveness, carrying with it a reluctance to share what one has with others. Among the teachers we interviewed, this was most overtly an issue when there were threats to ownership, when decisions about one's children might have to be shared with someone else. This happened in several cases when teachers had been required to meet and program with the special education resource teacher (SERT) for children in the class who had been identified as needing modified programming. As teachers talked about this consultation, they revealed the existence of conflicts in the early stages of their relationships. Who was responsible for these children? Who had the authority to make decisions? Power struggles appeared to have occurred over the ownership of special education students in a number of regular classes, although in most cases by the time of the interview, these seemed to be settling down. After describing initial difficulties with his SERT, one teacher summed up matters by saying:

> If classroom teachers have the greater responsibility—85 to 90 percent expectation that the programs will be modified to meet the needs of unique or individual learners—then the expectation must also be there to have available to them resource personnel, someone with expertise, someone that can share ideas, so that the time is well spent.

Notwithstanding consultation and complementary expertise, for this teacher it was absolutely clear where the ownership rested: with the classroom teacher.

If the divisions between care and ownership are unclear, so, too, are those between care and control. Sometimes, it seems we act as if we are being kind to be cruel. Control in social settings comprises the ability to regulate, determine, and direct the course of one's life or other lives and to avoid or resist intrusions and impositions by others that interfere with that ability. Control over one's own destiny and over the destinies of others has both positive and negative implications. The bounded classroom in which the teacher has almost exclusive contact with and responsibility for the development of impressionable young minds is rife with control implications. Indeed, there are elements of the control impulse that attract many teachers to that setting. The following interview extract illustrates some of the issues that are at stake here.

INTERVIEWER: So, what's the biggest difference that you've found, moving from special education to having a class of your own?
TEACHER: Control! I'm in charge. I'm the one that calls the shots, I'm the one that says what goes. As a resource teacher, you're with other people. You adapt to whatever style, method, philosophy the other teacher has.

Care, ownership, and control are in any one teacher's sentiments, often combined together in a complicated and subtle mixture. This complex mixture had important and unexpected implications for preparation time practice, particularly regarding the judgment of a subsample of teachers about the possible drawbacks of still further additions to their preparation time that were then being proposed by their federation representatives. In the collaboratively inclined board, teachers' and principals' observations on the value of further additions to preparation time were evenly divided between support for and opposition to additional time. Of the 10 teachers who gave clear views on the advantages and disadvantages of extending preparation time further, 5 were at least ambivalent about and, in many cases, strongly critical of the impact that additional preparation time would have on the coherence of their children's program, the stability of the classroom atmosphere, and the quality of instruction. Most of these teachers were genuinely torn in their commitments and their desires. They could do with more time, most of them said. But their worry and concern, which overrode this desire, focused on the negative consequences that extra time away from class would have for instruction and for what they called classroom flow. As one teacher put it:

A little bit of concern that I have is it's nice to have prep time, and I do appreciate it, but if you start to take more time away, take me away from the children more, then I do get concerned. Because one teacher has one set of standards that they can do, and then another has another set of standards. I don't think I would like to be away from them too much more, unless it's the same teacher. Even the one teacher that does come in, unless I specifically state what I want, the children don't work as well for her as they do for me.

Another teacher said:

I guess having taught when there wasn't any [planning time], I'm so grateful for having some. I think it's hard. I could say, "Yes, I could use more." But you've got to remember that the more time you're out of the classroom, they get different teachers. And there are three teachers right now in my class. To introduce a lot of kids—when they hit grade 4, they could still have a French teacher, two or three different teachers coming in for preps, their own teacher—is this too much for the kids? Is it too much for the classroom teacher trying to keep track of all these other people? I wonder if I had much time away if I would feel I was losing something with the kids. And yet I could certainly use the time.

A third was more vociferous in his reactions:

As [the time] was increased, I thought, "It's fine." But there's an amount you can increase it to and then you are missing your kids. This is what I said to [the principal] the other day. "It's fine having all these spares, but when do you ever get the kids?" I said, "That's what we're here for. To be with the kids, too."

At the end of the interview, he added:

I think when they're talking about prep time—I had a letter put in my mailbox the other day, and apparently there are some elementary teachers who are in quite a flap because they are teaching 10 minutes longer than the senior school teachers who are teaching [grades] 7 and 8. And they want this justified. They want that time. And I'm thinking, What are you here for? Teaching the kids or trying to find out how much time they don't have to teach them?

In the arguments and concerns surrounding the provision of additional preparation time, one can see how different but closely interrelated aspects of individualism—for example, care, control, and ownership—combine to play themselves out. There were concerns about fragmentation of the program for the students, about fragmentation of their contacts with adults, and about teachers' loss of being in touch with kids. Care, ownership, and control underpinned many teachers' attachments to their classes and underpinned their concerns about classroom relationships and program continuity being interrupted and damaged by too many visiting teachers. Nor beyond a certain point was working with other teachers viewed as being as valuable as spending time with the kids.

Teachers who were critical of additional prep time feared the consequences of the loss of continuous contact with their classes, the loss of their psychic rewards. The combined concerns of care, control, and ownership were paramount. Yet it is also interesting that these teachers assumed preparation time would necessarily mean time *away* from their classes. For such teachers, when arrangements regarding the use of additional preparation time are being discussed, it may be important to develop patterns of use that appeal to and build on these teachers' commitment to the ethic of care instead of threatening it. This could mean, first, that some additional preparation time might be spent *with* existing classes in different ways—perhaps with individuals and small groups (while a covering teacher takes responsibility for the rest)—deepening and extending the commitment to the ethic of care rather than weakening it. Second, schools and administrators may need to consider different principles for developing and different ways of justifying collaborative work relations among their teachers. At the moment, these are commonly organized and justified according to an *ethic of responsibility*, with appeals to professional obligations, instructional effectiveness, and the like. Yet a number of teachers, it appears, are motivated not by this ethic at all, but by an *ethic of care*. The challenge to administrators may therefore be to show in their deeds that relations with one's colleagues can also be organized according to the ethic of care: that care need not be confined to the classroom but can be extended to the collegial community also. Should this become a priority, it would be important, of course, for principals to develop and demonstrate such a commitment to the ethic of care in their own case as well.

Care is not necessarily tied to individualism. But partly because of its additional associations with ownership and control, the two do go strongly together. Many attempts to eliminate the habits of individualism also unintentionally threaten teachers' commitment to care. Some of the reforms just outlined may make it possible to unhinge care from its attachment to individualism and to classroom work alone. With that kind of loosening, it may be possible to change the culture of individualism without challenging the ethic of care that teachers hold so dear.

INDIVIDUALISM AND INDIVIDUALITY

Care is an often unseen and misunderstood component of what usually passes for individualism in our schools. Another commonly overlooked component is individuality. In his impressive treatise on individualism, Lukes (1973) notes how, from Balzac on, many writers and thinkers have more generally posited a fundamental opposition between *individualism* and *individuality*. For Lukes, the first implies "anarchy and social atomization" (p. 8). The second implies "personal independence and self-realization" (p. 8). *Individualism* leads to the relaxation of social unity—the traditional concern of sociologists like Durkheim (1956). But the extinction of individuality, perhaps in the name of removing individualism, creates only a spurious unity: surrender to public opinion (Swart, 1962, p. 84).

In his analysis of heresy, Szaz (1976) fascinatingly describes how its original meaning, derived from the Greek, was that of *choice.* Quoting the *Encyclopaedia Britannica*, Szaz describes heresy in its original sense as an act of choosing, which came "to signify a set of philosophical opinions or the school professing to them" (p. 1). The original meaning of heresy is one of independence of judgment, then. But over time, after its appropriation by Christianity, its meaning took on negative, pejorative associations of illegitimate dissent. By a similar process, the principled dissent and disagreement of *individuality* are commonly presented in the pejorative language of individualism. When what is thought to be individualism is eliminated, individuality may be the sacrifice.

The power to make independent judgments and to exercise personal discretion, initiative, and creativity through their work—what Schön (1983) described as the heart of professional action—are important to many teachers. If requirements for teamwork and collaboration seem as if they might be eliminating opportunities for independence and initiative, unhappiness and dissatisfaction may result. One teacher highlighted these concerns in some detail:

TEACHER: It's being encouraged more and more. They've been through all the schools. They want you working as a team.
INTERVIEWER: Do you think that's good?
TEACHER: So long as they allow for the creativity of the individual to modify the program. But if they want everything lockstepped, identical—

no, I think it would be disastrous because you're going to get some people who won't think at all, who just sit back and coast on somebody else's brains, and I don't feel that's good for anybody.

INTERVIEWER: Do you feel you're given that space at the moment?

TEACHER: With [my teaching partner] I am. I know with some others here, I wouldn't. . . . I'd go crazy.

INTERVIEWER: How would that be . . . ?

TEACHER: Basically controlled. They would want—first of all, it would be their ideas. And I would have to fit into their teaching style, and it would have to fit into their time slot. And I don't think anybody should have to work like that. . . .

This teacher, a self-confessed maverick like his partner, did not approve of sharing for sharing's sake. Indeed, to him, sharing sometimes seemed a way of closing down his options for teaching rather than opening them up. He described, for instance, a recent in-service experience he had undergone, in which:

We were just hearing philosophy. I wasn't hearing any practicality. And I like to see practicality and philosophy go together, so I'd like to try some of the ideas out, so if I have questions I can ask them about it, and I'm not getting that. . . . The philosophy has been that you share a lot of ideas, you get in contact with a teacher at [another school], and you talk about what they're doing there. And you get their ideas and you give them your ideas. To me, that's a waste of time. Why can't we just sit there with a consultant or whatever, and if we're having a meeting that night, plan a couple of sequential meetings where we're going to build up this fund of knowledge. It's not up to the person [at another school] to tell me!

In this kind of in-service experience, he went on, the fundamental questions he wanted to ask were not addressed. He was invited to go and share with someone else instead. He cited another recent case in which "there were a lot of questions, but they were just ramming everything down your throat." This was not only frustrating, but also a threat to his own classroom competence, he felt:

They'll say, "Well, if you have any questions, just let us know." Well, it's fine, but you're starting to go through this thing and you're saying to yourself, "What's the purpose for this? This does not make sense to me, and yet I've got to teach it." When you teach it, the kids are looking at you and saying this doesn't make sense either.

Another teacher described ways in which threats to autonomy had been associated with declining competence and sense of professionalism in her own case. In her previous school, she said, her principal had been committed to whole language teaching:

Exceedingly! Whole language. Totally. All day. You never had a reading group that sat down with a certain reader and a certain story all at the same time. That was forbidden. . . . "Whole language" was the current buzzword, and this one administrator could not allow any structure.

So vigilant was this principal that "you never knew when he was popping in," and "you must not have kids working quietly at the same task." "It was very difficult," she went on, and in the end she simply resorted to survival tactics:

You had to put out the work for them. The kids had to choose. They were all choosing different things, all different subjects, all of the time. . . . And I just found the children's skills were not developing.

These remarks are not criticisms of whole language per se, which does, of course, have many different definitions and meanings. They are criticisms, rather, of its particular implementation in this school. In important ways, this teacher felt her professional autonomy, her power and right to exercise discretionary judgment had been breached. By contrast, this teacher was overflowing in her praise for her new principal, who respected her autonomy and judgment and recognized that she had "solid workable ideas that are effective." "It's a tremendous reassurance," she said, "to realize that once more, there is someone out there who will trust you."

Individuality as the power to exercise independent discretionary judgment was therefore closely linked to competence. Indeed, threats to individuality and mandated requirements to carry out the less than fully understood judgments of others were closely linked to a sense of incompetence. Efforts to eliminate *individualism* should perhaps proceed cautiously therefore lest they also undermine *individuality* and the teacher's competence and effectiveness that go with it. In some school systems, the purge of individualism has become unrestrained, and the eccentricity, independence, imagination, and initiative that we call individuality have become casualties in its wake.

INDIVIDUALISM AND SOLITUDE

In teaching, if isolation is the destiny of the diffident, solitude is the prerogative of the strong. Isolation for many teachers is the permanent state of affairs for their teaching: the base of their occupational culture. Solitude is more usually a temporary phase in the work, a withdrawal to delve into one's personal resources—to reflect, to retreat, and to regroup. Isolation is either a prison or a refuge. Solitude is a retreat. One of the dangers in seeking to halt the pursuit of privatism is that often it is all too easy to argue that we are benevolently releasing teachers from their enforced isolation when all we are really doing is restricting them in their chance for solitude.

Teachers sometimes like to be alone—not with their classes, but with themselves. Not all teachers are like this, of course. Many thrive on collegiality and on collaborative planning. This can provide them with some of their most creative moments. Asked if she preferred to work with a grade partner, one teacher said, "Yes, I do. Because it lightens your work load, and if you bounce ideas off each other and compare, they benefit and you benefit and hopefully the children benefit." Brainstorming and bouncing ideas off each other—these were the benefits of collaborative work for many teachers and were their spurs to creativity.

In the majority of cases, however, preparation time—or planning time, as some people called it—was not at all the best time to plan and to work with colleagues. Preparation time, rather, was a way to cope with the immediate demands of instruction as they affected one's own students. In particular, it provided a way to cope with these demands in the context of internally driven and externally imposed expectations, which were high in standard yet diffuse in focus. Preparation time was precious. It was "my time," the teacher's own time, to be focused on the short-term practical requirements of the teacher's own class. Time spent in other ways—on relaxation or conversation, for instance—was in many respects regarded as wasted time, a distraction from the central task of classroom instruction. Indeed, so powerful was the emphasis on short-term classroom-focused practicality that almost no teachers we interviewed used preparation time for long-term planning. Long-term planning was instead done at home alone in quiet and privacy, away from the hustle and bustle of the school day.

The home or the car were the best places for many teachers to think, plan, and create for their classes. This might not be true for all teachers all of the time, but it affected most in some measure. The art specialist who otherwise thoroughly enjoyed working and planning with his grade partner nonetheless preferred to do his art alone, to create this most precious area of his work for himself. He was more productive and got better ideas that way, he said.

Selfish, precious, prima donnas: these are some of the ways we describe teachers who may often prefer the solitude of their own thoughts to the company of others when they are engaged in the processes of creation that give teaching its interest and its life. However, Storr (1988), in a thorough and searching analysis of the subject, encourages us to revise these judgments. Contrary to conventional psychological opinion, Storr points out that a preference for solitude can display one of the great and more unremarked qualities of intellectual maturity: the capacity to be alone. Solitude can also be sought by those who are in search of intellectual or biographical coherence and who have the capacity to converse with and record their own developing thoughts and work. This kind of solitude, says Storr, is often sought by great writers, who engage with and reformulate their work, or by the aged, who engage with and reconstruct their lives. Solitude for many people also expresses the legitimate principle that, for them, interests and work can be as satisfying as interpersonal relationships. Last, and perhaps most important, solitude can stimulate creativity and imagination. Storr concedes that exceptional creativity in adults may well result from enforced solitude in childhood. However, whatever its origins, Storr continues, once it is in place, creativity and imagination and the consuming interests and public acclaim that they generate can be their own spurs to further work. The chosen solitude of adulthood, it would seem, can be justified even when the enforced solitude of childhood cannot.

If most teachers in a school prefer solitude, this is probably indicative of a problem with the system—of individualism representing a withdrawal from threatening, unpleasant, or unrewarding personal relationships. If teachers prefer solitude only some of the time, however, or if solitude is the desired state for only a few teachers, then a school and its administration ought to be able to tolerate its presence. A system that cannot tolerate interesting and enthusiastic eccentrics, that cannot accommodate strong and imaginative teachers who work better alone than together, and that calls individualists prima donnas and turns creative virtue into nonconformist vice is a system devoid of flexibility and wanting in spirit. It is a system prepared to punish excellence in pursuit of the collegial norm.

CONCLUSION

One of the particular strengths of qualitative research is its capacity to identify the unexpected and illuminate the odd. In organizations driven by bureaucratic imperatives toward goal consensus and conformity, the unexpected is not easily noticed and the odd is all too easily persecuted or expunged. The social construction of heresy accompanying the narrowed visions that sometimes characterize organizational bureaucracies occasionally spills over into the research enterprises that work with those bureaucracies. Broadly speaking, much of the research associated with organizational improvement is concerned with reforming the faith, not reconstituting it.

This paper has undertaken just such a reinterpretation of teacher individualism. It does not claim that all of the foregoing research on teacher individualism and its alleged weaknesses is incorrect, only that much of it is unproven. It does not claim that the aspects of individualism discussed here are more typical of teacher individualism as a whole than those aspects discussed elsewhere in the literature. But it does identify and reappraise particular aspects of individualism that have a different character, serve different purposes, and have different consequences than has commonly been assumed until now. Care, individuality, and solitude, I have argued, have not been fully given their due and have not been sufficiently acknowledged and accommodated by reformers and researchers working to improve the quality of schooling. This paper points to the foolishness of presuming that all teacher individualism is iniquitous. It encourages us to think the unthinkable and actively consider some of its potential strengths before we rush to purge it from our school systems.

NOTES

[1] In Ontario elementary schools that have French immersion programs, the program is often divided into English and French components, each with a separate teacher. Here, the children rotate between their teachers for different areas of the curriculum, usually for half a day at a time.

REFERENCES

Ashton, P., & Webb, R. (1986). *Making a difference.* New York: Longman.
Campbell, R. J. (1985). *Developing the primary curriculum.* Easthbourne: Cassell.

Durkheim, E. (1956). *Education and sociology.* Glencoe, IL: Free Press.

Flinders, D. J. (1988). Teacher isolation and the new reform. *Journal of Curriculum and Supervision, 4,* 17–29.

Fullan, M. (1982). *The meaning of educational change.* Toronto: OISE Press.

Gilligan, C. (1982). *In a different voice.* Cambridge, MA: Harvard University Press.

Hargreaves, A. (1988). Teaching quality: A sociological analysis. *Journal of Curriculum Studies, 20,* 211–231.

Hargreaves, A. (1992). Cultures of teaching. In A. Hargreaves and M. Fuller (Eds.), *Understanding teacher development.* London: Cassell and New York: Teachers College Press.

Hargreaves, A., & Wignall, R. (1989). *Time for the teacher: A study of collegial relations and preparation time use among elementary teachers* (Final research report funded by Transfer Grant No. 51/1020). Toronto: Department of Educational Administration, Ontario Institute for Studies in Education.

Hargreaves, D. (1980a). A sociological critique of individualism. *British Journal of Educational Studies, 28,* 187–198.

Hargreaves, D. (1980b). The occupational culture of teachers. In P. Woods (Ed.), *Teacher strategies.* London: Croom Helm.

Hargreaves, D. (1982). *The challenge for the comprehensive school.* London: Routledge and Kegan Paul.

Jackson, P. (1986). *The practice of teaching.* New York: Teachers College Press.

Joyce, B., Murphy, C., Showers, B., & Murphy, J. (1989). *Reconstructing the workplace: School renewal as cultural change.* Unpublished manuscript, Booksend Laboratory, Eugene, Oregon.

Little, J. W. (1984). Seductive images and organizational realities in professional development. *Teachers College Record, 86,* 84–102.

Little, J. W. (1990). The persistence of privacy: Autonomy and initiative in teachers' professional relations. *Teachers College Record, 91,* 509–536.

Lortie, D. (1975). *Schoolteacher.* Chicago: University of Chicago Press.

Lukes, S. (1973). *Individualism.* Oxford: Blackwell.

McTaggart, R. (1989). Bureaucratic rationality and the self-educating profession: The problem of teacher privatism. *Journal of Curriculum Studies, 21,* 345–361.

Mortimore, P., Sammons, P., Stoll, L., Lewis, D., & Ecob, R. (1988). *School matters.* Berkeley: University of California Press.

Nias, J., Southworth, G., & Yeomans, R. (1989). *Staff relationships in the primary school.* London: Cassell.

Purkey, S. C., & Smith, M. (1983). Effective schools: A review. *Elementary School Journal, 83,* 427–452.

Rosenholtz, S. (1988). *Teachers' workplace.* New York: Longman.

Schön, D. (1983). *The reflective practitioner: How professionals think in action.* New York: Basic Books.

Seeley, J. R. (1967). The making and taking of problems. *Social Problems, 14,* 382–389.

Storr, A. (1988). *Solitude*. London: Fontana.

Swart, K. W. (1962). Individualism in the mid-nineteenth century (1826–1860). *Journal of the History of Ideas*, XXIII, pp. 77–90.

Szaz, T. (1976). *Heresies*. New York: Anchor-Doubleday.

Zahorik, J. A. (1987). Teachers' collegial interaction: An exploratory study. *The Elementary School Journal, 87,* 385–396.

Zielinski, A. E., & Hoy, W. K. (1983). Isolation and alienation in elementary schools. *Educational Administration Quarterly, 19*(2), 27–45.

Part II

COMMUNITY IN CONTEXT

The four papers in this section trace the contours of professional community among secondary school teachers: the claims they make on one another, the "consciousness of kind" they experience (or do not experience), the obligations they embrace or resist, and the mutual support they provide or withhold. Here we encounter roots of community that are both *multiple* (based not only on institutional or individual goals for students but also on other aspects of teachers' work and lives) and potentially *conflicting*.

The papers center on four principal contexts that combine to shape teachers' experience of teaching: students, subject, department, and school. (Absent from this rendering, although clearly deserving of closely situated inquiry, are dimensions of broader occupational community that extend well beyond the classroom and the school walls.) Echoing some of the themes of Part I, these papers reveal ways in which the immediacy and intimacy of the teacher-student relation shape teachers' orientation to their work and provide the circumstantial basis for teachers' professional community. Examining features of social organization beyond the classroom, these papers also show how special missions, subject and departmental affiliations, and dynamics of resource allocation unite or divide secondary teachers and give local meaning to the construct of professional community within individual schools.

3

Milbrey Wallin McLaughlin
Stanford University

What Matters Most in Teachers' Workplace Context?

What about the school workplace matters most to teachers? What dimensions of the school setting are most influential in shaping the ways in which teachers think about practice and what they do in the classroom? Questions about how to improve teaching have occupied public school reformers from the system's inception (Tyack, 1974), and over the years, ideas about what counts for the character and quality of teaching have varied substantially (Cohen & Ball, 1990; Cohen & Spillane, 1991).

Various strands of research and the reforms they have prompted have focused on numerous aspects of the teachers' workplace context in efforts to identify factors that shape teachers' practice and, by extension, student outcomes. For example, the effective schools literature identified five key factors: strong instructional leadership, a clear sense of school purpose, an emphasis on basic skills, close monitoring of academic accomplishment, and an orderly school environment as workplace dimensions related to student achievement (Edmonds, 1979). Somewhat ironically, in this line of research and the policy that flows from it, administrators are framed as the decision makers of greatest consequence; teachers are cast primarily as targets of effective schools policies.

The research reported here was conducted for the Center for Research on the Context of Secondary School Teaching (CRC) at Stanford University with funding from the U.S. Department of Education Office of Educational Research and Improvement (Grant No. G0087C0235). The comments and quotations in this chapter are, unless otherwise attributed, from CRC interviews with teachers during the 3 years of our field research. Respondents are not identified to honor the confidentiality of our interviews.

Other analysts have focused on structural and organizational aspects of the workplace as major determinants of teachers' attitudes and practices. Researchers have examined the physical, economic, organizational, and political aspects of schools in efforts to discover factors that influence what teachers do and how they think about their work (for an analytical review, see Johnson, 1990). Issues such as governance, class size, work load, leadership, safety, authority relations, and supervisory arrangements alternatively comprise explanations of "the problem" and suggestions for policy solutions (Corcoran, Walker, & White, 1988; Louis & Miles, 1990; Shedd & Bacharach, 1991).

Teachers' incentives and motivation have also received attention from policymakers and reformers. In particular, the relatively low pay and status afforded teachers have prompted reforms such as merit pay or career ladders to induce better performance from teachers and to bolster their commitment to teaching (Bacharach, Bauer, & Shedd, 1986). Better pay or reward for top performance, these strategies assume, will stimulate teachers to work harder and more effectively.

Other reforms targeted teachers' qualifications and sought to bring more rigorous standards to teachers' credentialing and preservice training (Darling-Hammond & Berry, 1988). More dollars for and attention to in-service education or staff development aimed to enhance the skills of teachers at work in the nation's schools (Little et al., 1987; McLaughlin, 1991). Teacher evaluation strategies moved to the fore as a way to monitor teachers' classroom effectiveness and to identify inadequate professional performance and teachers' competencies that need improvement (see the perspectives collected in Millman & Darling-Hammond, 1990).

Yet another approach to the problem of improving teaching practices moves from teachers' attributes variously considered to focus on the "technology" of teaching, on the content of curriculum and of teachers' classroom practices, and on student standards. State reform efforts during the 1980s and early 1990s focused on curriculum guidelines and frameworks and tougher standards for students as strategies to enhance academic excellence (Clune, 1989; Clune, White, & Patterson, 1989; Firestone, Fuhrman, & Kirst, 1989). Reforms of this genre strive to bring more academic content and higher standards of achievement, as well as enhanced coherence through curriculum frameworks and common conceptions of practice, to America's classrooms (Smith & O'Day, 1990).

The school workplace has been central to the Center for Research on the Context of Secondary School Teaching's (CRC) multiyear research effort aimed at understanding the diverse contexts in which teachers work and their significance for teaching and learning. The CRC's core research program involves 3 years of fieldwork and surveys in 16 public and private secondary schools located in eight different communities in two states. The CRC sample includes diverse secondary schools—magnet schools, small public high schools, elite independent schools, alternative schools, and large comprehensive high schools—located in a variety of communities— urban and suburban. Our sample schools serve quite different students. Student populations in the schools we studied range from predominantly middle- and upper-middle-class white students to "majority minority" schools that serve both neighborhood youngsters and students participating in desegregation plans.

A distinctive feature of our research is its bottom-up, teacher's-eye perspective on teaching within particular kinds of embedded contexts. This view of teaching and of the contexts within which teachers work differs from that of researchers and policymakers who look at practice from the outside in, considering teachers and their work within established frames of policy or social science paradigms. The teachers' perspective makes all of these structures and relationships problematic and considers teaching in terms of the daily communion of students, instruction, and dynamics of the school setting. A teacher's-eye view sees teaching as an integrating activity, intertwined and interdependent with students, subject matter, and features of the immediate workplace environment. The CRC's research, based on this different perspective, yields a strategically different conception of what matters most to teachers, of the factors that figure most prominently in their conceptions of practice, and of what transpires in the classroom.

STUDENT CHARACTERISTICS AND TEACHERS' PRACTICE

By teachers' reports, students are the workplace "context" of greatest consequence.[1] Students were the basic referents as teachers talked about their schools, colleagues, classrooms, and commitment to teaching. Teachers focused on their students' academic abilities, needs and interests, attitudes, and backgrounds as they explained what they do in their classrooms, how they evaluate their own effectiveness, and their sense of engagement or discouragement with teaching (McLaughlin, Talbert, & Phelan, 1990). To this point, we find that teachers discriminate their sense of professional efficacy on a *period-by-period basis* depending on their relationship with students in each class. Teachers' sense of efficacy is not a global trait, as it is considered in most research, but instead is constructed uniquely in terms of the differences in the characteristics of the different classes taught by the same teacher (Raudenbush, Rowan, & Cheong, 1990).

Teachers' comments about the aspects of their students that had the greatest impact on their classroom practices focused on the cultural diversity of students in their classes and on the demands, difficulties, and pressures associated with today's students. Teachers across our diverse secondary school sites accentuate the difficult world of the contemporary classroom. Teachers see today's students burdened and distracted as never before by various family dysfunctions, peer pressures, substance abuse, pregnancies, demands of jobs or other out-of-school responsibilities, and a general lack of support from family or the larger community.

Teachers in urban secondary schools also struggle to respond to high rates of student absenteeism; gang-related violence; and the needs of large numbers of immigrant children, youngsters with illegal status, or students with limited English proficiency. A registrar comments on the skyrocketing rate of student mobility in her secondary school:

> When I first started as registrar (about 5 years ago), I had on the average 50 kids in and out a year. Now, last year I had almost 700 students going in and out of this school. Just last week, I checked out as many kids as I checked in!

A science teacher, in what could be considered a typical high school, commented:

> It's nothing like it was 10 or even 5 years ago. It's worse, much worse. The kids live in incredibly stressful conditions. Their self-esteem is at the bottom. The pressures on teachers are horrendous.

An English teacher echoes the theme of today's students as critically different from those in teachers' personal and professional experience:

> They are facing different things than I ever had to face. I never had to face busing. I never had to face being completely uprooted, you know, and having my family leave and my mother commit suicide, and being raised by heaven knows who. I never had to face being caught up in such a bad crowd that I had to move to another state or was unable to come to school. These are serious issues that are becoming common. And then our expectations are that kids come to school and abide by all our rules and that they function like we think they should. I mean, it's really tough for these kids.

Such student factors, say teachers, determine the attitudes, energy, competencies, and motivation that youngsters bring to class, and these student factors have everything to do with how teachers construct instruction and consider their work. Classroom practices are forged in the up-close instructional relationships between teachers and their students (Pauly, 1991; Sarason, 1990). This perspective underscores the finding that teachers depend fundamentally on their students for their principal professional rewards and sense of identity (Lortie, 1975; Rosenholtz, 1985).

What has received less attention than this reciprocity between teachers and their students, however, is the *substantial diversity in teachers' goals* for students, a diversity that reflects differences in teachers' conceptions of the teaching task and of the needs of students.

GOAL DIVERGENCE AMONG SECONDARY SCHOOLS

Teachers' goals for students are diverse and contextually specific. The 1989 CRC survey of teachers included an item on goal priorities that captured these differences in schools and teachers. We asked teachers to rank each of eight general educational goals "in order of their importance for your teaching." The goals listed were basic academic skills, good work habits, academic excellence, personal growth (self-esteem, self-discipline), human relations skills, citizenship (knowledge of institutions), specific occupational skills, and moral or religious values.[2]

Teachers' responses were used to construct a goal profile for each school: average teacher ratings assigned to each of the eight goals. A comparison of these profiles for the CRC field sites yielded clusters of schools that represented five distinct goal profiles and embodied teachers' trade-offs among different possible goals for their students[3]:

- Assimilating high schools
- Alternative high schools
- Elite academic high schools
- Typical high schools
- Academic high schools

Assimilating high schools typically experienced significant shifts in goals, associated with rapid change in the character of a school's student body. (In the discussion that follows, pseudonyms are used for actual schools and districts.) For example, one school in our sample, Esperanza, in little more than 2 years changed from a school serving white, college-bound students to a school whose student body is 58 percent minority, most of whom are recent immigrants from Southeast Asia and have limited or no proficiency in English. The challenge that faced faculties in assimilating high schools involved decisions about the fit or lack of fit between existing courses and their students and about the development of new courses suitable for this dramatically different student population.

Alternative high schools also reflect their particular student body. One independent school that we studied, Greenfield, and the public alternative school in our sample, Prospect, serve students who have been unsuccessful in traditional secondary schools. The mission of these alternative schools, defined in terms of the needs of the student body for a personal environment, strong support, and attention to individual needs, assigns highest priority to the goal of personal growth.

Another independent school in our sample, Paloma, represents an *elite academic secondary school.* Paloma is at the other end of the spectrum from the alternative high schools and defines its objectives in terms of preparing its student body for admission to prestigious colleges. Its high-achieving, highly motivated student body makes this school elite both in terms of its academic content and its expectations for students.

These "mission" schools are distinguished by singular characteristics of their student bodies and thus have goal profiles that differ markedly from those of the average U.S. high school. The other schools in our sample have less dramatic or consistent stories of institutional response to the student population; their goal profiles reflect the mix of student characteristics and community expectations evident at the school. Three high schools serve an essentially typical student body in terms of ethnicity, socioeconomic status, skills, and interests and represent the *typical high school* profile.

The four high schools that fall into the *academic high school* category have a more homogeneous student body in terms of student academic interests, family expectations, and socioeconomic status. Thus, they are able to devote more attention to academic excellence and less attention to basic skills than the typical high school is. Even within these schools, however, important diversity of goals exists at the individual teacher level. Most particularly, student (and to some extent, teacher) tracking practices create substantively different student contexts and teaching challenges for teachers within the same school and department.

These divergent goal profiles, drawn by teachers with reference to the youngsters who attend their classrooms, reflect teachers' contextually defined conceptions of the teaching task. But in most school settings, the daily workplace reality is even more complex than these aggregate differences suggest. These school-level goal profiles mask critical between- and within-school differences in teachers' goals for similar students and in the ways in which workplace features generated dissimilar patterns of pedagogical response.

PATTERNS OF TEACHERS' PEDAGOGICAL RESPONSES

Excepting the mission schools in our sample, in which a pervasive and agreed-on school charter and a relatively homogeneous student body generated goal congruence at the school level, we saw that teachers *within* a secondary school can and do develop substantively different decisions about the kinds of content they will cover, how they will cover it, their instructional aims, and their expectations for students' performance and roles. These teacher responses to students comprise decisions about how to differentiate the curriculum in terms of specific classroom realities (Hemmings & Metz, 1990).

As we observed teachers and learned about their practices from interviews and surveys, their classroom responses to contemporary students fell into three general patterns:

- Maintain traditional standards
- Lower expectations for coverage and achievement
- Adapt practices and pedagogy

Some teachers *maintained traditional standards* and continued conventional instructional practices. Nontraditional students often failed in these classrooms; their teachers expressed cynicism about today's youth and about teaching and frustration at their lot. An English teacher proud of the literature curriculum that she had built over the years said:

> I never had this much trouble teaching Julius Caesar in the past. During the past few years, it's been worse, but never this bad in terms of students' failures. I don't know if I can go on with this. I am on my way out.

Commenting on the year ahead, a traditional social studies teacher in one of our assimilating secondary schools said:

> I don't know what's going to happen except that they're just going to have a miserable year and fail, and I'll have a miserable year. Everything's miserable. Folks just won't admit that we need to be more attentive and not put these kids in regular classes . . . that's not to put kids in boxes, but in all honesty, we know they can't make it. They just don't know how to pay attention, how to sit, even 2 or 3 minutes at a time. And the willingness. . . .

Other teachers *changed expectations* for many of today's students, lowering standards of coverage and achievement or "dumbing down" the curriculum. Whether motivated by best intentions for their students (for example, preserving students' self-esteem) or by disrespect for their students' motivation and ability ("I don't want to teach those kids! I don't want to be saddled with them!"), both students and teachers disengaged in these classroom settings. Many teachers with whom we spoke agonized over these responses:

> I will do whatever I can to get their grades up, to have them feel better about themselves . . . sometimes to the point that I think I am rescuing them instead of enabling them. But then if I had the kind of home life that some of these kids have, maybe I'd want a teacher to not be so rigid, you know? There's a fine line between instilling responsibility and being flexible and teaching them what they need to know to be able to negotiate.

Other teachers, who believed that their students could not handle academic work, exempted themselves from having to teach it. A social studies teacher with more than 25 years' experience commented:

> I can say with a lot of confidence [that changes in students today] have changed the idea of teaching from academic orientation to survival. . . . And the idea of lecturing—I hear fewer and fewer people are even trying it. It's more hand out, do this, do that. Unfortunately, this gets misconstrued as a laziness on the part of the teachers, but this is not the case. It is a question of pragmatism. You're doing what you can do with the clientele you have. I spend perhaps an entire semester using a book that I used to open in a sophomore class for maybe a couple or three weeks. And now it's a semester. You just can't do much more.

Students learned less in these classrooms because they were exposed to less, and teachers derived fewer rewards from their practice. Dispirited instructional settings such as these have been called a "classroom conspiracy between alienated students and equally disaffected teachers [and the] major source of the bad pedagogy that pervades so many of the nation's public schools, especially in bottom-track courses" (Toch, 1991, p. 243; see also Sedlak, Wheeler, Pullin, & Cusick, 1986).

Whether choosing to enforce traditional ways of doing things or electing to lower expectations, teachers who adhered to these conceptions of practice tended to bitterness and on-the-job retirement. They located the problem of the contemporary classroom almost entirely in the student and generally felt that things would only get worse in terms of students' academic interests and accomplishments and their own professional satisfaction and sense of effectiveness. This social studies teacher's assessment is typical:

> It's a harder job, and you get less out of it. And that's why—that's why everyone would love to be retired. Not because they just want to sit home and watch soap operas, you know, but just so you don't have to do this anymore. It's just so hard, just so hard managing. [Teachers] would rather go to work at the [local hardware store] and manage nails. Nails are easy to manage. Teenagers in the 1990s are hard . . . there is so little payoff. I don't think there is one teacher in a hundred who would say [he or she likes this job].

A third general response to the challenges of teaching in contemporary classrooms involved *changed practices.* This response framed the problem of effective instruction in today's classrooms in terms of disjunction between canonical views of content and pedagogy and the interests and character of today's students. Teachers who had this perspective developed broadened but not lowered definitions of achievement, new classroom arrangements (such as group work and cooperative learning), and construction of an active role for student learners. Such changes are almost always difficult, especially for veteran teachers:

> A lot of the stress [that teachers] deal with is self-imposed, trying to deal with different kinds of problems than we have ever confronted before. I have to make some fundamental changes in what I do. For example, I never used to want to have kids work together because I was afraid all they would do was copy. Now I see that by just talking with each other, some of the minority kids are able to ascertain some of the concepts better. I have made all sorts of changes in how I run my classroom. Five years ago, I never would have done that. But, you know, when you see that somebody's trying to meet you halfway in terms of accomplishment—when they're trying to learn what you [are trying to teach]—you know you have to make some changes.

The consequences of teachers' attempts to rethink and adapt their practices to better meet the needs of today's students differed critically. Students, most especially nontraditional students, generally prospered in these classrooms (McLaughlin, Talbert, & Phelan, 1990; Phelan, Davidson, & Cao, 1991). These teachers recognized the enormous challenges of their culturally diverse student body and were highly critical of their colleagues who were, in their view, insensitive to the particular needs of ethnic minority or immigrant students. For example, an angry English as a second language (ESL) teacher comments:

> We've got a tremendous amount of work to do on insensitivity among teachers, who still flunk these kids, [who don't think they can do the work. School] doesn't work the same way with these kids. But many teachers don't see the inside of these students as truly intelligent, giving—you know, good kids. They think they are the baddest, the leftovers, the scum.

Outcomes for teachers who attempted to rethink their strategies in terms of the contemporary situation and make changes in their classroom activities varied substantially. In many settings, teachers were exhausted by their efforts; they either resorted to a kind of triage, finally selecting specific students with whom they would work closely and essentially leaving others to their own devices, or left teaching altogether. For example, a weary English teacher told us:

> I get so frustrated. If there is a word that describes me, that's it. I've only got so much energy. I can't just go, go, go. And I just had to say, "Okay, these are the ones who are going to get the attention." I just have to draw a line somewhere with regard to my work.

Such exhaustion and frustration were not always a consequence of efforts to respond to today's students with new practices, however. Some teachers reported not exhaustion, but exhilaration and satisfaction as a result of efforts to respond to today's students. A math teacher with 30 years' tenure of teaching in an assimilating high school said:

> To be honest, I was ready to retire and was really bored with teaching until we tackled the problem of being more effective with the kids we see today. The planning, the discussions, the challenges . . . I am excited and turned on again. It is like a renaissance in my teaching.

Or a teacher in a challenging alternative high school setting said:

> We all work together to meet the needs of our kids. It is exhausting, but it also is a high. How often do you get to be a hero? We

know we are reaching these kids; we know we are making a difference. And it requires our own growth and change, too.

What made a difference in teachers' responses to students? Why did some teachers elect to maintain standards? To dumb down? Or to revise practice? Why were some teachers burned out and discouraged, while others were energized and hopeful? The critical point to stress here is that teachers *within the same school or even within the same department developed different responses to similar students depending on the character of their collegial environment.* Which response a teacher chose was a product of his or her conception of task as framed and supported by a particular school or department community.

WORKPLACE FACTORS THAT SHAPE TEACHERS' RESPONSES TO STUDENTS

Workplace factors that influence the ways in which teachers respond to students and the ways in which teachers think about their work operate at both school and department levels. The nature of these workplace factors depends on school mission, departmental structure, and patterns of communication.

SCHOOL-LEVEL DIFFERENCES

Two dimensions of the school-level workplace that play an important part in the responses to students that teachers develop are the extent to which teaching objectives fit with dominant school-level conceptions of goals for students and the extent to which supports exist for practice as teachers conceive it. For example, teachers who work with the ethnic minority students transported to affluent Onyx Ridge High School as part of a desegregation effort complained of insufficient support for their efforts to address basic skills and personal growth goals within the school's controlling mission of academic achievement for the majority college-bound student body. Teachers who work with this nontraditional student population felt that their efforts were neither valued nor understood at the school level. For example:

> I think there is a tremendous reluctance to address any improvement in areas having to do with lower-achieving kids or ethnic diversification. It doesn't happen here. This school is concerned with keeping a pristine reputation and doesn't want to address the fact that some of the kids are racist, that some of the teachers are

racist, that kids [who come from the other side of the city] don't feel like they are being encouraged.

At Scholastic, an academic magnet school, teachers whose classes are filled with minority youngsters from the neighborhood, rather than majority students transported from a wealthy section of the city for purposes of racial integration, express similar concerns. Their students typically have limited English proficiency and low academic skills, based on prior education. Goals for these students are framed in terms of basic skills development and personal development objectives that stand in marked contrast to those of colleagues who teach advanced courses and focus on the academic accomplishments of their academically talented students. Scholastic serves two very different student populations, yet academic excellence defines the magnet mission. Teachers with other objectives feel cut off and deprived of the extra resources and assistance that poured into the school to build a strong academic program.

Teachers in such workplace environments report that general lack of support at the school level often forces them to retreat from the practices and objectives they would like to pursue for their students and instead to focus on activities that are less demanding in terms of personal resources and workplace supports. These experiences caution that when teacher-student relations are forged under conditions that are alienating for teachers, few teachers will extend themselves—or will continue to do so.

In secondary schools in which the student population comprises primarily students who bring all of the challenges of today's economic, demographic, familial, and community realities to the classroom, teachers' goals for students can differ significantly depending on the presence or absence of problem-solving structures at the school level. For example, Valley, one of the schools that we labeled an assimilating high school, lacks a coherent or positive school-level professional community, problem-solving structures, or opportunities for rethinking practice.

Teachers at Valley High School have seen their student body change dramatically in recent years, from primarily majority college-attending students to ethnic minority students bused across town. The absence of effective organizational supports at Valley is exacerbated by the incongruence between the school's mission as remembered and the reality of most teachers' classrooms. Many teachers at Valley, upset and embittered, see the failures of their classrooms in terms of the new students and defend their traditional practices in terms of professional principles and standards. For example, a veteran mathematics teacher complained:

Oh, man, you sit here and you think, How can anyone be this damn stupid? What [policymakers] have got to do is work on the kids, not [the curriculum, and so on]. They just keep churning and churning at the end of the material. They never churn at the end of the students . . . but the kids here are where the problem is today. There's nothing wrong with the curriculum. If I could just get people who wanted to learn, I would teach and everything would be wonderful.

This same teacher, who had both advanced placement courses and basic math courses, requested lower-level classes for the upcoming academic year so he "wouldn't have to do so much preparation for the lesser kids." He maintained standards with a vengeance, regularly ejecting students from his classes and awarding a preponderance of Ds and Fs. This teacher's talk, like that of other teachers who shared his view of students as the problem, was filled with military metaphors—combat pay, front line, kick butt, line of fire—which reflect his general view of the classroom as a battlefield.

There are no effective school-level structures for solving problems or sharing information at Valley. Teachers have no way of knowing about the experiences of their problem students in other classes or in other areas of school life, except when individual teachers initiate a focused inquiry. Teachers' personal beliefs about the needs and abilities of their students and about best practice or even feasible practice largely go unchallenged and unexamined at Valley. Even departments are only marginally supportive environments. Most of Valley's department chairs decline to hold meetings beyond the mandated semester gathering. By their own report, chairs occupy effectively symbolic, bureaucratic positions for want of effective authority or school-level leadership.

Esperanza High School provides an illuminating, strategic contrast to Valley. Esperanza, an organizational match for Valley in many ways, is approximately the same size, has a similar academic tradition, and faces similar challenges from today's ethnically diverse student body with limited English proficiency. Like Valley's faculty, most teachers at Esperanza were teaching advanced placement and other college preparatory classes only 3 years ago. Unlike the demoralized Valley faculty, however, the majority of Esperanza's faculty express excitement about plans for new courses and engage in continuing discussion with colleagues and school administrators about how best to serve its new student body. A math teacher noted:

We have a supercompetent faculty here, and everyone who works with us says that. And there's a can-do sense. We can fix this problem. Let's roll up our sleeves and figure it out and go to work on it.

A paramount difference between these schools lies not in faculty talent or professionalism, but in the school-level structures set up to foster planning and problem solving and the consequent development of a supportive school-level professional community and opportunities for reflection. Whereas most of Valley's faculty feel helpless and alone facing their changed classroom contexts, many of Esperanza's faculty feel both stimulated to examine their practices and a part of a collective effort to fashion effective responses. Whereas many of Esperanza's faculty recognize the need to examine and to change traditional practices in light of the students they teach today, many of Valley's faculty continue entrenched routines and cling to canonical conceptions of practice and standards, even though they are incongruent with Valley's current student body. Valley's mission is stuck on old student contexts and fails to align with many teachers' classroom-based realities and needs for support. This discrepancy dampens energy for change at Valley and feeds frustration and pessimism. At Esperanza, however, explicit attention to changing the school mission has energized faculty and fueled efforts to develop new practices.

DEPARTMENT-LEVEL DIFFERENCES

Equally powerful if not more so than these school-level influences are the influences of department and of the professional community it embodies. Positive, supportive collegial relations comprise an acknowledged, important role in the Byzantine world of schools in which teachers are segregated by assignment and by physical space (Grant, 1988; Lieberman, 1990; Little, 1982; Rosenholtz, 1989). Yet beyond breaching professional and personal isolation, we saw that the nature of collegial relations and the up-close professional community in which teachers operate played a critical role in determining the ways in which teachers thought about classroom practices. For most of the secondary schools we studied, the department was the professional community of greatest significance to teachers' norms of practice, conceptions of task, and attitudes toward teaching and students (Siskin, 1990). Further, we saw that the character of the departmental professional community varied significantly within the school. For example, Figure 3.1 illustrates the significant differences in departmental collegiality within a high school even though the mean collegiality score for the school is above the national average. This substantial variation means that teachers who work literally across the hall from one another but work in different departments experience their workplace in critically different ways. For example, teachers who work in the highly collegial department 01 experience a workplace buzzing with daily conversations about joint projects, new materials to share, and plans for next week, next

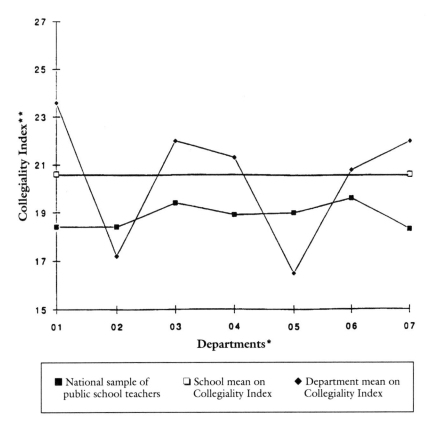

Figure 3.1. *Department variation in collegiality at site 10.* *Subject areas are represented by codes to protect the anonymity of teachers' responses to collegiality questionnaire items. Means are plotted only for departments with ≥5 teacher scores. **The collegiality index combines five survey items to construct a 5–30 scale.

year, or tomorrow. Teachers in department 02 interact only in mandated department meetings, where they generally sit in sullen silence through the chair's announcements and pronouncements. So noncollegial is this department that faculty members have been unable in a year to craft a vision of instructional goals to guide the department's response to the new state frameworks. Within-school differences in department culture and collegiality were evident in all but the mission schools in our sample.

The character of the up-close department community—its norms of collegiality, of practice, or of professionalism—has much to do with how teachers respond to students and how they construct their practice: whether they choose to maintain traditional standards, to adjust expectations and content, or attempt to change practices in ways that enhance students' learning and classroom role. Our 1991 survey data show that professional communities that are cohesive, highly collegial environments are also settings in which teachers report a high level of innovativeness, high levels of energy and enthusiasm, and support for personal growth and learning. Teachers who belong to communities of this sort also report a high level of commitment to teaching and to *all* of the students with whom they work. These features characterize department communities such as department 01 in Figure 3.1, in which teachers struggle collectively to examine their practices and to devise new ways of meeting students' needs and of supporting one another in efforts to change. In other words, norms of collegiality and collaboration signal more than supportive social relationships among teachers; collegiality, our survey data show, indicates a professional community with norms of innovation and learning in which teachers are enthusiastic about their work and the focus is on devising strategies that enable all students to prosper.

In contrast to these collaborative communities of teacher-learners stand settings in which teachers report strong norms of privacy (and thus low collegiality). In these workplace environments, another sort of syndrome operates. Teachers who characterize their workplace in terms of norms of privacy also say that they see their job as routine, their workplace setting as highly bureaucratized, and their subject matter as static or unchanging. Teachers who describe their workplace settings in these terms are less likely to innovate and to report support for learning. Teachers who sketch this profile of their professional community are also more likely to lower expectations for students, especially nontraditional students, and to report low levels of commitment to teaching.

Comments about the frustrations of isolation were common in professional communities of this stripe. Teachers expressed feelings of having to "do it all themselves" with no help or support from colleagues. A discouraged, experienced social studies teacher grappling with the demands of swift change in classroom demographics observed quietly: "Here you have to do it over and over again by yourself, and you do it every day, forever. Why did I go into teaching? I don't know; not smart, I guess."

Teachers who work in these sequestered and noncollegial settings receive neither challenges to their conceptions of practice and to their assumptions about students nor support for trying to do something different in response to today's students. Teachers who work in this kind of professional community tend to stick with what they know, despite a lack of student success or engagement and despite their own frustration and discouragement. These are the teachers who burn out, who believe teaching has become an impossible job.

Departmental communities with positive norms of collegiality and high levels of innovativeness, learning, and professional growth share many of the features that characterize the strong professional communities of the charter schools described earlier. Like these mission schools with their guiding objectives, departments with high levels of collegiality and support for teachers' growth had an *express conception of what the department was about: a vision.* A vital English department drew energy and focus from a collective concern for writing and the collaboration it engendered. A mathematics department with strong norms of collegiality and innovation established express goals of devising new strategies to work more effectively with the immigrant and nontraditional students who were filling their classes. The energy of critical examination and development invigorated the department and led not only to changed practices but to changed norms of faculty relations. A science department adopted a similar focus and worked as a group to examine their practices in light of the motivations, abilities, interests, and needs of the students in their science classes today.

A word of caution is in order, however. Strong professional communities, by themselves, are not always a good thing. Shared beliefs can support shared delusions about the merit or function of instructional orthodoxies or entrenched routines. This collective agreement can generate rigidity about practice and a "one best way" mentality that resists change or serious reflection. *Capacity for reflection, feedback, and problem solving* were essential to communities of professionals endeavoring to respond effectively to today's students and to the mission schools in our sample.

Supporting collective efforts to address a shared objective in the mission schools and the collegial department environments were explicit *problem-solving structures and norms.* Within the mission schools, particularly the alternative schools, commitment to ongoing problem solving and to examination of practice was fundamental to the success of the enterprise. Problem solving at our two alternative high schools, Greenfield and Prospect, involved intense, time-consuming deliberation about the nature of a child's difficulties and the effective responses available to the school. Greenfield's faculty meetings illustrate collective problem solving and responsibility of the highest order; they support faculty efforts to turn around difficult students by providing information and by framing the problem in terms of the responsibility of the whole rather than of individual faculty members.

Greenfield's extensive and intensive investment in problem solving and in collective responsibility reflects the reality and special mission of the school, and the basic elements of this strategy are evident in strong collegial department environments as well. An especially cohesive, dynamic, and innovative English department meets every day at lunch to discuss practice and to share ideas and materials. A social studies department characterized by extraordinary collegial spirit and innovative practice meets once a week to review events, exchange classroom stories, or even present sample lessons. A science department blessed with a central space has established norms of ongoing problem solving and of discussion of practice, abetted by frequent visits to each other's classes as observers or participants.

The professional communities created in these departments and in the mission schools were also characterized by a sense of fair play and *democratic decision making*. For example, teacher tracking was either eliminated or avoided, if possible, in these highly collegial departments. Advanced placement courses were not the entitled domain of senior faculty, with newer teachers assigned to the basic courses. All teachers taught all levels of content in most of these departments, and all teachers had a say in which courses they would prefer to teach.

When teacher election failed to result in course coverage in such collegial settings, most department chairs consulted the group rather than simply assign the unwanted courses. A social studies chair comments on the many benefits of this policy for both faculty and students:

> I invited the department to analyze the situation in which the majority of the teachers indicated they would "kill" to avoid freshman social studies and suggest a solution. The response was to make the freshman course the top department priority, involve the strongest teachers in an augmented planning team for the upcoming year, and to recruit student teachers to bring added enthusiasm to the program. The department, in essence, decided to construct an outstanding curriculum so that most members would want to teach it in the future. Democratic decision-making turned a potential disaster into a new opportunity for collaborative growth. (Hill & Bushey, 1992, pp. 10–11)

All of the settings that exhibited high levels of collegiality and norms of professional growth made critical reflection a norm and made development of effective instructional practices for *all students* the top priority. Within these collegial environments, instructional practices that were ineffective for students or demoralizing for faculty were not allowed to stand. This strategy made critical review and construction of practice a necessity; adaptation to students was a by-product of this constant revision of practice in the context of a broader instructional mission. The professional community provided an opportunity for content- and student-specific mirrors of practice, letting the workplace *be* a teacher and enabling teachers to be learners. All of these departmental communities established norms of collective responsibility—of mutual support and mutual obligation—for practice and for student outcomes.

These strong communities also created small-scale environments in which human relationships could be formed and nurtured, settings in which information about students served as a resource to practice. And with this scale and the personal knowledge it assumed came fewer rules and regulations defining roles and responsibilities. Teachers who worked in these settings located the sources of their professional control and decision making in their community, not in supposed bureaucratic routines or disciplinary orthodoxies, as did teachers who functioned in settings characterized by strong norms of privacy and individual isolation. The significant within-school variation and within-department variation in the extent to which teaching jobs are perceived as routine and the environment viewed as bureaucratized suggest that the function of rules or management controls are in the eye of the beholder. It is not surprising that isolated teachers, with no resources to support adaptation or change or to take effective control of their practice, blame organizational routines—structures beyond their control—as significant constraints on practice.

Departments and schools characterized by professional communities of this sort—discourse communities and learning communities—instilled and enabled teacher autonomy of the most fundamental and meaningful variety: control posited in the up-close workplace and collegial context and in attitudes of "we can do it" and of collective expertise. Teachers in such settings do not cede their authority to rules, unexamined conventions, or the challenges brought to the classroom by today's students. Strong professional communities establish a locus of control in the profession and locate a capacity to initiate action in problem-solving routines and norms of reflective practice. To this point, almost every teacher we encountered who pursued notions of alternative practices for his or her classroom on a sustained basis, who felt excited about workplace challenges and engaged in issues of practice and pedagogy, and who expressed energy and continued enthusiasm for the profession was a member of a strong collegial community, a community of learners. And every teacher we encountered who was engaged in the active, demanding form of pedagogy called "teaching for understanding," in which students and teachers construct knowledge together, belonged to such a community (see Cohen, McLaughlin, & Talbert, in press, for an elaboration of what teaching for understanding is and what settings enable it). Not one teacher who had evolved this form of pedagogy and conception of classrooms was an isolate.

CONCLUSION

Teachers construct different goals for their students, objectives that reflect conceptions of practice rooted not in the latest entry in the education fashion parade or even in state or district policy pronouncements but in teachers' decisions about how to respond to the students in their classrooms. Teachers are brokers who construct educational arrangements that acknowledge the goals of society, the characteristics of the students with whom they work, their professional judgment, and the character of the workplace context (Hemmings & Metz, 1990).

Not all teachers respond in the same ways to similar students, and not all teachers' responses lead to positive outcomes for either themselves or their students. Teachers' classroom choices are a product of their conceptions of subject matter (fixed or malleable?) and their conceptions of their students as learners (motivated, academically able, proficient?). These relationships between teachers, students, and subject matter are the stuff of schooling. The way in which this stuff plays out in particular classrooms or school environments depends most of all not on factors popular with policymakers, but on the character of the up-close professional community to which teachers belong.

Classroom practices and conceptions of teaching are not predetermined or invariate but emerge through a dynamic process of social definition and strategic interaction among teachers, students, and subject matter in the context of a school or a department community. The character of the professional community that exists in a school or a department—collegial or isolating, risk taking or rigidly invested in best practices, problem solving or problem hiding—plays a major role in how teachers see their work and their students and in why some teachers opt out, figuratively or literally, while many teachers persist and thrive even in exceedingly challenging teaching contexts.[4]

Effective responses to the challenges of contemporary classrooms require a spirited, reflective professional community of teachers—a workplace setting that allows examination of assumptions about practice, focuses collective expertise on solutions based on classroom realities, and supports efforts to change and grow professionally. Strong professional communities allow the expression of new ideas and innovations in terms of specific curricula and student characteristics. Energetic professional communities at the school or department level actually generate motivation to roll up one's sleeves and endeavor to meet the unfamiliar and often difficult needs of contemporary students.

Strong professional communities of this stripe are essential— especially for veteran teachers—to changing norms of practice and pedagogy in ways that benefit both students and teachers. Inadequate workplace stimulation reinforces teachers' propensity to plateau or continue with stale practices. The embittered, frustrated teachers who spoke in these pages all existed in professional communities with powerful norms of privacy and unchallenged sacred principles or personal beliefs. Lack of contact with others who held different views or struggled with similar problems deprived these teachers of critical feedback about their practices and beliefs, as well as exposure to possible responses or alternative practices for contemporary classrooms. Teachers' collective experience composes a rich pool from which new practices or changed conceptions can be fashioned. Classroom challenges beyond the reach of an individual teacher may yield to collective reflection and development.

And for professional communities, what made the difference between communities rigidly vested in one right way or in unexamined orthodoxies and communities that could play this teaching function was the existence of norms of ongoing technical inquiry, reflection, and professional growth.

The school workplace is a physical setting, a formal organization, an employer. It is also a social and psychological setting in which teachers construct a sense of practice, of professional efficacy, and of professional community. This aspect of the workplace—the nature of the professional community that exists there—appears more critical than any other factor to the character of teaching and learning for teachers and their students.

This conclusion suggests that the metaphors of the school workplace that motivate policy and frame research on schools and teaching may misdirect rather than enlighten (Talbert & McLaughlin, in press). Metaphors of school as a formal organization direct attention to incentives, management structures, oversight and accountability, governance, technology, and material aspects of the workplace. Shifting to a focus on the school workplace through a metaphor of community highlights strategically different aspects of the school environment and fundamentally different levers for policy and topics for research. The community metaphor draws attention to norms and beliefs of practice, collegial relations, shared goals, occasions for collaboration, and problems of mutual support and mutual obligation. The community metaphor also draws policy attention to conditions in the school context that enable the community and stimulate the up-close professional contexts that support and stimulate reflective practice.

Moving from metaphors of formal organization to a metaphor of community directs research to examine questions of transforming and supporting a vital professional community. How do strong professional communities come about at the school level or within schools? How can professional communities be transformed from cultures dominated by norms of privacy and rigid orthodoxies to cultures that value sharing, reflection, criticism, and invention? How can communities be formed so that student success is considered a collective responsibility rather than an individual teacher's challenge? The research reported here suggests that the metaphors that presently dominate illuminate less important aspects of the school workplace and relegate to shadows what matters most to teachers and teaching: the character of the workplace as a professional community.

NOTES

[1]Curiously, much of the school workplace literature ignores students. Exceptions are work by Pauly (1991), Sarason (1990), and Johnson (1990). This research documents the ways in which relationships between teachers and their students determine classroom practices and goals for schooling. See also Lortie (1975) for evidence that teachers secure most satisfaction and most professional rewards from successful associations with students.

[2]This item replicated a question from the 1984 Administrator and Teacher Survey (ATS), which was administered to teachers within a nationally representative sample of schools from the High School and Beyond study. Thus, we are able to locate the responses of CRC respondents and schools in a national sample and to compare CRC goal profiles with those from the ATS sample.

[3]The U.S. school averages defined a typical school goal profile and served as a yardstick for the CRC analysis (Talbot et al., 1990).

[4]Nias (1989) develops this important idea. To this point, no faculty in our sample of secondary schools works with a more difficult student body than does the Greenfield faculty. Yet in our 1989 survey, that faculty's rating of professional satisfaction was the highest in our sample of schools. The faculty explains this response in terms of their school community—their ability to draw on the strength of the whole to make a difference, the freedom to act on their professional judgment, and expectations that they can make a positive difference in the lives of their students.

ACKNOWLEDGMENTS

My thanks to Joan Talbert for her many contributions to this chapter as CRC colleague, fieldwork partner, and collaborator in ongoing conversations about the many meanings of the school workplace; to David Cohen for his thoughtful reading of an earlier version of this chapter and helpful suggestions for the next iteration; to Rebecca Perry for careful reading of the penultimate draft and useful comments; and to Juliann Cummer for managing the various data bases on which this essay depends.

REFERENCES

Bacharach, S. B., Bauer, S. C., & Shedd, J. B. (1986). *The learning workshop: The conditions and resources of teaching.* New York: Organizational Analysis and Practice of Ithaca.

Talbert, J. E., Eaton, M., Ennis, M., Fletcher, S., & Tsai, S. (1990). *Brief report on goal divergence among U.S. high schools: Trade-offs with academic excellence* (Report No. R90-2). Stanford, CA: Center for Research on the Context of Secondary School Teaching, Stanford University.

Clune, W. H. (1989). Three views of curriculum policy in the school context: The school as policy mediator, policy critic, and policy constructor. In M. W. McLaughlin, J. E. Talbert, & N. Bascia (Eds.), *The contexts of teaching in secondary schools: Teachers' realities* (pp. 256–270). New York: Teachers College Press.

Clune, W., White, P., & Patterson, J. (1989). *The implementation and effects of high school graduation requirements.* New Brunswick, NJ: Center for Policy Research in Education, Rutgers University.

Cohen, D. K., & Ball, D. L. (1990). Relations between policy and practice: A commentary. *Educational Evaluation and Policy Analysis, 12,* 331–338.

Cohen, D. K., McLaughlin, M. W., & Talbert, J. E. (in press). *Teaching for understanding: Challenges for practice, research and policy.* San Francisco: Jossey-Bass.

Cohen, D. K., & Spillane, J. P. (1991). *Policy and practice: The relations between governance and instruction.* East Lansing, MI: Michigan State University.

Corcoran, T., Walker, L., & White, L. (1988). *Working in urban schools.* Washington, DC: Institute for Educational Leadership.

Darling-Hammond, L., & Berry, B. (1988). *Evolution of teacher policy.* Washington, DC: Center for Policy Research in Education, Eagleton Institute of Politics at Rutgers University and The Rand Corporation.

Edmonds, R. (1979). Effective schools for the urban poor. *Educational Leadership, 37*(October), 15–24.

Firestone, W. A., Fuhrman, S. H., & Kirst, M. W. (1989). *The progress of reform: An appraisal of state education initiatives.* New Brunswick, NJ: Center for Policy Research in Education, Rutgers University.

Grant, G. (1988). *The world we created at Hamilton High.* Cambridge, MA: Harvard University Press.

Hemmings, A., & Metz, M. H. (1990). Real teaching: How high school teachers negotiate societal, local community, and student pressures when they define their work. In R. Page & L. Valli (Eds.), *Curriculum differentiation* (pp. 91–111). Albany, NY: State University of New York Press.

Hill, D., & Bushey, B. (1992). *Building a learning community: The challenge of department leadership.* Unpublished manuscript, Stanford, CA: Center for Research on the Context of Secondary School Teaching, Stanford University.

Johnson, S. M. (1990). *Teachers at work: Achieving success in our schools.* New York: Basic Books.

Lieberman, A. (1990). *Schools as collaborative cultures: Creating the future now.* New York: Falmer Press.

Little, J. W. (1982). Norms of collegiality and experimentation: Workplace conditions of school success. *American Educational Research Journal, 19,* 325–340.

Little, J. W., Gerritz, W. H., Stern, D. S., Guthrie, J. W., Kirst, M. W., & Marsh, D. D. (1987). *Staff development in California.* San Francisco/Berkeley: Far West Laboratory for Educational Research and Development and Policy Analysis for California Education, University of California, Berkeley.

Lortie, D. (1975). *Schoolteacher.* Chicago: University of Chicago Press.

Louis, K. S., & Miles, M. B. (1990). *Improving the urban high school.* New York: Teachers College Press, Columbia University.

McLaughlin, M. W. (1991). Enabling professional development: What have we learned? In A. Lieberman & L. Miller (Eds.), *Staff development for education in the 1990's: New demands, new realities, new perspectives* (pp. 61–82). New York: Teachers College Press.

McLaughlin, M., Talbert, J. E., & Phelan, P. K. (1990). *1990 CRC Report to field sites* (Report No. R90-4). Stanford, CA: Center for Research on the Context of Secondary School Teaching, Stanford University.

Millman, J., & Darling-Hammond, L. (1990). *The new handbook of teacher evaluation: Assessing elementary and secondary school teachers.* Newbury Park, CA: Sage Publications.

Nias, J. (1989). *Primary teachers talking: A study of teaching as work.* London: Routledge.

Pauly, E. (1991). *The classroom crucible.* New York: Basic Books.

Phelan, P. K., Davidson, A. L., & Cao, H. T. (1991). *Students' multiple worlds: Negotiating the boundaries of family, peer, and school cultures* (Report No. P91-129). Stanford, CA: Center for Research on the Context of Secondary School Teaching, Stanford University.

Raudenbush, S. W., Rowan, B., & Cheong, Y. F. (1990). *Contextual effects of self-efficacy of high school teachers* (Report No. P90-124). Stanford, CA: Center for Research on the Context of Secondary School Teaching, Stanford University.

Rosenholtz, S. J. (1985). Effective schools: Interpreting the evidence. *American Journal of Education, 93,* 352–388.

Rosenholtz, S. J. (1989). *The school workplace.* New York: Longman.

Sarason, S. B. (1990). *The predictable failure of school reform.* San Francisco: Jossey-Bass.

Sedlak, M. W., Wheeler, C. W., Pullin, D. C., & Cusick, P. A. (1986). *Selling students short: Classroom bargains and academic reform in the American high school.* New York: Teachers College Press.

Shedd, J. B., & Bacharach, S. B. (1991). *Tangled hierarchies.* San Francisco: Jossey-Bass.

Siskin, L. (1990). *Different worlds: The department as context for high school teachers* (Report No. P90-126). Stanford, CA: Center for Research on the Context of Secondary School Teaching, Stanford University.

Smith, M. S., & O'Day, J. (1990). Systemic school reform. In *Politics of Education Association yearbook* (pp. 233–267). London: Taylor & Francis Ltd.

Talbert, J. E., & McLaughlin, M. W. (in press). Understanding teaching in context. In D. K. Cohen, M. W. McLaughlin, & J. E. Talbert (Eds.), *Teaching for understanding: Challenges for practice, research and policy.* San Francisco: Jossey-Bass.

Toch, T. (1991). *In the name of excellence.* New York: Oxford University Press.

Tyack, D. B. (1974). *One best system.* Cambridge, MA: Harvard University Press.

4

Mary Haywood Metz
University of Wisconsin

Teachers' Ultimate Dependence on Their Students

Analysts repeatedly find that teachers stress the intrinsic rewards of their work (Ashton & Webb, 1986; Jackson, 1986; Lortie, 1975)—an emphasis that emerges in part from the lack of other rewards for teachers. Few extrinsic or auxiliary rewards are differentially distributed by merit or gained by persistent effort. Therefore, all that teachers can control are intrinsic rewards (Lortie, 1975). Still, even their dependence on these kinds of rewards is undercut and rendered uncertain by a host of factors: the lack of reliable, clearly effective strategies for accomplishing classroom work; the difficulty of judging long-term effects on students; and the prospect of collegial criticism.

More fundamentally, teachers who depend on intrinsic rewards to make their work worthwhile are extremely vulnerable to their students. Students can confirm or destroy such teachers' pride of craft. As the results of teaching reside in the minds and characters of students, students have ultimate control over the fruit of teachers' labors. Teachers cannot obtain the satisfaction of a job well done through their own efforts alone; they can obtain them only through the cooperation of their students—the very

The research on which this material is based results from a project entitled The Effects of the School As a Workplace on Teachers' Engagement, supported by the National Center on Effective Secondary Schools at the Wisconsin Center on Educational Research with funds from the Office of Educational Research and Improvement (Grant No. G-00869007).

students they are supposed to discipline, lead, transform, or even reform. To rely on intrinsic rewards in teaching is to build one's house on shifting sands.

At the same time, because it is the teachers' responsibility to guide and change their students and the students' responsibility to obey and follow their teachers, such vulnerability is paradoxical and socially unacceptable. Both as adults relating to children and as professionals relating to clients, teachers are expected to be in control and in charge. Teachers are given authority to demand behavioral conformity. Students who persistently refuse to display such conformity can be disciplined beyond the classroom. However, actually to teach, to make learning happen, and especially to transform or develop the thinking of another person, a teacher must have that person's assent and cooperation. Anyone who has had close contact with a child of 18 months or older knows that although children are socially subordinate to adults, children have sufficient independence of mind and will to make teachers as well as parents crucially vulnerable to their decisions about cooperation. To be dependent on clients who are children for the accomplishment of one's own success is both technologically paradoxical and socially demeaning. But in teaching—or in any other kind of work in which professionals try to change the inner states of people of lower status than themselves—it is inescapable.

Despite this inherent relationship, students may have so many reasons to cooperate with teachers that an observer would never notice teachers' dependence on students. In many circumstances, even teachers may be able to dismiss it from consciousness. Such willing and reliable cooperation from students can stem from several sources. The social legitimacy of teachers' leadership may be so pervasive that a student senses that to be uncooperative would evoke the anger of many significant others. A form of this legitimacy that is particularly common in childhood inheres in many young people's innocent inability to imagine the viability of a disobedient, defiant, or indifferent posture in a relationship with an adult outside their family who is in a position of legitimate authority. More pragmatically, high school students may be consistently cooperative with teachers because teachers exert control over rewards that students are eager to seek.

The rewards and punishments attendant on students' cooperation with their teachers are neither constant nor randomly distributed among the population. At the high school level, especially, they are closely related to the social class of the child. As U.S. schools are heavily segregated according to social class as well as race, whole student bodies differ radically in the rewards they anticipate from cooperating with teachers (Eckert, 1989). Collective attitudes and expectations reinforce individual ones.

In consequence, teachers' vulnerability in the face of their students' interpretation of the role that school and its teachers play in their lives varies widely according to the social class of school populations. The effects of social class variation in schools on *teachers'* experiences in those schools have been too little studied.

This chapter employs data from a year-long study of high school teachers in eight high schools to examine the dynamics surrounding teachers' dependence on their students, giving special attention to the mediating influences of students' socioeconomic status (SES).

EIGHT ORDINARY HIGH SCHOOLS

The research for this chapter took place in eight high schools whose student populations spanned the social class spectrum. They were otherwise ordinary schools in the sense that they were comprehensive high schools with the typical departmental organization and range of curricular and extracurricular activities. None was engaged in any special program of school improvement or teaching innovation.

We visited each school in teams, usually with two people spending more than 2 weeks and a total of about 30 person-days in each school. All the schools were in Midwestern metropolitan areas. Six were public schools, and two were Catholic schools. Of the six public schools, two were in high-SES areas (Maple Heights, Cherry Glen), two were in middle-SES areas (Quincy, Pinehill), and two were in low-SES areas (Charles Drew, Ulysses S. Grant). (All of the names for the schools are pseudonyms.) One school, Quincy, which was in a small industrial city, drew mostly middle-income students not bound for college but with some diversity. Another, Charles Drew, was in a very poor, all-black section of one of the 10 largest cities, which we call the Metropolis. The rest of the schools were in and around one of the 30 largest cities in the country, which we call the City. Two, Maple Heights and Cherry Glen, were in suburbs where the population was highly educated and a large proportion held professional or managerial jobs. Pinehill was in a blue-collar suburb, with a student body roughly like Quincy's. Ulysses S. Grant was in a changing area of the City where income was low, but not as low as in the neighborhood surrounding Charles Drew in the Metropolis. The two Catholic schools were located in the City. At St. Augustine's, the student body was large and predominantly middle class, but at St. Theresa's, it was small and predominantly working class.

In each of the eight schools we studied, we met with the principal and collected a set of documents about the school that ranged from student test scores to faculty and student handbooks and the master schedule for teachers. We then visited the classes of six students, half underclassmen and half upperclassmen, with one high, one middle, and one low achiever in each group of three. We thus saw a range of classes at the outset and got to know a varied group of teachers. We then spent a full day with each of eight teachers of core academic subjects, who were chosen to constitute a sample diverse in age, gender, race, experience, and philosophy. We interviewed these teachers at length after observing them. We used a standard, but open-ended, interview guide. We also conducted shorter interviews with 10 other teachers in each school, chosen because they had special perspectives as chairs, union leaders, informal faculty leaders, new teachers, and teachers in special education and vocational education. At each school, then, we gathered notes based on our observation of classes and on our informal conversations with teachers, as well as on 8 long, standardized interviews with teachers and 10 shorter, less formal interviews. There were 64 long interviews and 80 short interviews with teachers, for a total of 144 teacher interviews. Although our fieldwork in each school was too brief to be genuinely ethnographic, the strength of the design lay in its comparative potential. We attended classes and interviewed teachers in situations that were formally parallel across the eight diverse schools. We could see their differences in clear relief.

It is probable that there are biases in our school sample. All the schools are in two Midwestern states, states that for the most part lightly regulate high school curriculum and evaluation. Because these were Midwestern states, most students were in public or parochial schools. No school served a really elite clientele, even though Cherry Glen is well up among the 10 highest-income school districts in its state. It serves three separately incorporated communities, of which one, Glen Hollow, is a genuinely wealthy enclave. Charles Drew comes closer to the opposite extreme. It is in a strikingly poor, racially isolated area. Although we tried to find a large school and a small school in each of our categories, there was rather little variation in size among the schools. None of the schools was larger than 2,000 students. Only two were smaller than 1,000: suburban Maple Heights with about 750 and tiny St. Theresa's with about 250 students.

There was also some bias in our selection of teachers to observe for a day and then interview. We made a conscious decision, after following students' schedules, to exclude from our sample any teachers who seemed to us to be incompetent. We reasoned that a teacher who cannot handle the subject matter or the demands of classroom management is facing such important difficulties that other factors affecting engagement would be overwhelmed. We tried not to exclude teachers who seemed discontent or in some way alienated, but because alienation can lead to incompetence and vice versa, we doubtless undersampled alienated teachers. Furthermore, individual teachers had the freedom to refuse to be observed and interviewed, and some of our candidates for "alienated but competent" respondents did turn us down.

Our sample is thus biased toward teachers who feel relatively productive and take a positive attitude toward their school environments. It is certainly in no way proportionally representative of teachers across the country. Its ability to inform us about teachers in general lies in the lessons we learned about how processes in the school and the classroom can affect teachers' personal responses to their work. We cannot speak to the frequency with which the varied processes that we saw occur. We can illuminate only the nature of social processes surrounding teachers' work and show the coherence of certain social patterns.

THE PARADOX: AUTHORITY AND VULNERABILITY

Because teachers' work consists of creating rather complex changes in children's cognitive understandings and skills on the one hand and in their developing characters on the other, it is nearly impossible for teachers to be effective without at least passive acquiescence from students. To be fully effective, teachers need each student's hearty cooperation. Furthermore, as students are responsive to each other as well as to teachers and classrooms are small and crowded spaces, teachers cannot be effective with some of their students while other students are engaging in activities designed to distract them or to disrupt the lesson.

Consequently, teachers' ability to control the class enough to get attention to the task and their ability to win assent or active cooperation with actual learning from each student are crucial parts of teaching. The common sense way in which most members of our society—and most educators with them—think about this issue is not teachers' dependence on students for their cooperation but teachers' duty to control and engage their classes. It is one of the universals of human societies that children have a duty to obey adults. Certainly, this society condemns both teachers and students if teachers are not firmly in control of their classes. Principals also expect such control. Lack of such control is the first and most likely cause for a principal to seek to assist or to discipline a teacher.

Not only must teachers control their charges, but they must also set the agenda for the efforts they make. Teachers, not students, are given responsibility for deciding what students should learn, how they should learn it, and how fast they should assimilate it. An audience of parents, employers, and college admissions officers knows what should be taught, in what way, and to what standard of accomplishment if teachers and students are to be considered competent. In this view, teachers who do not determine what will be done and see that it is done are simply not skilled in the art of teaching. It is part of that art to see that students cooperate with teachers' directives and that students learn material in which they may have no spontaneous interest.

If we look analytically rather than evaluatively at the relationship of teachers and students, however, the situation looks a little different. Although teachers certainly vary in the personal skill with which they elicit students' cooperation and interest, there is much more to the relationship than this skill. There are more students than there are adults in a school. Ultimately, the teachers' control depends on winning the students' assent. Students may be persuaded, dominated, intimidated, bribed, or manipulated, but in the end, they decide whether to grant the teacher control.

Fifty years ago, Waller (1932/1965) wrote about the small-town schools that most of us now consider part of an idyllic past and described the fragility of teachers' control in those schools and the desperate concentration of young teachers on the primary task of controlling their charges. Waller understood that students are always able to break away from the control of adults. Teachers' control is a social construction that is constantly fragile and constantly rebuilt. While the individual teacher builds it within the single classroom, he or she does so within the framework of society's structural supports and cultural meanings. If those do not support the teacher's individual efforts, the teacher's ultimate dependence on the assent of the many students surrounding him or her will rapidly become visible.

Writing shortly after Waller, Barnard (1938/1962), an executive in the telephone company, propounded a classic analysis of authority that makes this dilemma plain. Barnard defines authority as the acceptance of a command by a subordinate. He argues that subordinates will give such acceptance when a command furthers the common goals or values on which an organization centers, as the subordinate understands them. In other words, even persons with societal legitimacy behind their commands, like teachers, can expect subordinates to inspect their directives for consistency with the organizational purposes that justify them. If the commands seem to be inconsistent with those goals or if they demand more personal sacrifice than that agreed on between the organization and the relevant group of subordinates, obedience may not be forthcoming.

It is the perspective of the subordinate on the validity of the command and the superordinate's definition of the enterprise that determine action. Put differently, anyone in charge in a relationship of authority can exert control only if subordinates agree that the directives given are sensible and reasonable means to agreed-on ends or are expressions of common values or other bases of authority in a social order. Ultimately, superordinates are dependent on subordinates' willingness to cooperate. As adolescents are at a period of life when they are investigating the limits and possibilities of social arrangements, they are especially likely to test their elders' directives. Teachers, more than most bureaucratic superordinates, will feel the force of their dependence on their subordinates.

This paradoxical dependence of teachers on students whom they must control and for whom they must set tasks that students have little desire to perform was as much a fact of life in the schools of 1930 as it is in those of 1990. It is a classic but not a frequently discussed problem in the teacher's role. However, although it is always present in principle, the likelihood that students will act to make teachers feel their dependence or force them to shape their commands to students' desires varies across time and across groups of students. Students may be more or less disposed to cooperate with teachers, and teachers may have more or fewer resources with which to win their cooperation. There is good evidence that the problematic character of teachers' authority over high school students has been increasing since World War II and deteriorating noticeably within the last few years (Hurn, 1985). Furthermore, the problem is much more severe in schools that serve poor children and children who are not planning to attend college, especially those who doubt their ability to find work as well.

Many scholarly and literary descriptions of school life describe the complexity and difficulty of the task of winning students' assent to learn in a variety of times and places. However, because the public and their peers consider good control a necessary quality of a good teacher, most teachers find it difficult to discuss their travails in winning students' commitment to their efforts. In our interviews, an explicit question about how difficult it was to get students' cooperation generally drew short, upbeat answers. But in other parts of the interview, these teachers talked at length about what were, in fact, efforts to win students' cooperation, which was by no means easily forthcoming. Furthermore, when asked whether teachers changed what or how they taught to get students to cooperate, the majority of teachers answered in the affirmative. Often teachers said, in essence, "of course." They defined this adjustment as a flexible teaching strategy, not as a difficulty in controlling students.

Teachers have very limited resources with which to persuade unwilling students to accommodate to them. Although teachers have a measure of authority from their adult status and their legitimation by the institution of the school, students will always challenge and test that authority in face-to-face relations. An earlier study (Metz, 1978) explored this process at length. Successful authority in a school setting rests on teachers' and students' agreement that their efforts together lead to the education of students. The legitimacy of the school and its staff's authority rest on their contribution to students' education. Students will test teachers' academic and social competence and the relevance of their commands to educational ends. Teachers who pass these tests will receive considerable cooperation from students who are seeking an education. However, although students will fairly universally grant the societal legitimacy of teachers' roles and the good faith of those who play them competently and fairly, they may not value education in and of itself; thus, they may not be willing to expend any effort in its pursuit.

Teachers must then turn to ways of providing students with something in exchange for their cooperation. Those heading for college or for work that requires a diploma at least value education for its contribution to these desired ends. Within that framework, in schools in which students are heading for college, good grades are a powerful reward for cooperation for many, but not all, students. When students at least want a diploma, passing grades bring some reward. But when students do not plan college and have few occupational hopes for which grades or even graduation will provide assistance, teachers have a limited stock of rewards to give.

Sedlak, Wheeler, Pullin, and Cusick (1986) have vividly described the increasing lack of tangible rewards for students that are available to schools whose clienteles want only to graduate. Ogbu (1978, 1987) has described the discouragement of minority students who fear—on the basis of others' experience—that not even graduation will get them a job. The principal of Ulysses S. Grant, one of our schools located in a poor, racially mixed area, gave an account that illustrated this problem. He told us, in frustration, of a conversation with a black student about to drop out. When the principal urged the boy to stay in school for the sake of his earning potential, the boy asked cynically why he should do so when his three older brothers, all with diplomas, were all unemployed.

If teachers cannot command obedience with authority or barter it with an exchange of goods, what about coercion? Isn't it their right to demand obedience and cooperation and to punish those who don't give it to them? In theory, it is. But the increasing number of legal limitations on schools' use of coercive sanctions, from paddling to suspension, are well known. Furthermore, even when such sanctions are freely available, they must be applied sparingly or they lose their effect on day-to-day interaction. Fear of possible coercion is a more effective curb to action than coercion itself. Finally, coercion is more helpful in preventing some disruptive actions than in generating active cooperation.

Given teachers' limited resources for control over students, teachers must adjust both their strategies for control over order and civility and their strategies for instruction to the resources they have available to induce cooperation in both realms. Fieldwork done 20 years ago in junior high schools with diverse student bodies, (Metz, 1978) revealed that the same individual teachers used very different methods for behavior control and for instruction in classes at different track levels. Students pushed them into these adjustments. Similarly, political scientist Morgan (1977) noted very different patterns of control and instruction that indirectly teach different conceptions of citizenship depending on the social class of a school and the track level of its students. Lacey (1970), in an English grammar school, and Hargreaves (1967), in an English secondary modern school, also noted the interaction of students' class background and their track level in shaping their cooperation and teachers' strategies of control. Concentrating on students' side of the issue of classroom diligence and cooperativeness, Schwartz (1981) found very different classroom dynamics in working-class schools depending on the track level to which students were assigned. Track level seems to reflect and shape students' aspirations and hopes for adult status—and thus the rewards that they hope to get from school—in ways that may work with or against their class background, making them like or different from other students in a school.

There is some evidence that teachers' resources for control have been weakening over the last 20 years. Hurn (1985) recently argued that such a change has been taking place with increasing legal constraints on teachers' and schools' coercive powers by courts and legislatures. Furthermore, as the economy ceases to grow and opportunities for children of the working class, especially, not only cease to be expansionary but actually begin to look bleaker than their parents' prospects at a similar age, cooperation with schooling ceases to promise these young people utilitarian gains. As Sedlak, Wheeler, Pullin, and Cusick (1986) point out, the justification for schooling for the vast majority of students in this country has always been cast in terms of its reward in better and more rewarding employment. As that promise fades, so does students' willingness to be subordinate to school officials and teachers.

A spate of recent studies of high schools has found classroom patterns in which teachers turn to negotiation (McNeil, 1986), treaties (Powell, Farrar, & Cohen, 1985), or corrupt contracts (Boyer, 1983) with students, as teachers' bargaining with students for their cooperation has been recently labeled. Teachers lessen their demands for academic work, for time on task, or for conformity in return for students' cooperation. Teachers thus generate resources for exchange by failing to enforce the rules or to make demands that students know they have the legitimate right to make. McNeil (1986) gives the fullest analysis of this process, showing how students' unwillingness to put out effort leads teachers to make fewer demands but also to make the work less interesting as they simplify it. Students have even less reason to become engaged with it, and a downward spiral ensues.

Sedlak, Wheeler, Pullin, and Cusick (1986) summarize a recent flood of descriptions of schools that have documented such arrangements. We saw the kind of negotiations described by these authors most clearly in our blue-collar schools. Such bargains, in which reduced academic demands are exchanged for order and minimal academic effort, seem to reflect conditions in the broad middle band of society, in which students are headed toward nonselective colleges or toward openings for the steady but unselective jobs available in offices, factories, and the more stable parts of the service industry. Most students in these schools were able to do the work normally expected in high school, and they seemed to protect their progress toward graduation and a diploma. However, teachers found them by and large unwilling to put out more than minimal effort.

EFFECTS ON TEACHERS' CONFIDENCE

As we talked with teachers, the abstractions of the uncertainty of teaching and of the lack of a reliably effective technology appeared in the form of human experience, often of poignantly painful human experience. In preparing a presentation for practitioners and policymakers, I used two portraits to convey that pain:

> A pretty young teacher from a European country is teaching for a year in the comfortable Midwestern suburb of Maple Heights, where over three quarters of the students will go to college, many to prestigious ones. She perches uneasily on her chair to be questioned by an American researcher. Asked where it is easier to teach, she hesitates and says a comparison is hard to make. "I have wonderful things here," she says, "many more facilities. The gym is much nicer. I have a tape recorder and a filmstrip machine in my own classroom [for foreign language instruction]. I have access to a videotape player anytime I want it. But I have been disappointed to find the students are just as lazy here. They come to class already tired. The first-year students especially want to know if we are going to do something fun today. Fun, always fun they want. I find this puzzling because I am a serious person and I expect some seriousness from them.

Asked whether teachers in her home country encourage their children to be teachers, she becomes reflective. . . . Her voice grows quiet and contemplative, and she gradually starts speaking almost to herself as she says, "You are never at peace, always questioning yourself about whether you did something right. Asking whether there is a better way. Whether the teaching you have done is really good quality. Your never know whether you have done a good job or not. You question yourself all the time." She shakes her head as she considers such a job for her child, who does not yet exist, and says softly, "No, I wouldn't."

On another day, not far away in a poor neighborhood of the City, for which Maple Heights serves as a bedroom community, a seasoned social studies teacher talks to the same researcher, who is visiting his classes. He is eager to tell about the plan he has developed to get complex concepts across to his freshman and junior students in upcoming days. Despite his careful planning, as the researcher watches classes that she finds to be thoughtfully presented, interesting, and even absorbing from her own perspective, students sit passively. The teacher says that often, as he gets well started on a lesson he has planned with thought and care, he watches students' heads lower on their desks, one by one. On other days, some classes become restless, and he can barely keep order. In answer to the questions of her interview, he says, "You've got to have a relationship where you're fair, and they can trust you, and [they] can have some success. They feel they're getting some progress here; therefore, the guy must know what he's doing. . . .

"They have to trust you to have control, that somebody isn't going to walk over you, that kind of thing. . . . A trust that comes from a person who's serious.

"You've got to get into your subject, you've got to get impassioned about it. And that's sometimes where I lose my temper. When somebody goofs off, I just can't stand that. I called a kid a shithead once: 'Get out of here, I don't want to see you,' and so forth. 'Jesus Christ,' and so forth. And I was quite sincere. And so, I think that builds up a regard, an ethical appeal that you've got to have."

These quotations seem apt not only because these two teachers expressed so vividly the painful consequences of the dilemma of teaching but also because their different circumstances convey the universality of their dilemma. Nonetheless, this dilemma is far more intensely experienced by teachers whose students do not want to cooperate with regular school agendas or who cannot do the work well because of a lack of skill. When children who are unable or unwilling to learn what teachers have to teach come to dominate the classroom, this dilemma becomes acute.

By no means did all the teachers speak to us openly of the dilemma of their dependence on students. Especially in the three schools in which most students were realistically headed for college—Cherry Glen, Maple Heights, and St. Augustine's—skillful teachers often received good enough performance and cooperation from their students and accommodated to uncertainties well enough that the issue receded to the back of their consciousness. In the other five schools, although there were clearer signs of the painful dilemma of teachers' dependency, teachers defended themselves against it in a number of ways.

Some anesthetized themselves successfully—most of the time—like a resigned science teacher from the same school as the second teacher quoted earlier, Ulysses S. Grant, an urban school in a low-income, racially mixed, deteriorating neighborhood. Asked to think about the best and worst things in the last week, she had this to say:

> Well, I really don't know how to answer that. My days, I don't feel, are out of the ordinary. Every day is pretty much the same. You find success when the experiment goes well or the kids are busy. The busier they are, the more they must be enjoying what they are doing. If you have greater feedback, this type of thing, then you feel successful. If I don't—now, today was OK. It really wasn't that bad, but there have been days where it was just like pulling teeth and you felt very discouraged. . . .
>
> The test I gave [my advanced class] last Friday ended up being very discouraging. The period had hardly started when they were handing these papers [in] that showed total lack of study. You don't want to take it personally, but you are immediately thinking, "I didn't handle this material right." For some reason, I didn't motivate them or whatever it was. When you think about it and you look over the test and you think about the past years, you realize it's not really your fault. They are not doing anything. Most of the kids told me when I went up to them personally [and asked,] "What was wrong here? What happened?" "Well, I didn't study, Mrs. Gardiner, I had to work," or "I forgot all about it," or "The fight was on." . . . I suppose you are looking for something to make you feel a little better when the whole class fails a test.
>
> [This week] has been pretty routine. I'm not depressed. I'm

not burned out. Really, if anything, it's going above average as far
as I'm concerned, but there are days that are not as nice as other
days because you don't feel successful.

Some teachers respond to their dilemma with active cynicism, like a
veteran social studies teacher at Pinehill High School in a suburb of the
City, where most parents had never attended college and about half the
students also would not. He spoke of his initial belief in the importance
both of history and of his ability to affect students. But disillusionment set
in at the very beginning of his teaching career. When he was asked how his
ideas about teaching compared with those of other teachers in the school
now, the following exchange took place:

MR. EVENS: We've got some teachers here who think that their teaching
    job is going to save the world. They are world savers. And if they
    don't save the world, they'll probably jump off the edge of a cliff.
    Then, of course, we've got some teachers who don't give a rat's ass
    about anything. And then, of course, probably a whole bunch who
    come in-between on the scale. I think I come somewhere right in-
    between. I like my job, but it's not going to save the world. You see
    kids, wave hello, say good-bye. We've got some teachers, they actually
    think they are saving the world. I know better.
INTERVIEWER: What do you think they mean by saving the world?
MR. EVENS: I'm trying to find some words to describe it. They're here at
    6:30, and they don't leave until 5:00 at night, and they're always drag-
    ging 9 thousand tons of books home, and all this sort of stuff. And
    when kids leave in June, [these teachers] say good-bye, but they have
    the feeling that their job is the most important job in the world. Now,
    maybe that's the right attitude to have, I don't know, but I don't have
    that particular attitude. 'Cause I don't think that I have that great of an
    effect on kids. But I think they think they have that great of an effect on
    kids—that, you know, they take their job, in my estimation, too seri-
    ously. It's important, obviously, but I don't think it's that important.
INTERVIEWER: What do you mean by having an effect on kids? I'd like to
    talk about that a little bit because you said you've learned better . . .
MR. EVENS: Did you ever have biology?
INTERVIEWER: Yes, in high school.
MR. EVENS: You had biology in high school. What did you learn about
    biology in high school that helped you later on in life?
INTERVIEWER: Well, I don't know.
MR. EVENS: I can't think of a thing. I think biology is probably one of the
    most useless courses in the world. What do you remember about biol-

ogy?! Now, if you're going to go on to be a biologist or perhaps a doctor, or maybe in the health field, maybe something like that would help you. What I'm trying to say is that some teachers think that their subject matter is so godly important that if these kids don't get this idea that I'm trying to put across, they're not going to be better people and they won't grow up to be good citizens and mothers and fathers and productive people in the community.

INTERVIEWER: What effect do you think you're having by teaching the subjects that you're teaching?

MR. EVENS: Very little. Very little. Maybe on down the road. But I know that if I would give the kids a test on what I taught 6 weeks ago, they'd all flunk it.

Other teachers who found their jobs difficult admitted to no self-doubt at all. They blamed the travails of teaching on specific others, on students, on parents, or on administrators. They did this sometimes in what seemed to be viable but not easy circumstances. Pinehill, where Mr. Evens taught, was a solid blue-collar and lower-white-collar suburb with a nearly all-white student body. Only 11 percent of students scored in the bottom quartile on standardized tests in the eighth grade, and 38 percent scored in the top quartile. Yet Mr. Marsch, who taught English, was boiling over with rage at students and parents when he was interviewed. Although he seemed to teach for only a few minutes of each class period in the semester-length course he had just recently started, he saw it differently:

MR. MARSCH: This semester it's been really strange. [In] practically every one of my classes, with the exception of my 9th-hour seniors, they walk in, they sit down, they listen, I teach. I haven't done that for a long time. . . . But it's not typical. Had you been here last semester and seen my classes, you would have seen the difference.

INTERVIEWER: What do they do? What keeps you from walking in and teaching?

MR. MARSCH: Well, it's their attitude. I was just talking to a girl. She couldn't understand why she failed [first semester]. Well, she would walk in and sit down—and she's typical of many of the students here, at least 30, 40 percent. I would be explaining something to them up in the front of the class, and she would be turning around talking to her friend about her date last night. And when I'd say, "Okay, Sharon, pay attention," she'd turn around and in effect say, "Don't bother me with your dumb-assed education bit. I'm more interested in what happened last night."

And that's the attitude. Well, if you have an attitude like that, you can imagine what it's like walking into six classes in a day's time and listening to that boring teacher talk about academic stuff that you could care less about. And as a result, a million things can happen. Not paying attention, flunking tests, not making a justifiable effort on any given assignment, etcetera, etcetera, etcetera, etcetera. And ultimately failure for the course. . . .

[And] the low levels, you have to work on the social problem. Just getting them to understand that, "Hey, accept the other person's point of view. You might completely disagree with it. Okay, but at least listen and accept it." They'll have the attitude, "He's an adult. What the hell does he know?"

Why should they listen to me, because they probably go home at night and the old lady's telling the kid to get lost because she's shacking up with some other guy. And the kid doesn't know up from down. So, no one listens to her, why the hell should she listen to her mother or you, the teacher? That's what you face. And it's very difficult to get to the kid.

These words convey some sense of teachers' experience of the problems of uncertainty as well as of the problems of control inherent in teachers' dependence on students. As some of the teachers quoted make very clear, many teachers hold themselves fully responsible for the effects of their efforts even though they cannot fully control that work because it consists of transforming the minds and perhaps the characters of their students. As the European teacher said so clearly, it is even impossible to know whether one has done a good job, whether the quality of one's own work is good. Its result is buried in the minds, characters, and bodies of 100 or more young people. Whether they have actually learned is difficult to see—tests notwithstanding—and whether they have or have not, as Mrs. Gardiner says in attempting to reassure herself, it is difficult to know what share of the credit or blame should be assigned to the teacher and what share to the student.

Furthermore, as Mr. Evens tells us, teaching is future-oriented work. If teachers are to accomplish their ends, students must perform well or act with wisdom and integrity, not just during the year they spend in the teachers' classes but over the many years of their further educational careers and their future lives. The result of teachers' craftsmanship, the product of the daily work that the vast majority of the teachers we talked with set at the center of their careers, is like a seed buried in the ground. But teachers do not have control over whether the ground is watered and fertilized; the students—and all the many other people and influences they encounter—control the conditions under which the seeds grow. Worse, in modern mobile communities, the garden metaphor breaks down because the ground is not fixed or stable; the plants are mobile. They are scattered beyond the teachers' ken before the seed can do barely more than sprout.

Some teachers protect themselves from this uncertainty by ceasing to care about the plants that come up; they scarcely look to see if any green is showing above ground. Others, like Mr. Marsch, find it barely worth the effort to scatter seed.

EFFECT ON TEACHERS' PRIDE OF CRAFT

Consistent with the emphasis in the literature on the importance of intrinsic rewards, we were impressed with teachers' emphasis on the work itself as they talked about their working lives. Asked what were the best and worst things that had happened the previous week, the most common responses concerned a class or an individual's learning that had gone well or poorly—or a relationship with a student in the same way.

Most teachers did not volunteer statements of uncertainty as direct as those quoted concerning the effects of their teaching on students. Yet the importance of students as evidence on which teachers must build their own sense of craftsmanship was made vivid in teachers' answers to a question asking them to name the most satisfying experience of their whole career. There was more consensus in answers to this question than in response to any other. A majority of those questioned told of some convincing evidence of students having learned. Many named students who wrote, called, or returned as adults to thank them for an effect on their lives or simply to compliment them for a good course. They also spoke of encountering former students who were now successfully pursuing careers.

Teachers of freshmen and sophomores were less often rewarded by returning students than were those who worked with upperclassmen, but some of them found rewards in the success or compliments of former students as they progressed into their last years of high school.

The frequent mention of the rare event of seeing or hearing from adults who had been students many years ago as the most satisfying part of a career underscored the lack of experiences that confirm teachers' competence in their ordinary round of life. Although students' success at some task or new insight might be the best event in a week, current students were not fully competent to testify to teachers' efficacy. It was only when students became adults that they had progressed far enough for the effects of teachers' efforts to be fully confirmed. Furthermore, although changes

in students were the fruit of teachers' labors and students were the benefi-
ciaries and in a sense the best observers of those changes, only as adults did
they become fully credible judges of educational quality. Teachers of
younger students had to make do with half a loaf in the testimonials of
juniors and seniors or young college goers about the effects of their early
high school work.

HOW TEACHERS RESPOND TO STUDENTS' SOCIAL CLASS

The schools we visited varied significantly in ways related to social class.
This variation in part reflected teachers' dependence on students and the
adjustments that teachers made to keep students' goodwill and to set
themselves goals that seemed attainable given the students they taught.
However, the variations among the schools did not reflect only this dependence. The communities in which the schools were located exerted pressures on the schools through many channels; students were only one such
channel. Parents and the wider communities surrounding the schools had
quite different ideas about the proper purposes and conduct of the
schools. They expressed those expectations in varied ways that shaped the
school through board and central office directives, through the principal's
interpretations of the best way to run a school for the community, and
through teachers' interactions with the school hierarchy and directly with
parents, as well as with students.

The satisfaction of students' later accomplishments was very unevenly
distributed among schools in the metropolitan areas where our eight
schools were located. Teachers who sent many graduates to college were
provided with a much richer crop from which some might return to show
themselves as successes than were those teachers whose students went
straight from school to the factory floor, the office steno pool, the infantry,
or the unemployment lines. Yet the talent, skill, and dedicated effort of the
teachers were not necessarily related to these destinations of their students.

There was only a slight overlap in the futures awaiting students at our
highest-SES schools and those awaiting students at our lowest-SES
schools. As a result, teachers' criteria for what constituted satisfaction in
signs of craftsmanship diverged between schools. For example, Ms. Etude,
at Cherry Glen in an affluent suburb, told us she was pleased when a former student who had become a Broadway producer took the trouble to
call to tell her that she had played a role in his success. Both Ms. North and
Ms. Colwin at Charles Drew, located in a desperately poor neighborhood,
mentioned encountering a former student as a doctor in a hospital as the
most satisfying experience of their careers. Each was thrilled to learn that

one of her students had become a professional—a doctor—something that might well be taken for granted by Cherry Glen teachers, where most students go to college and a large proportion of parents are professionals.

Not only did teachers come to adjust their ideas of success as they faced different group outcomes at different schools, but many also adjusted their sense of responsibility for students' accomplishments. The principal at Charles Drew complained that some teachers would say, "I taught it. I've done all I can; it's up to them, not me, whether they learn it." She chastised such teachers, telling them they could not claim to have taught material unless they taught in a manner that induced students to learn. We saw more teachers who had withdrawn into cynicism or venial passing of time in class at the low-SES schools than at the middle-SES schools and more at the middle-SES schools than at the high-SES schools. Teachers who did not withdraw often switched their goals, seeing success in the passing of competency tests that tested low level skills, in the mere fact of graduation even with a tenuous record, or in a few students' return to class attendance and reasonably steady classroom effort as a result of teachers' intense personal relationships with them.

The teachers we talked with found their own worth affected by the accomplishments of the school's students as a whole, but even more by those of their own students as a group. In each school, there was at least minimal competition for and jealousy over the school's stronger students. These students' interests, abilities, and performance not only made teaching easier, but they also gave an impression that the teacher had done a better job. At several schools, resulting competition was tempered by informal agreements that all teachers should teach at least one section of the school's lower achievers. Access to strong middle achievers was also evened out at several schools. The very strongest students, especially upperclassmen, still often went to what were perceived to be the best teachers, thus creating a self-fulfilling prophecy. Sometimes these classes went to department chairs as rewards, but chairs were usually also perceived as strong teachers—perhaps in a circular fashion. Occasionally, seniority was taken so seriously in the assignment of classes that the strongest students went to the most senior teacher (Finley, 1984).

The performance of both individual students and of whole student bodies reflected not only their skills but their willingness to cooperate with and engage in the academic work of the school. That willingness varied with the social class of the students. It affected teachers' sense of accomplishment at least as much as did students' skills and aspirations. The outlook of whole faculties was affected by the performance of student bodies as a whole, just as the outlook of individual teachers was affected by the performance of their own collection of students.

Teachers' Response to Students at High-SES Schools

Three schools in which most students planned to attend college and in which the better students sought admission to at least moderately selective colleges had important similarities. Maple Heights and Cherry Glen were public schools located in upper-middle-class suburbs, and St. Augustine's was a Catholic school that drew a predominantly but not exclusively middle-class clientele. At these three schools, most students' skills were good, and most students expected later rewards for effort and good grades. Furthermore, teachers who tried could elicit some intrinsic interest in the material from their students, especially at Maple Heights and St. Augustine's, where such efforts were in keeping with the expectations of the communities and the schools as a whole. The teachers were thus able to follow standard school practice and get comprehending and diligent responses from most students most of the time.

Most teachers worked very hard at all of these schools. Most took home a lot of work and spent long hours on preparation and grading. Also, most worked with extracurricular groups and invested themselves in that aspect of the job as well. Most teachers at these schools received significant intrinsic rewards from this work. Many spoke of watching students' skill development with pleasure and pride. Many said they experienced a sense of accomplishment as students' character and relationships changed and matured with the healthful challenges that the school—and they as individual teachers—provided.

There were loci of tension in all three of these schools. There were students with poor skills or serious emotional problems and teachers who felt detached from their work and made minimal efforts. However, most teachers found the organizations fundamentally supportive of their efforts and most of the students responsive to them. Although teachers worked hard to make their courses both solid and interesting, they did not have to depart from the standard practice of high schools to draw students into the enterprise. The majority of responsive students whom they encountered in each day's work made their efforts seem worthwhile—despite daily frustrations and failures with particular lessons or particular classes or students.

St. Augustine's provided teachers with the most rewarding relationships with students. Intrinsic rewards had to be high to keep teachers because pay was significantly lower than that at public schools. The school had flexible scheduling that allowed and indeed pushed teachers into small group meetings and individual conferences with students. It was also expected that students would be allowed to raise questions and that moral issues would be explicitly treated in all classes, not just religion classes. These expectations were generally realized in the practice of the teachers we saw, and they constituted departures from practice in the public schools. They seemed to work to draw students into the educational enterprise and to cement bonds between teachers and students. They helped teachers to be responsive to students without having to bargain away portions of the curriculum. The strength and positive character of most teacher-student relationships at St. Augustine's were supported not only by a predominantly college-going clientele that anticipated future rewards from high school learning but also by students and staff alike sharing membership in a religious community that strongly supported the legitimacy of the teachers' and administrators' leadership.

TEACHERS' RESPONSE TO STUDENTS AT MIDDLE-SES SCHOOLS

Our schools in the middle of the SES spectrum, Quincy and Pinehill, were the most diverse. The majority of parents in both communities were employed in blue-collar jobs, although until the recession of the eighties at least, many had been well paid. At Quincy, about a quarter of students failed to graduate with their class, and less than a quarter went on to higher education. At Pinehill, nearly half went on to higher education, but most of them stayed close to home at relatively nonselective institutions. Catholic St. Theresa's served a similar clientele in a working-class but declining area of the City, although its student body also included children of members of the church who had moved out of the neighborhood to the suburbs.

Most students entered these high schools with reasonably good skills that should have enabled them to master the high school curriculum but perhaps not to distinguish themselves. Most of the students wanted to graduate but had little sense that their later purposes required more than the minimal effort required to obtain a diploma. They did not show intrinsic interest in what they were learning unless teachers made extraordinary efforts to elicit such interest. At Pinehill, where there was a slightly higher level of parental education and ambition for students, students were more conscious of grades than at the other schools. Often, anxious parents pushed for better grades by asking that their child be moved to a less demanding track or class. In most classes, students were polite but uninterested. In classes for less skilled students and in a few for those with average or even above-average skills, students were not always attentive and were sometimes rude and disruptive.

At all three of these schools, there was some sense that the teachers and administrators were holding a line, trying to hold students to academic and behavioral standards in which they were becoming less interested with the passing years. At small, personal St. Theresa's, the staff was split over the problems that these changes raised. Some teachers thought they should change their teaching approach and the orientation of the school to accommodate a student body that they saw as less skilled and less interested in the curriculum and less supported by home than earlier students had been. Others sought to stress traditional school standards, embodied in dress codes and rules for behavior, and to demand that students cleave to traditional school patterns. The latter group was more powerful, but enrollment was declining. It seemed possible that maintaining standards in this way would mean closing the school in a year or two. Indeed, that prediction quickly came to pass. The school closed in 1988, although suburban parents who had been connected to the church opened a new school with the same name in the suburbs. Simply closing or seeking a new clientele is an option for private schools but is not an option for public schools that have trouble finding common ground between school standards and routines and their students' capabilities and values.

At these schools, teachers were expected to be firm in maintaining order. The task was demanding but possible because most students were willing to cooperate as long as expectations for effort were moderate. There was less pressure for teachers to keep up with their field or to learn new approaches than at the higher-SES schools—and less support for those who wished to participate in such activities. Individual teachers were given wide autonomy in shaping the curriculum; there was less pressure or opportunity for collegial decision making in these matters than at the higher-SES schools.

In these schools, the forms of school rested on the fragile support of students' desire for a diploma, their willingness to behave in a generally orderly and compliant fashion, and their adequate, if unspectacular, skills. However, students' lack of spontaneous curiosity about material offered in the standard high school curriculum and their belief that only minimally adequate performance was needed for their career goals created pressure for them and their teachers to move through the forms of standard school practice with minimal effort expended.

Teachers and administrators stressed the maintenance of good order and cleanliness in the school at large. They also stressed hard work for work's sake. There were systems to ensure that work was completed even when students were absent, but much less attention was given to the substance of students' learning. The vast majority of students were prompt, did assigned work, and behaved in an orderly fashion. At Pinehill more than at any other school, students demonstrated a certain expressive distance from the school. Student couples engaged in expressions of affection in public—in fact, the most public places they could find, such as the doors of classrooms between classes. Students also chattered persistently about their private affairs and had to be quieted for any class to start. The theme of valuing private life ran throughout the community and the adults at the school as well. Students used it in many ways to oppose adults' pressure on them or to express their psychic distance from academic affairs.

At Quincy and Pinehill, teachers made adjustments in the classroom. At Quincy, they tried to "be realistic"; several taught standard subject matter with a practical cast that might appeal to students going straight from school to work. At Pinehill, most teachers and students struck a tacit bargain not to ask too much of each other. The majority of teachers assigned limited homework and did not present complex material. Many teachers routinely set aside class time for students to work on homework and allowed this time to become a social hour. There was a tacit trade of quiet attention to a shortened lesson for an opportunity for time with friends. At both schools, some individual teachers tried curricular modifications designed to engage students' intrinsic interests and also to challenge them, and some used personal charisma or the development of personal intimacy to lure students into involvement with the subject matter.

With this tacit bargain, acceptable to the majority in both groups, neither students nor teachers were pushed to seek possible cures for the psychological distance from and discomfort with schooling that students expressed in their marginal commitment of effort and involvement. A few teachers brought tremendous energy and imagination to an attempt to elicit more active student interest. A few expressed rage and dismay or withering cynicism about students' unwillingness to engage in serious learning, although they felt helpless to break the pattern. Most teachers at the public schools, like the students, limited their effort and spent much time with other teachers in card playing or talk about their private lives, although they might exhibit a mostly unspoken malaise.

These faculties developed good personal relations. They had active social lives inside school in continuing card games and outside school in faculty social events or informal get-togethers with good friends. But they did not talk about school practice in these relationships. In fact, among the men at Pinehill, the subject was informally forbidden both in school and outside it.

At St. Theresa's, where faculty included several members of religious orders and salaries were so low that most lay teachers were there for only a few years due to a motivation of service, many teachers worked very hard to engage students. With a student body of fewer than 300, relationships could be very personal. Some students were appreciative and supportive of faculty efforts; others teased them and carried on a disruptive counter-theme in classes. As already noted, the more powerful faction reacted repressively. Enrollment fell, and the school was eventually closed.

TEACHERS' RESPONSE TO STUDENTS AT LOW-SES SCHOOLS

At the low-income schools—Charles Drew, in a part of the Metropolis that had been black for a quarter century, and Ulysses S. Grant, in a racially mixed, changing area of the City with some black students bused in from other neighborhoods—there was visible, acute dislocation between the skills, aspirations, and attitudes of the students and the routines and curriculum standard in U.S. high schools. This disjunction produced severe problems for the staffs of both schools. The two staffs had different perspectives, were subject to different district pressures, and used different strategies to deal with similar difficulties. Still, both had to struggle to bridge the gap between standard high school routines and the skills, expectations, and values that students displayed.

Drew had a dedicated set of administrators and many energetic teachers who were genuinely concerned with helping their students. The majority of the teachers and all of the administrators were black. Most did not condemn students for what others might consider deviant lifestyles; many were in teaching due to a motivation of service. The principal was determined that students would receive an education that offered as much opportunity and challenge as that of any high school in the state. She therefore stressed the academic curriculum and set requirements for academic courses for graduation above the district minima.

Despite the presence of drugs, gang activity, and episodic violence in the community, the administrators and teachers created a school in which students and teachers felt safe and in which there was not only order but a grave courtesy in the interactions of almost all students and adults. Still, checks of identification cards at the front door and in the lunch room and the presence of security guards with walkie-talkies in the halls reminded one that the environment was an unsettled one.

Many students entered the ninth grade badly equipped to meet the demands of a high school curriculum. Their basic academic skills were very weak; nearly 60 percent of those who got as far as the sophomore year scored in the bottom quartile on nationally standardized tests. The majority of students were deeply discouraged about their academic prospects. The school attempted to help these students with remedial classes and a policy of substituting "pending" for failing grades for a full year for freshmen, giving them opportunities to recover from early difficulties. However, many students still read their situation as hopeless. The all-black community within which most of them led their whole round of life was ravaged by the high levels of unemployment that their city shared with most others. What students saw around them gave them little reason to think that expending the intense effort required to catch up academically would reap them extrinsic rewards later. Approximately half the students who began at Drew did not enter the senior class.

Because many students' alienation was visibly dramatic and even committed students who were eager and grateful for attention needed large doses of technical assistance, Drew's teachers could not see their job as one of routine teaching. They were caught between the severe academic deficiencies and economic discouragement of the students and the perspective furthered by the administration and shared by a large part of the faculty: that the students were inherently as able as any student body and so deserved the opportunity to assimilate a standard high school curriculum. For the sake of their own pride as well as their students' welfare, teachers wanted to teach and help students to learn the "real" high school curriculum, which is offered to more fortunate students across the country (for a more complete discussion of this issue, see Metz, 1990). The issue of skills aside, this curriculum made few points of contact with Drew's students' daily lives, and only the most skilled and persistent would be able to use it to gain college entrance or a good job. It provided few intrinsic incentives or immediate rewards for most students.

Drew's teachers were divided. Many were dedicated teachers who respected the students and wanted to help them. For the most part, they tried to develop personal relationships with students that would lead students to trust them and then to learn, based on that trust. The task was a demanding one. It was further complicated because the formal curriculum that teachers were expected to teach was often beyond the students' skills. They moved back and forth between simple skills that the students needed to work on and material included in the formal curriculum. The task was very different from that of teachers at Maple Heights or Cherry Glen, who could set a brisk academic pace, confident that skilled students eager for college entrance would follow them.

Other teachers at Drew considered the task hopeless or considered it possible to "save" only a few students. The first of these made minimal teaching efforts, simply going through the motions of teaching without serious effort to attract students' attention or to have an impact on them. The latter group taught to the part of the class that was most willing and able to stay with a moderately demanding regimen, and ignored the rest.

At Ulysses S. Grant, students as a group were more skilled than at Charles Drew. About a third scored in the bottom quartile on nationally standardized tests, only slightly over half as many as at Drew. The community was less economically depressed, and almost 40 percent of the students were white. However, the vast majority of students still had low skills and lacked economic hopes compared with students at Quincy, Pinehill, and St. Theresa's (although there was overlap in economic circumstances and skills between this school and the lower end of the students at the middle group of schools).

At Grant, the overwhelmingly white, middle-class faculty, most of whom lived in City suburbs, felt overtaken by events because the student body had changed. It had changed from solid working class and lower middle class to poor and from predominantly white to predominantly black. Neither the district nor the school administration had given teachers systematic assistance in understanding the experiences, perspectives, or problems of their students. They had to develop such understanding along the way while instructing students in geometry, American literature, or secretarial skills. Compared with Drew's staff, Grant's staff had much less extensive and successful relations with parents and the surrounding community. Many fewer had any faith that students' inherent abilities were adequate to help them overcome their deficits even if they could be persuaded to try and were assisted in the effort.

The attitude of the faculty toward the students' future was expressed by the secretary to the counselor responsible for helping students to plan college entrance or seek jobs. When asked for a list of destinations of the previous year's graduating seniors, she replied with flippant anger, "Our students aren't going anywhere," although after some searching she was able to find the list. At this school, when two of our team introduced themselves to a group of teachers in the lunchroom, one replied by saying that we would get an eyeful of the worst there is at this school. Another teacher told an interviewer that a recent valedictorian had been dismissed for academic failure from the local branch of the state university. She produced this fact as a sign of the poor quality of the school and its students, assuming that the student's dismissal had reflected poor skills, not his diligence or emotional state.

Many teachers at Grant bolstered their sense of their own abilities as teachers, in the face of students who discouraged them, by desperately insisting on the maintenance of standards. They graded according to what they perceived to be national criteria. More than half the grades at the school were Fs and Ds. The principal at the school was under pressure from the central office to improve achievement but more proximately to see that grades rose. To this end, he circulated a list of each teacher's average grades from the previous semester. He had hoped to put pressure on those who gave the lowest grades to give higher grades. Instead, teachers who spoke with us about the list and conveyed discomfort were those at the high end of the distribution—teachers whose average grades were in the C range, 2.0 or above. Even a teacher teaching mostly upperclassmen in relatively advanced work thought she should probably be giving lower grades after reading this list. The principal had not reckoned with the strength of informal agreement among many faculty about maintaining standards, an agreement that supported these teachers' sense of themselves as teachers whose capabilities were better than the performance of their students.

Many teachers at Grant continued to make active efforts to teach but made little effort to accommodate their style or the content of their teaching to students' abilities or interests. In interviews with us, teachers expressed enormous frustration with the inability or unwillingness of their students to cooperate and to learn as these teachers thought they should. Other teachers became discouraged and withdrew into routines that minimized demands on themselves and the students, such as showing movies several times a week. Some teachers made adjustments of various kinds to the students and sought to build personal relationships that would support their efforts to draw students into academic work.

Staff resentment of students seemed to contribute to students' estrangement from the school. There was more tension between students and teachers at Grant than at Drew. Although Grant's neighborhood was less economically depressed and less dangerous than Drew's, teachers described several small incidents of physical confrontation between students and teachers inside the school—mostly in the halls or with students who came into classes from the halls. One male teacher we interviewed had sustained a minor injury in a scuffle with a student shortly before our interview; another told us of an invader from the hallway knocking the telephone out of his hand when he was going to call for backup after the invader refused to leave. There were signs that teachers—especially those on the halls serving freshmen, where trouble seemed most heavily concentrated—were uneasy about their physical safety. One male teacher told us that he avoids being in the halls at certain times. A woman was obviously relieved to have company walking through the halls to her car after a postschool interview. We also witnessed some students being threatening in their manner and saw some students enter a classroom and start questioning other students in a menacing way, although they left when firmly told to by the adult in charge.

At Drew, we heard of no such incidents involving students and adults, although we did hear of anger between students boiling up in hallway confrontations. Asked directly about safety, Drew's teachers told us they considered the school and parking lot safe. That they were not simply reluctant to discuss safety issues in our presence was reflected by the fact that we heard many discussions among teachers of safety problems for students passing through the neighborhood. Teachers rarely kept students for activities after dark because they worried about students' safety in getting home.

CONCLUSION

It is inescapable that teachers' work requires them to create changes in their students—to have effects on their students that will leave them different. Sometimes these changes are relatively superficial, as students learn to solve quadratic equations, to put commas in the correct places, or to list and describe the systems of the human body. But if teaching is to go beyond superficial skills—for example, inducing students to think more critically or awakening an active curiosity about a subject—it requires more than a passing involvement between teacher and student. When students are skeptical that more than minimal learning in school will be of benefit to them, teachers must change attitudes reinforced by peer attitudes and community experience before they can expect students to make serious efforts in their courses. To create such changes in students, teachers must think deeply about their teaching strategies and must become personally involved with their students to at least some degree.

Such a task requires a great deal of effort. More important, it requires constant checking of results and corresponding large or small modifications in approach in response to students' responses. A teacher cannot be effective without careful attention to students and to their responses to his or her efforts. This is more true the more resistant the students are. In such a job of give and take, it is almost necessary that success in the task—intrinsic rewards—be valued if one is to keep up with the demands and the cognitive and emotional investments that these tasks require. Good teaching requires not only enormous skill and energy but also probably some visible confirmation for those efforts—and a sense that effective teaching is important and valuable—to support a teacher in persisting in making the investment required. Although extrinsic rewards can doubtless also bolster a teacher's commitment and willingness to persevere in the task, intrinsic rewards are probably indispensable.

Because teachers' work consists of affecting their students, they are dependent on their students both for the actual success of their work and for evidence of that success. Even in the best of circumstances, this inescapable characteristic of the work makes teachers dependent on people whose status is inferior to theirs because of younger age and lesser knowledge. It also makes them dependent on people they are charged to direct and control. Their situation is always paradoxical, even when students are eager and able to learn and the teacher is effective—although probably no one will notice the fact under such circumstances. However, when students come to school mistrusting the institution of the school or even hostile to it, teachers' situations become far worse. There is mounting evidence that, as a group, high school students who are not going to selective colleges—who constitute a majority—see little to gain from high school except a diploma. Although we did not study students directly, both our own classroom observations and teachers' descriptions of their experiences in the middle-SES schools as well as the low-SES schools were consistent with that analysis.

At the five schools that served mostly students who would complete their education with high school, teachers' dependence on students was the cause of frustration at best and deep anger, cynicism, or self-doubt at worst. Although a visiting analyst might say that the cause of these teachers' troubles was students' detachment from or distrust of school, based on larger social patterns that separated them from the school and from the parts of society to which it promised access, teachers experienced that distrust or hostility in a much more concrete and immediate form. From data discussed in this paper, teachers had to deal with students' heads going down on their desks during a carefully prepared presentation, a whole class failing a test on material that had been faithfully taught, students who passed a test giving no sign of remembering the material if it was referred to 6 weeks later, students turning their back on the teacher's lecture to gossip with friends, or even small violent confrontations and a nagging sense of a lack of safety. These problems were only exacerbated by the clear social understanding in our society that adults should be in charge and responsible for all that happens in their relations with children. Part of the art of teaching is supposed to lie in persuading the unwilling learner to learn.

With the partial exception of those who worked with the most capable and willing groups, teachers at these five schools were thus in constant danger of failing not only to get their students to learn but also to have respect for their own abilities as teachers. Their feelings of endangered self-respect found a variety of forms of expression. Cynicism, anger, and self-doubt were the most common.

Two marked kinds of interaction between the characteristics of teachers and students were significant. First, dependence on unwilling students was more galling for men than for women. There is a greater societal expectation that men will be in charge in their relations with the young than there is for women. The violation of men's roles as adults as well as teachers was greater than that for women. Although the correlation was far from perfect, we saw more men who responded to unwilling students with cynicism or anger and more women who responded with openly expressed self-doubt. At Pinehill, where the male and female faculty segregated themselves socially, these gender differences were institutionalized.

The insult to teachers' pride from students who were not respectful and obedient was strongest of all for teachers who held to a form of authority that was more like the traditional authority of the parent than the rational authority of the expert. These teachers were more often men—in fact, most were men from blue-collar backgrounds—but some women took a similar perspective. For these teachers, who did not differentiate their persons from the material they were teaching or from their role as teachers as much as other teachers did, students' restlessness was read as a lack of respect for them more personally. When such a perspective assimilated the teacher's role to that of a traditional patriarchal father whose word should be law, students' disrespect could be devastating to teachers' pride as teachers, as adults, and as men—all three. Such teachers frequently expressed strong anger or cynicism and withdrew from serious effort in their teaching. For women, the results were somewhat less devastating because their identity as women, at least, did not hinge on their ability to control the class. They most often experienced strong self-doubt rather than anger or cynicism. This feeling could lead to diminished effort but could also lead to a redoubling of effort.

Second, teachers responded differently to their dependence on students according to the degree to which they shared or understood students' background and culture. Here, it is important that minority teachers in schools with minority student bodies were much less likely than majority teachers to regard their students as morally tainted with the values of what teachers regarded as an illegitimate community lifestyle (Hemmings & Metz, 1990). They understood or even sympathized with students' skepticism about school as a whole and about a style of teaching that was foreign to them. Often they were able, in fact, to elicit better cooperation and more diligence from students than were other teachers. Although they also were often frustrated with students' behavior, skills, and progress, they understood enough of the roots of students' resistance so that they could take these things less personally than did other teachers. Because minority teachers were more likely to find their students morally acceptable than were other teachers, they were less likely to reject them in cynicism or anger. In some cases, blue-collar teachers were similarly supportive of blue-collar students, but the many teachers of blue-collar background who thought absolute parental authority should be part of their prerogatives found blue-collar students' tendency to take school lightly and bargain for the least work possible to be an attack on their person, to which they responded with cynicism, anger, or scorn. Teachers did not have to share students' background to develop an understanding of their perspectives. Some individual white teachers of middle-class origin were knowledgeable about and accepting of students whose backgrounds they did not share; they were able to work with them more constructively than most other teachers did.

As these differences among the teachers suggest, to say that teachers are dependent on their students does not mean that teachers are helpless before students. On the contrary, our data clearly show—both at the level of whole faculties and at that of individual teachers—that teachers can have a significant impact on students' behavior in school and on their learning despite strong social influences from their previous schooling, their families and communities, and their place in the larger society. In our study, this was most dramatically evident in the greater safety and good relations at Drew than at Grant, despite Drew's students' much lower skills and the more depressed and dangerous conditions in Drew's neighborhood. However, the impact that teachers can have is limited. Despite the able efforts of Drew's administration and much of its faculty, the dropout rate was very high, and most seniors' skills continued to be very low. For the staff of Drew, with its very low-SES students, to create a school that was more effective than it might have been was not to create a school like middle-SES Pinehill, let alone like high-SES Cherry Glen or Maple Heights.

To see teachers as dependent on their students runs against the grain of both society in general and education in particular, however much teachers might acknowledge the reality of the insight in an intuitive way. Furthermore, it is discouraging to educational policymakers because they have little if any control over the conditions that alienate from school not only the poorest students but also those in the middle range of society.

Nonetheless, this argument does have some policy implications. First, it teaches us something about the potential of policy initiatives currently being proposed. It suggests that changes intended to improve schools solely by changing teachers' roles—by giving them more time to plan curriculum, fewer hours spent with students, career ladders, and so forth—will not have much impact on the major condition of their work—the students—and thus will have limited effects, although perhaps beneficial ones. To change the balance of teachers' experience, one must change their intrinsic rewards in working with students.

Second, should it be possible to move the discourse about education into the arena of larger social policy, the experience of these schools indicates that the sorting of populations into housing that is homogeneous in class and race with connected schools that are equally homogeneous has demoralizing effects not only on students in lower-SES and middle-SES schools but also on their teachers. The policy implication is that schooling at the least and preferably housing as well should be reorganized to create a better mixture of class and race. A few urban areas have instituted metropolitan school desegregation that mixes class, although it mixes race with beneficial effects on housing as well as schooling (Rossell, 1978). Magnet schools in cities that draw students in ways not connected to housing can have similar effects if they are not designed to attract an elite (Metz, 1986). Such schools present some organizational problems of their own and require some innovative technical arrangements (Metz, 1986; Schofield, 1982), but the problems are less severe than those in low-SES schools.

Some policy implications of these findings stay within the current parameters of school organization and policy debate. First, it should be evident from this account that teachers' pride is rubbed raw by their daily experiences in middle-SES and low-SES schools. We found teachers very aware of the sometimes blatant, sometimes subtle tone in much of the current reform literature that suggests that recruiting better teachers is the key to school reform. Our analysis presents a sociological perspective that indicates that many—even though not all—of the failings in current teachers' behavior result from social conditions that teachers cannot control and that current policy initiatives will not remedy. If this view is correct, looking for better teachers as a solution to schools' problems will not solve the most important problems with teachers' performance. "Better" teachers will still leave or begin to look like the teachers we have now. If that is true, it might at least be helpful to stop the public drumbeat of criticism of teachers, which only hurts their already sensitive pride, with generally negative effects on their performance.

Finally, as the discussion of Drew and Grant illustrates, the attitudes of teachers and other school staff toward their students significantly affect—although they do not transform—the attitudes and behavior of students. At Drew, with a student body with poorer skills and more depressed circumstances, teachers built more positive relationships with students and were more persistent in trying to help students because they had more knowledge of students' community, considered it more morally legitimate even if not a good place for students to stay, and so had more empathy with students. One policy implication of these differences is the need to recruit more minority teachers. However, it is also important to develop programs to increase majority and middle-class teachers' empathy with minority and poor students. Such efforts have to go beyond 1- or 2-day in-service programs. Both teacher-training institutions and school districts should consider models from Peace Corps and Vista training or church-sponsored work camps and service projects that acquaint teachers with communities that differ from their own. Such programs should aim to teach aspiring or current teachers enough about the way of life of these communities to give teachers some respect for their integrity and for enough of their cultural styles to facilitate teachers' communication with students from these backgrounds.

REFERENCES

Ashton, P., & Webb, R. B. (1986). *Making a difference: Teachers' sense of efficacy and student achievement.* New York: Longman.

Barnard, C. (1962). *The functions of the executive.* Cambridge, MA: Harvard University Press. (Original work published 1938)

Boyer, E. L. (1983). *High school: A report on secondary education in America.* New York: Harper & Row.

Eckert, P. (1989). *Jocks and burnouts: Social categories and identity in the high school.* New York: Teachers College Press.

Finley, M. K. V. (1984). Teachers and tracking in a comprehensive high school. *Sociology of Education, 57,* 233–243.

Hargreaves, D. (1967). *Social relations in a secondary school.* New York: Routledge and Kegan Paul.

Hemmings, A., & Metz, M. H. (1990). "Real teaching?": How high school teachers negotiate societal, local, community, and student pressures when they define their work. In R. Page and L. Valli (Eds.), *Curriculum differentiation* (pp. 91–112). Buffalo, NY: SUNY Press.

Hurn, C. (1985). Changes in authority relationships in schools: 1960–1980. In A. Kerckhoff (Ed.), *Research in sociology of education and socialization* (Vol. 5, pp. 31–57). Greenwich, CT: JAI Press.

Jackson, P. W. (1986). *The practice of teaching.* New York: Teachers College Press.

Lacey, C. (1970). *Hightown Grammar: The school as a social system.* Manchester, England: The University Press.

Lortie, D. (1975). *Schoolteacher.* Chicago: University of Chicago Press.

McNeil, L. M. (1986). *Contradictions of control: School structure and school knowledge.* New York: Routledge and Kegan Paul.

Metz, M. H. (1978). *Classrooms and corridors: The crisis of authority in desegregated secondary schools.* Berkeley: University of California Press.

Metz, M. H. (1986). *Different by design: The context and character of three magnet schools.* New York: Routledge and Kegan Paul.

Metz, M. H. (1990). Real school: A universal drama amid disparate experience. In D. Mitchell and M. Foertz (Eds.), *Political Education Association Yearbook, 1989: Education politics for the new century* (pp. 75–91). Philadelphia: Falmer Press.

Morgan, E. (1977). *Inequality in classroom learning: Schooling and democratic citizenship.* New York: Praeger.

Ogbu, J. U. (1978). *Minority education and caste: The American system in cross-cultural perspective.* New York: Academic Press.

Ogbu, J. (1987). Variability in minority school performances: A problem in search of an explanation. *Anthropology and Education Quarterly, 18,* 312–334.

Powell, A. G., Farrar, E., & Cohen, D. K. (1985). *The shopping mall high school: Winners and losers in the educational marketplace.* Boston: Houghton Mifflin.

Rossell, C. H. (1978). *Assessing the unintended impacts of public policy: School desegregation and resegregation.* Washington, DC: National Institute of Education.

Schofield, J. W. (1982). *Black and white in school: Trust, tension, or tolerance?* New York: Praeger.

Schwartz, F. (1981). Supporting or subverting learning: Peer group patterns in four tracked schools. *Anthropology and Education Quarterly, 12*(Summer), 99–121.

Sedlak, M. W., Wheeler, C. W., Pullin, D. C., & Cusick, P. A. (1986). *Selling students short: Classroom bargains and academic reform in the American high school.* New York: Teachers College Press.

Waller, W. (1965). *The sociology of teaching.* New York: John Wiley. (Original work published 1932)

5

Judith Warren Little
University of California, Berkeley

Professional Community in Comprehensive High Schools: The Two Worlds of Academic and Vocational Teachers

An occupational community comprises "a group of people who consider themselves to be engaged in the same sort of work; whose identity is drawn from the work; who share with one another a set of values, norms, and perspectives that apply to but extend beyond work-related matters; and whose work relationships meld work and leisure" (Van Maanen & Barley, 1984, p. 287). At one level, teachers might be said to form an occupational community distinct from other occupations. But within teaching, there are also distinct communities of teachers. Beyond the formal distinctions made by categorical labels are the connotative dimensions that "lead some members to separate themselves from others who do denotatively similar work" (p. 295).

This chapter concentrates on aspects of professional identity and community in five sites, all comprehensive public high schools in a single state. Insights into teachers' worlds are derived from a comparison between

This research was supported by the National Center for Research on Vocational Education, University of California at Berkeley, with funds from the U.S. Department of Education, Office of Vocational and Adult Education (Grant No. G0087CO235), and by the Center for Research on the Context of Secondary Teaching, Stanford University, with funds from the U.S. Department of Education, Office of Educational Research and Improvement (Grant No. VO51A80004-90A).

teachers of the core academic subjects (English, social studies, science, mathematics, and foreign language) and those in three traditional vocational subjects (industrial arts, business, and home economics). To what extent are these high school teachers members of the same professional community? In what ways do their respective orientations to the work of teaching unite or divide them? Foster closer integration of their work or inhibit it?

Academic and vocational teachers share certain realities that demarcate the occupation of teaching from other work. Both rely on the ebb and flow of life in a classroom to yield "craft pride," a sense of accomplishment. Both spend their workdays surrounded by throngs of adolescents and speak in parallel ways about their concerns for students' accomplishments and aspirations. Among both groups, there are those who bring to teaching a passion for their subject and an enthusiasm for the students they teach, and there are those for whom teaching is no more than a job. In these and other ways, the teacher of American literature and the teacher of occupational auto dwell in the same world. But there are also important differences.

Academic and vocational teachers occupy two separate worlds in comprehensive high schools. Not all teachers and not in all schools, to be sure, but the "two worlds" phenomenon is sufficiently pervasive and sufficiently embedded in habitual ways of thought and deed to command attention. It is also a phenomenon that has remained nearly invisible in the mainstream research on secondary schools. That is, the discoveries of the past decade regarding school context, teachers' professional development, and teachers' career commitment are derived nearly exclusively from teachers in the core academic curriculum or are presented in ways that obscure within-school differences.

SUBJECT STATUS AND PROFESSIONAL RESPECT

Persistent stereotypes paint high school teachers as resolutely subject centered. Until very recently, there have been few efforts to penetrate that stereotype to discover the meaning that teachers attach to subject specialization. The studies that do exist are devoted almost exclusively to the nature of subject affiliation among teachers of traditional academic subjects. Among the examples are Elbaz's (1983) study of the English teacher "Sarah," Ball and Lacey's (1984) portrait of subject subcultures in four English departments, and Siskin's (1991) exploration of the academic department in comprehensive and magnet high schools. Together, these closely situated accounts of subject specialism help us to penetrate the stereotype. To these examples we now contribute a view of subject affiliation expressed by teachers of conventionally defined vocational curricula.

THE STATUS OF SUBJECT SPECIALTIES

The social organization of high school subjects mirrors the subject matter organization of higher education. Fields that are organized as recognized disciplines, holding departmental status in the academy, tend to command greater institutional respect and compete more successfully for institutional resources in the high school. This is not to deny that there are local variations responsive to local community character and priorities or to argue that the imprimatur of subject expertise is impervious to the relationships and reputations established by particular teachers in particular circumstances. On the whole, however, subject hierarchies favor those in the academic tradition (Ball & Lacey, 1984; Goodson, 1988).

Vocational studies in the U.S. high school have typically been treated as nonsubjects. (This phenomenon is not uniquely American; see Burgess, 1983, 1984; Connell, 1985.) Vocational teachers respond to subject hierarchies in part by campaigning for academic legitimacy. In Connell's (1985) words:

> Marginalised curricula can gain space, status, and resources in the school by redefining themselves as part of the hegemonic curriculum.
> . . . The pressure on a marginalised subject to do this can be quite serious (pp. 98; see also Little & Threatt, 1992).

Some vocational teachers argue that their preparation has been intellectually demanding and academically rigorous: "Home economists have a lot of scientific background." At the same time, they contest the singular standard of the *university* as that against which subject worth is properly assessed. When they identify alternative grounds on which status ought to be acknowledged, they point to the *economy*—the world of work and commerce—rather than the world of schooling. These comments from a home economics teacher typify the arguments we heard from many teachers:

> All of the nutritionists and dietitians come out of [home economics]. The fashion industry comes out of our field. . . . Interior design is our field. . . . People have always thought of us as "stitch and stir," but when you think of the world of work, we probably represent one of the largest segments of society's jobs.

Such alternative claims for status on the basis of real-world considerations have gained little hold in these comprehensive high schools. The power of subject differences to enhance or undermine teachers' professional identity is reflected in the differing degrees of confidence with which an English teacher and a home economics teacher parade their occupations in the world beyond the school. The English teacher celebrates her affiliation with English and with this English department in particular when she boasts, "You know, I've had people come up and say the Oak Valley English department is the best place in the county. . . . And I think English . . . is a subject that allows us an opportunity to really get to know kids. . . ."

A home economics teacher, by contrast, feels moved to hide her subject identity:

> When I go places and people ask, "What do you do?" I always say I teach high school students, I teach teenagers. I always know the next question is, "What do you teach?" You know, I really don't want to tell them anymore. "Oh, home ec! Oh, is that still around? Oh! I didn't know they still had that!"

Subject status arises not only from the perceived rigor of one's undergraduate education and professional preparation, but also from the perceived intellectual demand of course content in the secondary curriculum. According to vocational teachers, others consistently denigrate the cognitive or intellectual worth of curricula officially designated as vocational. A drafting teacher comments, "It's taken about 15 years for some people to actually give us any credibility that there's any intelligence in manipulative skills. Most of the time, the only intelligence [they] will accept is the reading-memory skills, which are the academic skills." Implicit here are the assumptions that work in the vocational areas requires fewer intellectual resources than work in academic subjects and that both the adults and the young people who dwell in the workshops are lower in native abilities than are those who populate academic classrooms.

Along with perceptions of intellectual substance comes a parallel set of perceptions regarding teacher work load: the intellectual, interactive, and pragmatic demands of teaching in one subject rather than in another. Among the academic domains, teachers make fine (if not always well-informed) distinctions regarding one another's teaching demands—observing, for example, that the load is easier in math, where the curriculum is highly standardized and evaluation of student work is straightforward.

Vocational teachers are generally convinced that their academic colleagues believe vocational courses to be easy on teachers as well as on students. As one home economics teacher reports, "I think a lot of them, probably many of them, feel that what we do is make cookies." Most put forth counterarguments, cataloguing the hours of outside preparation required to organize classroom projects and demonstrations and to assemble and maintain the necessary equipment and materials. These hours, they claim, equal or exceed the hours required to grade papers and examinations in the academic classes. Here, a home economics teacher describes the burden of preparing for food classes compared with what she thinks is required to prepare for a math class or any class that is teachable from a textbook:

> With home ec . . . there's so much preparation, there's so much. It's not like you're just opening a book and "Okay, guys, we're going to do Chapter 13 today. Let's read and discuss." That type of thing . . . I mean, that seems kind of cut and dried, where here there's so much activity and so much [material] and you have to consider your budget. . . .

And a business teacher said:

> I have had comments from at least one English person that I happen to have a prep period with that [showed] she had no idea that we worked as hard as we did in the business department. She thought that all we did was go in and say, "Okay, do this." And the kids did it, and you took no papers home to grade and etcetera, etcetera.

Ironically, these comments also underscore the way in which status differences are perpetuated by the relative privacy of teachers' work. Neither the academic teacher nor the vocational teacher whose exchanges we glimpse here has a complete and realistic grasp of one another's classroom practice or work load burdens.

Yet the specific relations among categorical subject status, the locally meaningful status of particular subjects in particular schools, and the realities of teachers' work remain to be worked out. For example, the advantage that generally accrues to academic teachers in these schools is diminished at Valley High School, where rapid changes in the student population have frustrated many academic teachers; the same changes have consolidated the position of the vocational programs. And at Oak Valley, the esteem that teachers derive from their association with a strong *school* may only intensify the status problems that accompany membership in a vocational *department*. A business teacher who says, "I think it's a great school," also declares, "Had I to do it over again, I probably would not have become a vocational ed teacher. I would have been in one of the academic subjects. . . . The counselors and everybody else, it's like they just say, 'Well, that's an elective and it's not that important.'"

In sum, the status differences between vocational and academic teachers originate partly in the status hierarchy of the subject disciplines in higher education and in the perceived intellectual demands posed by academic and nonacademic fields of study in the secondary curriculum. They are sustained, too, by the value attached to the student clienteles with whom academic and nonacademic teachers work.

SUBJECT STATUS AND STUDENT CLIENTELE

Throughout the service professions, the status of practitioners is closely linked to the status of the clients they serve. On the whole, professionals who work with children rank lower in the status hierarchy than those whose clients are adults. Work with older children confers greater prestige than work with younger ones; hence, many of these teachers tell of careers improved by a move from junior high school to high school or by the opportunity to work part-time in a community college.

Within high school teaching, still finer distinctions are made. The status order of subjects, aligned as it is with the subject hierarchy of the university, is responsive to the college-bound or non-college-bound status of one's students. One wins accolades by association with students who achieve success in the academic curriculum or in highly visible extracurricular activities that are also valued components of university life (athletics, band, or other performing arts). Conversely, an academic teacher's standing is eroded by exclusive affiliation with low-achieving students. Talbert (1990) estimates that about one quarter of U.S. high school teachers could be considered "tracked" by assignments to teach low-achieving students. (A still smaller percentage of teachers work exclusively with high-achieving students, teaching a steady diet of advanced placement or honors classes.) Talbert's analysis of the 1984 High School and Beyond data, together with Finley's (1984) ethnographic study of teacher tracking in a large high school English department, suggests that consistent assignment to low-track classes has a deleterious effect on teachers' orientation toward their work. According to both studies, low-track teachers less often perceive themselves as well supported by administrators and colleagues, are less likely to enjoy opportunities for professional growth, are less successful in the competition for instructional and organizational resources, and feel less efficacious in their work with students. The consequence, argues Talbert, is to exacerbate the inequalities experienced by students.

The teacher tracking phenomenon affects a relatively small segment of academic teachers in these schools. It is a circumstance in which *some* academic teachers find themselves, and one that varies widely within schools by department. Teachers most vulnerable to low-track assignments are those newest to the school and those held in lowest regard by administrators or department heads. Although there is, no doubt, a performance threshold below which a department cannot fall and still retain its legitimacy as an academic enterprise, academic departments retain their privileged position even when some individual teachers find themselves confined to remedial classes. And the affected teachers continue to identify more firmly with their departments than with similarly situated low-track teachers in other departments (Talbert, 1991).

However, the low-track designation well describes the *majority* of vocational teachers and, indeed, entire vocational departments or programs. In all five schools, student placement patterns concentrate the "low" and the "special" in nonacademic classes. In some very real sense, these are vocational teachers without vocational students. That is, they receive few students who are clearly dedicated to a vocational course of study (Little & Threatt, 1992). Presumably, students enthusiastic about pursuing a program of work education would soften or eliminate the stigma of external status attributions. A drafting teacher compares his former life in a specialized vocational center with his present work in a comprehensive high school, recalling, "My most enjoyable teaching assignment was over at the vocational center . . . because the students had a direction. . . . I was teaching kids to become drafters and designers and engineers. . . ."

Teachers who cultivated a craft because it held genuine appeal for them and who entered teaching in the hope of finding students with similar inclinations now find themselves viewed not as skilled craftspeople but as caretakers of marginal students. Neither their own subject expertise nor their accomplishments with academically marginal students yields much recognition. To vocational teachers, the link between the prestige accorded teachers and the academic standing of their students often represents a poor alignment of effort and reward. Some teachers respond with equanimity. Others respond with resentment:

> So, you begin to feel real unaffirmed. . . . So, who gets the awards? It's the ones that are glitzy or the ones that have all the top-notch students who can stand up and say, "Because of this teacher, I got into Stanford or I got into Yale." Well, what about people down here who every day are putting up with all of the riffraff, who are putting up with the discipline problems, who are really working in the trenches? And I guess that's maybe where we see ourselves. We're in the trenches.

Both kinds of responses, however, confirm the link between a teacher's identity and status and those of the clientele, reinforced and perpetuated by a schooling organized to distinguish between college-bound and non-college-bound students and to bracket preparation for work from academic endeavors. Such distinctions also constrain the ways in which teachers might contribute to one another's work by engaging in cross-disciplinary ventures, teaching one another's students, or acknowledging one another's achievements.

Teachers' subject commitments and subject philosophies are thus separated only with difficulty from concerns for students. Teachers are united or divided by the priorities they express and the views they hold regarding "what's best for kids" (see, for example, the description of competing teacher subcultures in Ball, 1987; Hargreaves, 1986; Metz, 1978). In this respect, academic and vocational teachers share a concern for students' command of basic academic skills, their overall level of academic achievement, their personal maturation, and their social development. Nonetheless, it is the differences rather than the similarities in their orientation to teaching that most seem to mark the relations between vocational and academic teachers. Academic teachers more often sound the recurrent theme of subject mastery and college preparation and derive their sense of individual and institutional pride (or frustration) from the number of college acceptances. Vocational teachers are more often set apart by their concerns for preparing students for employment. Their views do not always receive the enthusiastic approbation of administrators. The principal of one school confides, "I have to tell you that even personally I am not convinced that our job should be training kids for jobs in high school. I think we're doing a disservice to kids by having them shut down their options too soon. . . . [Preparing for jobs is] an aspect of what we're about, but I don't believe it's our primary purpose." The collegial environment in which vocational teachers work is shaped in part by the school priorities voiced by administrators and in part by the general disposition toward college preparation that teachers in the school express.

THE SATISFACTIONS OF SUBJECT SPECIALISM

Teachers' continued enthusiasm for teaching is bound up with opportunities to find both intellectual stimulation and emotional satisfaction in the classroom. Teachers judge their careers in part by the success they experience in getting to teach the subjects that they know and like, in the schools they want, with students they consider both able and interested, among colleagues they admire. On semester-by-semester and year-by-year bases, their pleasure in teaching is calibrated by the combination of classes configured in a six-period teaching day.

Teachers typically place subject commitments amid broader conceptions of what it means to be a teacher. That is, they place loyalty to the subject alongside loyalties expressed in "working with kids." Many, for example, cite involvement with one or more student activities. They view with ambivalence colleagues who know their subject but who "can't connect with kids" or "don't really like kids." Many construct their teaching task in terms of supporting the general maturation of young people: "helping them become independent." Such teachers paint the subject as a medium, not an end in itself. Certainly, subject enthusiasms alone cannot compensate for troubles with students or always help to resolve them. Nor do subject enthusiasms and subject commitments ensure teaching that is substantively lively or pedagogically inventive. Nor, finally, do all teachers evince genuine interest in the subjects that they teach, or invest equally in extending their subject expertise.

Nonetheless, enthusiasm for the subject is one major contributor to teachers' engagement in teaching. The passion for subject that many of these high school teachers bring to their work is exemplified in their stories of deciding to teach. Math teacher Charles Ashton considers geometry his favorite course and recalls his first introduction to it as a student:

Geometry was the thing that really turned me on to mathematics. For me, it was a critical course, and I guess I now interpret it the same. . . . It was so logical and so obvious, I thought God had given me the answer to the universe. It's kind of like listening to a Beethoven symphony in a way; this is the way it's supposed to be.

Hannah Naftigal started out as an elementary education major and switched to home economics after a course she found inspiring. "Something clicked in me when I took that course," she recalls. "It felt like I had come home." Both of these teachers came to teaching with a commitment to the subject, and both retain a certain subject loyalty. For them and for others like them, the most attractive reform proposals are those that would intensify the pride and pleasure to be found in subject expertise.

To some extent, both Mr. Ashton and Ms. Naftigal must struggle to experience the rewards of subject specialism in their comprehensive high schools. Both are affected by the ethnic, linguistic, and academic diversity of the students they teach, leaving them uncertain how to use the medium of the subject to reach all students. Both are affected by the tedium that may result from many years in the same assignment and the urge to find intellectual stimulation. As one of Mr. Ashton's math colleagues sums it up, "You know, the 300th time you've explained angle-side-angle [theorem in geometry], it's really boring." And both are sensitive to the ways in which particular teaching assignment configurations—the combination of good or tough classes in a five- or six-period day—can enlarge or diminish the satisfaction they find in their subject matter.

However, despite the similarities in the subject commitments that Mr. Ashton and Ms. Naftigal bring to their teaching and despite some commonalities in the teaching environment they encounter, these two teachers differ in the opportunities that each finds to derive craft pride from subject matter teaching. Recent reforms combine with the traditional subject hierarchy to place the satisfactions of the mathematics teacher more readily at hand and to render those of the home economics teacher more uncertain. Such externalities—the increase in academic graduation requirements and the corresponding restriction on electives, for example—account for part of the story. Another part is bound up with dynamics internal to the school, especially those that govern teaching assignment.

Academic teachers: subject specialism and the politics of seniority. Nearly all of the academic teachers in these five schools teach full-time in their area of specialization; they can legitimately and comfortably lay claim to being an English teacher or a math teacher. This is not to say that they look upon their course configuration with equal satisfaction and confidence or that they attain the same measure of success in each class (Raudenbush, Rowan, & Cheong, 1990). However, whatever the combination of subject and student they seek, academic teachers are generally able to forge it in the context of their primary subject specialty.

For academic teachers, seniority in the subject department is a major factor in determining whether the specific assignment that one receives is a good fit with one's preparation and preferences. To varying degrees, teachers compete over what Finley (1984) termed "the good schedule," one that represents, from the teacher's perspective, a desirable fit with favored subjects and students. Status considerations figure prominently in Finley's analysis; teachers earn prestige when they teach subjects and students highly valued by the larger institution and the community, and their prestige is eroded by teaching low-achieving students and remedial content.

The dynamics of the seniority system have perhaps best been uncovered by Neufeld (1984), who finds teachers able to describe its features and consequences in considerable detail: how long it takes to get seniority, the maneuvering within a personalized hierarchy, the appeals to fairness that help weaken the power of seniority, the frustrations of waiting out your turn, and the disposition to lock in a good course once in possession of it.

The English department and science department at Oak Valley High School represent contrast cases in the use of seniority to decide teacher assignments. In the English department, the effects of seniority, although not completely absent, are greatly muted by the presence of a department policy that calls for the regular rotation of remedial courses and for widely distributed responsibility for the department's course offerings. In addition, the chair makes a well-publicized effort to grant each teacher his or her first-choice class. The rotational principle is visible in the master schedule; only one of the department's 25 regular teachers shows a heavy load of remedial classes 2 years in a row. (This contrasts with Finley's [1984] English department of equal size, in which nine teachers were consistently assigned to low-track classes.) Of the department's 24 teachers, 5 dominate the honors and advanced placement classes (accounting for all such sections in 1989–1990 and 10 of 13 sections in 1990–1991). In no case do honors classes make up a teacher's entire teaching load.

In the science department, a different picture emerges. The chair of this department, too, maintains that the department bears a responsibility toward low-achieving students. However, there is no equivalent norm for rotating the assignment of remedial classes among teachers. In a 3-year period, the chair once acquiesced to pressure from the administration to take a turn at teaching a basic science course, but the experiment was short-lived (one section taught one time). He and other experienced teachers consistently dominated the advanced courses and courses enrolling juniors and seniors. The department's newest members teach full loads of the lowest-level basic science, life science, and physical science classes.

Academic teachers, then, are very likely to be teaching within their subject specialization but are less certain to be matched consistently with courses and students with whom they feel most efficacious. Career trajectories and fluctuations are linked to what teachers individually and collectively come to view as "the good schedule." The good schedule, in turn, is shaped by the demands, opportunities, and rewards presented by both the subject and the students.

Vocational teachers: subject specialism and the politics of electives. The opportunities for vocational teachers to demonstrate their subject expertise and to indulge their subject-related enthusiasms are less powerfully shaped by the dynamics of seniority than by factors associated with course-taking patterns and student placement policies: the decline of enrollment in nonacademic electives following shifts in high school graduation requirements, and student placement practices that populate vocational classes with students whom teachers see less as work oriented than as academically marginal.

The pattern across the five schools shows a steady record of decline in total numbers and in full-time assignment of vocational specialists. Most resilient have been the home economics (or consumer/family studies) and business departments; most diminished have been the trades-oriented industrial arts departments. Increasingly, teachers preserve full-time teaching assignments by teaching outside their primary subject area or by converting traditional courses to serve the purposes of basic skills instruction in academic areas. Departments maintain teaching positions by developing a marketable combination of vocational courses and courses that might be termed personal interest electives. Common among the vocational teachers is a pattern of survival-oriented entrepreneurialism—scrounging and hustling—by which individual teachers retain sufficient resources to carve out a full-time schedule of courses.

The decline in teaching staff is matched by a decline in the number of course offerings and by a shift in the types of courses available. At the beginning of our study, all five of the schools offered fewer vocational courses than their staffing permitted. That is, teachers whose background and experience lay in industrial arts, business, agriculture, or home economics were teaching fewer than five periods a day in those areas. Over the 3-year period, all schools reduced the total number of offerings still further. Thus, the range of course offerings that would communicate a subject specialty and provide like-minded colleagues for teachers is missing. Increasingly, teachers confront a compressed curriculum that bears little resemblance to the coherent program in which many once participated and from which they draw their professional identity. Wood shop teacher Ed Gordon describes a series of program cuts that have left him "teaching art this year for the first time." Mr. Gordon calculates that he has 12 years before retirement. He says, "I still love wood and I believe in it. But I'll hang on."

Mr. Gordon is resigned to hanging on, but one cannot help but gain the impression of curricula steadily weakened and careers derailed. Not all vocational teachers respond with the same equanimity. Such career fluctuations take their toll on teachers' commitment and performance. Greg Zeller, some years younger than Mr. Gordon, resists the prospect of "going backward" in his career. When his small engines program was cut, he entered aggressively into a district-level project to develop an applied technology course sequence. He tells us that if his plans are thwarted, he will leave teaching altogether. Short of that, he implies, he will curtail the energy he devotes to his teaching. And he will be more skeptical about new proposals in the future.

Subject identities and the teaching priorities to which they are tied remain a fundamental part of professional community for most of these teachers. The subject designations of departments count in the competition for resources, and subject expertise counts in the view that teachers have of one another. The opportunities for colleagueship among teachers and for the reconstruction of purposes and programs within schools reside largely in the resources of subject expertise. And teachers' subject affiliations are given prominence by the departmental organization of the high school.

DEPARTMENTS

Departments linked to established subject matter disciplines are a significant organizational feature in these comprehensive high schools and are the primary frame of reference for most teachers. Despite assaults on segmented curricula and departmental organization (Hargreaves, 1988; Sizer, 1984, 1992), subject matter departments continue to dominate the social and political organization of secondary schools. These comprehensive high schools are no exception. At four schools, subject matter affiliations are rendered organizationally salient through a formal departmental structure; at a fifth school, efforts to build and sustain an alternative structure organized around learning units are gradually giving way to restored subject matter boundaries (Siskin, 1991). Among the five schools, no fewer than 86 percent and as many as 97 percent of regular classroom teachers were teaching full-time in a single-subject department. In recent experiments to realign vocational and academic curricula, schools preserve subject matter groupings even while organizing new multidisciplinary "houses" or "career clusters." To some extent, schools are driven by external circumstances to do so. The state's curriculum frameworks are subject specific, as are testing protocols, state-approved textbooks, university admission requirements, and regulations governing teacher licensure and assignment.

Given the dominant subject-matter organization of high schools, departments represent a naturally occurring ground for teachers' interactions and satisfactions (or frustrations). The department is the most prominent domain of potential interdependence among teachers. In seeking meaningful arenas for interaction and interdependence among teachers who work largely as "independent artisans," Huberman argues in Chapter 1, "I would look instead to the department [not the school] . . . as the unit of collaborative planning and execution in a secondary school. This is where people have concrete things to tell one another and concrete instructional help to provide one another; this is where the contexts of instruction actually overlap."

The relationship between academic and vocational teachers is thus inescapably linked to the history of subject organization in high schools. Our survey data include reported levels of departmental identification across the five schools. On survey measures, all schools report moderate to high levels of departmental affiliation. In interviews, too, teachers make the department or subject a prominent part of the stories they tell. They do so even at Rancho, where the faculty has made a concerted effort to displace departmental organization. Across all five schools, departments and subject affiliation are meaningful components of teachers' work life. One measure of the competitive strength of academic and vocational subjects, then, is the individual and collective strength of their respective departments.

Departments define themselves and are defined by others as strong or weak. The definitions have multiple referents. When the chair of an industrial arts department judges his department to be very strong, he is referring to the members' long-standing friendships and to their shared support for the nonacademic student. When an administrator judges the same department to be weak, he is recording his criticism of the department's slim record of initiative in program innovation. Thus, internal and external judgments do not always coincide, nor do insiders and outsiders, teachers and administrators, always assess the salient elements of departmental strength in the same way. For some vocational teachers, congenial relations among peers are sufficient to outweigh low institutional prestige; for some teachers in academic departments, being rich in resources does not compensate for the absence of intellectual and professional accord. Overall, however, some conditions could be said to contribute to departmental strength and others to erode it.

DEPARTMENT COMPOSITION

One of the major contributors to departmental strength among the four English departments studied by Ball and Lacey (1984) was full-time participation by a cadre of subject specialists. Most academic departments in our five schools were able to preserve the full-time instructional services of their subject experts. That is, most teachers of math, science, social studies, and English taught full-time assignments within their subject specialty. Indeed, most of the drain of subject expertise from academic departments in these schools occurs not in the form of out-of-subject teaching but in the form of commitments to the school's athletic program.

Vocational teachers, especially those with general secondary credentials, are more vulnerable to assignments outside their primary field. Sometimes those assignments require teaching as many as four periods a day in another subject (often math or science); in other instances, they require traveling between schools. In 1989–1990, for example, 21 teachers in the five schools were assigned to teach in two departments (exclusive of coaches). Of these, eight (38 percent) were from vocational subjects, although vocational teachers constitute only 12 percent of the teacher work force. An additional three vocational teachers maintained their full-time assignment in their specialty by traveling between two schools.

In a heavily departmentalized structure, to lose subject specialists from a department is to weaken the social cohesion and programmatic unity needed to compete for resources; similarly, to admit to the department full- or part-time members who are not subject specialists is to weaken the department's professional standing. One might envision an alternative configuration in which a group's competitive standing is contingent on interdisciplinary strength rather than on single-subject strength. Such a shift cannot be managed on a subject-by-subject or department-by-department basis, however. It requires a uniform shift in the principle of organization—for example, to a house or career cluster model. Rancho High School did attempt a variant of a house configuration, but competition over resources within learning units remained tied to subject specialties.

Among academic departments, a shift in the composition of the department membership (more part-time teachers, for example) may occur independent of shifts in department size. In a case study report entitled "Are core subjects becoming a dumping ground for reassigned high school teachers?" Gehrke and Sheffield (1985) observed that in times of declining enrollment, academic courses are maintained through "reassignment" while courses that require special technical skills (for example, instrumental music and wood shop) are cut from the school program altogether. In our five schools, we found a similar phenomenon of teaching assignment following the shift in high school graduation requirements. In the wake of such developments, the remaining vocational teachers, especially in the industrial arts, tended to become vocational generalists (for example, teaching isolated sections of wood shop, metal shop, and drafting).

Thus, academic departments maintain or increase their size but lose their claim to subject expertise, while vocational departments lose both size and specialist depth. Each of the five schools has at least one one-person vocational department. At Oak Valley, the largest of the schools, the largest vocational department numbers 6, while the four core academic departments range in size from 14 to 25. At the remaining four schools, the maximal size of the vocational departments is 4; the maximal size of academic departments in the same schools is 14. And as vocational departments dwindle in size, little remains to link teachers together or to serve as a platform for cross-departmental work. A home economics teacher at Valley says:

> As much as I would like to see the department growing, it seems to be diminishing. We really don't have a full-time teacher. We just have the two courses. Possibly [if we had] a teacher and a half, that

would give you somebody to share your ideas, communicate with, that type of thing. . . . It would be different having somebody in the school, actually sharing what's happening.

The school's only business teacher compares her present isolation with past circumstances, in which she could count on others for stimulation. At a previous school, she says, "I had three other teachers, and we could bounce off each other. Here I don't really have anyone yet. Because I'm the only business teacher, you know."

The programmatic strength of a department thus begins with its membership: the pool of knowledge and experience available in the teachers who make up the department's roster. In Oak Valley's English department, all teachers are full-time members of the department who bring to their work extensive formal preparation in English. All members of the department are available to devote the majority of their time and energy to the teaching of English and the refinement of the English curriculum. The department's policy of encouraging teachers to tackle a new course every couple of years has resulted in a faculty with a collective ability to teach widely in the department's curriculum and across grade levels. In the industrial arts department, by contrast, only one of six teachers continues to teach a full-time load in his or her main area of expertise. The teachers pursue very separate specialties, ranging from electronics to auto and metal work, which add to the difficulty of relying on flexibility in staffing to achieve curriculum depth and continuity.

DEPARTMENT LEADERSHIP

The power of departments in secondary schools is enhanced by a formal provision for department leadership and is correspondingly diminished when no such provision is made. Two of the three districts that serve as home to our five schools support the position of department head; in both districts, the position is potentially one of substantial organizational and collegial leadership (although it is not always enacted in this way). The third district, in which Esperanza and Rancho are located, eliminated formal support for department heads several years ago. However, even within the former two districts, resources to support departmental leadership are not uniformly distributed and do not go uncontested. An industrial arts teacher typifies comments that we heard frequently regarding the vocational departments' claim on resources for department leadership:

A lot of people think because we have [only] six people and because our department doesn't have papers to grade, that the department chairman doesn't have the load that the other department chairs do. But if you look at all the equipment that we have, to make sure that it stays [in repair]—you can't just come in and write a work order and expect it to happen. You've got to follow through.

An important influence on the department's professional and organizational presence is the leadership stance assumed by the department chair. In Oak Valley's English department, three successive chairs of the English department sound a common theme: The role of the chair is to sustain both the coherence of the curriculum and the cooperative spirit among teachers. Teachers compete for the position of chair on the basis of substantive expertise and ability to lead a group of respected experts. (There were three internal candidates for the position when it last came vacant.) The present chair of the industrial arts department, by contrast, describes a rotation in which "we all take our turn in the barrel." The main job of the chair in that department is to ensure appropriate and timely expenditures of the equipment budget. The chair of the business department reports that her position is "strictly a liaison with administration." A generally permissive or timid stance toward department leadership may prove detrimental to any department, but more so to those without other forceful advocates in the organization.

COMPETITION FOR RESOURCES

Departments in the same school may differ dramatically in the material resources that they command: space, equipment, up-to-date texts, supplemental materials, professional development monies, and the like. To some extent, the differences are felt within both academic and nonacademic arenas. As Siskin (1991) relates, for example, science departments are typically favored in the resource competition in ways that social studies departments are not. She traces the disparities between these academic departments in part to the external prestige of science, the tightness of scientific paradigms compared with those of social studies fields, the perceived legitimacy of claims regarding laboratory facilities and materials, and the relative scarcity of science teachers. Nonetheless, she concludes:

> The status differences among these academic departments, however, are small, and often lie not in the automatic link to the discipline, but in the cultivated links to the administrators. The most intriguing glimpses of consequential differences in disciplinary status come from the departments not studied here, such as Industrial Arts. (pp. 207–208)

Siskin speculates that the most dramatic status differences and resource differences are to be found between the academic and nonacademic fields (vocational education, the arts, and special education). Her speculations are borne out in our interviews with vocational teachers, who are united in their view that their school's discretionary resources go most readily to develop academic programs. At Rancho, the science chair confirms the status differential, observing that the math and science departments have received "the lion's share of the funding." He would not be surprised to hear an industrial arts teacher in the school lament, as he did to us:

> We sometimes feel like we're second-class citizens, probably because the English department, the math department, or social studies department, or science department can yell for more money, and they seem to get more money or more of the pie than their fair share, plus some.

Departmental strength is reflected in and maintained by successful claims to valued resources. Among the forces that contribute to a departmental presence in a school, neither department size nor subject prestige weighs on the side of the vocational departments. With regard to control over material resources, there is little doubt that academic departments reign in these five schools. However, departmental presence can also be felt by the intellectual and moral stance that a department adopts, individually and collectively, toward the work of teaching.

DEPARTMENTAL ETHOS AND BOUNDARIES

Departments provide very different kinds of collegial homes for the teachers who inhabit them. A small number of prior studies offer widely varying portraits of departments and department leadership. The department heads and teachers interviewed by Johnson (1990) claim that department members are engaged extensively in joint activity on matters of curriculum and instruction. However, in his study of staff networks in two Midwestern high schools, Cusick (1982) concluded that departments were principally instruments of administrative convenience. They offered neither pressure nor support for teachers to adopt a coherent stance toward curriculum and instruction; indeed, they had little to do with the intellectual and professional lives of the teachers assigned to them. Both of these portraits come to life again in our own data (see also Bruckerhoff, 1991). Teachers and administrators in these schools readily and vividly define individual departments by their characteristic stance toward subject, students, and schooling. Here, for example, an English teacher and a social studies teacher who teach in the same school present drastically different portraits of their respective departments.

ENGLISH TEACHER: I came here [to interview], and I was really impressed right away with the teachers that were here in the English department. . . . They were really energetic and involved in what they were doing . . . sharing ideas about what they were doing in class, what was working, showing students' work. . . . It's very cooperative.

SOCIAL STUDIES TEACHER: There is no agreement in the department on what is important, no agreement on standards, no agreement on priorities. The faculty is out there floating. People are just putting in time.

In the English department office, one finds a group picture prominently displayed on the wall, and teacher traffic is heavy throughout the day. Conversations among teachers are frequent and lively. The social studies office, located nearby, is nearly empty of teacher traffic, and there is nothing in the physical environment that would suggest close personal or professional relations among the department's members.

Of course, there is no necessary relation between personal closeness in a department and a disposition to act collectively in regard to teaching. Nonetheless, social cohesion may dispose a department more readily to cooperate on educational pursuits when the occasion arises. The English department prides itself on being open; it is not unusual to find substitute teachers gravitating to the English department to have lunch, regardless of what subject they are covering for the day. The department members also welcomed members of our research team, making time for us to have informal conversations and making room for us at the lunch table. Student teachers and other teachers new to the department commented on the warm and cooperative environment they discovered. This large English department promotes a sense of belonging among its immediate members, but its boundaries remain permeable. Other departments, including social studies, preserved a more formal stance toward strangers and newcomers, as well as toward colleagues from neighboring departments.

This English department represents perhaps the clearest case of a department dedicated to a coherent program of studies to which most or all teachers contribute. Individual autonomy exists within the context of collective agreements regarding curriculum emphasis and, to a lesser extent, instructional preferences. Teaching assignments traced over a 3-year period reveal a departmental commitment to displace conventional patterns of individual course ownership with teachers' widespread knowledge of and participation in the broader curriculum. The chair explains:

> We started something a couple of years ago where every teacher is not forced but encouraged to pick up a new prep every other year. And the idea behind that one is that courses didn't become so specialized to teachers that if a teacher were to leave the department and all of a sudden the course, you know, somebody's stuck teaching it and doesn't really know how it's supposed to go and all that. [We] tried to remove the idea of special-interest classes and say, "Look, if it's in our department then it's worth being taught, and so let's have people who can teach it."

Course offerings, staffing patterns, and course coordination all serve as policy mechanisms that may spur or impede collaborative activity within or across departments. Despite the large size of this English department, teachers attain a remarkable familiarity with one another's teaching and a remarkable level of genuine agreement about their departmental priorities. They are supported in this achievement by their inclination to see themselves as engaged in a common task (college preparation), to underplay their subspecialties and concentrate on commonalities in the broader discipline, and to promote strong curricular leadership from within their own ranks.

In some respects, the differences between strong departments and weak departments appear to be quite independent of subject matter. The English department at Oak Valley is a powerhouse; the same subject department at Esperanza is badly polarized. Our investigations of life inside departments over the past 3 years have led us to believe that school-level measures of departmentalization and collegiality are likely to be misleading or at best they offer an incomplete picture of the various bases of colleagueship in a secondary school. Within the same school, we find some departments that are powerful instruments of curricular policy and other departments that provide no more than an administrative label for a loose assemblage of individuals. (Indeed, reducing the wide range of variation and increasing the normative power of collegiality would appear to be crucial elements of a reform strategy.) Vocational departments appear no more or no less inclined than academic departments to take a collective stand on curricular priorities or to supply one another with professional support.

There remain, however, certain systematic differences between academic and vocational departments. That is, there are forces that tend more often than not to weaken vocational departments compared with academic departments. Academic and nonacademic departments are positioned differently to act as instruments of curriculum policy and as guarantors of staffing and program configurations. At Oak Valley High School, for example, the consumer/family studies (home economics) department bears a certain resemblance to the English department in its effort to achieve a certain curricular coherence. The department's course offerings reflect a decision to employ state funds to develop a set of occupationally oriented programs in restaurant management, early childhood education, and fashion merchandising. However, unlike the English department, where teachers set out to learn courses across the department's curriculum and where teacher turnover would have only marginal impact on the course offerings or core content, the consumer/family studies department relies on individually developed one-person programs. It is therefore less flexible in its options for staffing, and its program continuity is vulnerable to teacher turnover. (Indeed, the fashion merchandising program was abandoned when the teacher who organized it left the school.) In the industrial arts department, too, each of six teachers pursues a single specialty. Faced with declining enrollments, the department has devoted resources to helping individual teachers develop alternative courses but has made no collective moves to reconsider and consolidate its curricular priorities.

Across all five schools, academic departments appear stronger than vocational departments in the overall competition for symbolic, human, and material resources. In schools where academic achievement and preparation for college attract the greatest concentration of symbolic and material resources, vocational departments are seen as backwaters. Vocational teachers are more vulnerable to split assignments and are more likely to travel between schools than are teachers in academic departments. Vocational teachers' motivation and opportunity for intensive participation in a department are diminished as their vocational departments are less able to act as guarantors of preferred teaching assignments, breadth and depth of course offerings, and full-time department membership.

Departments exude a certain spirit, one that varies widely both within and between schools. They also confront quite different conditions of teaching. The conditions supportive of departmental collegiality include a full complement of subject specialists; a subsidized and meaningful department head position; a budget adequate to encompass both program development and professional development; a coherent stance toward curriculum policy; and norms supportive of collective problem solving, innovation, and intellectual growth.

AMONG COLLEAGUES

Subject affiliation and departmental membership powerfully define professional community in these comprehensive high schools. They do not, of course, exhaust the possibilities. In a six-period instructional day, most teachers spend five periods in the classroom. They come together in the moments before the school day begins or in the passing periods between classes, in an assigned preparation period, at lunch, and at the occasional after-school meeting. Against a backdrop of departmental preoccupations and classroom privacy, one can detect considerable variations in the nature and extent of teachers' professional and personal relations with one another. Some teachers can be found in their classrooms throughout the day, even at lunch. They venture out only to collect mail from the office or to attend required meetings. Others seem not isolated at all; when not in class, they are immersed in a round of lively and nearly continuous exchange with colleagues on topics ranging from student work or classroom activities to family matters, sports, and the state of the economy. Greetings exchanged in passing and stories told in the moments between classes convey some sense of a backstage life among the school's adults. Some individuals and groups exude openness; others exude a stiff reserve. Some colleagues supply one another with primarily a warm and congenial personal environment; others provide professional advice, ideas, or collaboration on new ideas or projects. Friendships and occasionally feuds may span decades and may extend well beyond the school walls.

The collegial environment is in many ways more dynamic, fluid, and complex than might be anticipated by dwelling on the closed classroom door or on the boundaries constructed by subject and department loyalties. Yet in the relations between academic teachers and their vocational colleagues, the dominant theme is one of division: a general physical, social, and educational isolation that separates vocational from academic teachers and a pattern of competition over student enrollment and other resources. Overall, the organization of time, space, curriculum, and students tends to separate individual teachers from one another, further separate teachers considered academic from those in nonacademic specialties, and intensify the departmental basis of professional community.

Teachers do not all respond to isolation and subject segmentation in the same ways. It would be a mistake to think of the vocational teachers as chafing for greater involvement while academic teachers serve as obstructionists. Indeed, the themes introduced by the vocational teachers are consistent with those sounded throughout the secondary teacher population. For some, the privacy of the classroom engenders a sense of entrepreneurial pride—a sense that one's program is an individual accomplishment and the basis for professional esteem. For others, programmatic iso-lation is offset by satisfactions achieved elsewhere. Thus, one business teacher chooses to remain in her computer lab most of the school day but finds sufficient opportunity for collegial exchange in regularly scheduled department meetings. Others settle for a version of benign neglect or the absence of overt conflict. One home economics teacher says of her school's faculty, "There's not too much that we have in common, but I have no complaints about the other teachers." And still others pursue an idiosyncratic but cosmopolitan array of relationships and activities.

The general congeniality and warmth among teachers at most of these schools do little to relieve an underlying competitive reality that centers on student enrollment. As Connell (1985) and others portray the situation, such competition is not grounded in individual dispositions but in a pol-icy orientation that favors the academic curriculum. State and local policy developments throughout the past decade have expanded the academic course requirements for high school graduation and have narrowed the time available for students to pursue elective courses (especially electives deemed nonacademic).

Vocational teachers compete with one another and with academic teachers for sufficient student enrollment to sustain a full-time teaching assignment. In doing so, they often underscore the separation of academic purposes and nonacademic purposes. In the competition for enrollment, courses that meet requirements or courses that can offer academic credit are advantaged. When the art department refused to award art credit to a photography course taught in the industrial arts department, the industrial arts teachers were at risk of losing photography altogether. To maintain their class sections, they were pressed toward a course description that emphasized a vocational orientation:

> It was vocational skill training. We geared them in that direction.
> . . . This is for professional ends. These are the vocational areas
> that you want. For us, we believe time lines in getting stuff in are
> as important as the composition and the color and the lines and
> the repetition, the value, the art structure. We've all pretty much
> agreed in that area.

Relegated to the marginal realm of an electives department, voca-tional teachers employ a variety of means to market individual courses and programs to administrators and students. Vocational teachers are left largely to their own devices to sustain a full-time teaching assignment composed of courses that both they and their students find satisfying. Observers of high schools have drawn attention to the ways in which aca-

demic teachers' own entrepreneurial activities could result in small empires
or market niches of quite idiosyncratic course offerings that preserve student enrollment and maintain teacher interest but compromise broader
purposes. To the extent that we find collaboration, we find it turned
inward, with members of a department working together to consolidate a
favored position in the competition over students and other resources.
That is, a survival orientation drives collaboration internal to a department
and constrains collaboration across departments.

In principle, entrepreneurial ventures or crossover assignments might
provide the occasion for joint planning, might foster more extensive and
intensive forms of collegial exchange, and might open up possibilities for
experiments with an interdisciplinary curriculum. We have no evidence
that they have done so in these cases. Broad questions of institutional purpose are thus obscured, and capacities for curriculum policy at the district,
school, and departmental level are diminished.

CONCLUSION

Three aspects of professional community underscore and sustain the two
worlds of academic and nonacademic teachers. Each is a potential guaran-
tor of the status quo or a potential lever of change. First is the legacy of
subject specialization and the conditions surrounding subject expertise
and subject status. Second is the departmental organization of the high
school and the way in which it opens up or closes down opportunities for
a more unifying construction of secondary schooling. And last is the generalized pattern of patchwork involvement among colleagues and the collegial dynamic fostered by competition over student enrollment and other
resources.

In increasing numbers of local communities, one finds a creeping
unease about the failures of secondary schooling. Some proposed remedies, to be sure, tend in the direction of doing more of the same. They
intensify pressures on teachers and students by specifying more time, more
courses, more homework, and more tests. Other remedies require a reexamination of fundamental purposes, practices, and structures. They call
into question aspects of schooling on which secondary teachers' identity
and community have been based, among them subject specialism, age
grading, and differentiated curricula. It is within this emerging field of
debate that one best locates problems in the integration of vocational and
academic education.

We undertook this analysis of teachers' professional community—or
more precisely, communities—in part to discover on what basis such inte-

gration of purposes and subjects might be founded. In these schools, at least, we find the language of subject specialisms dominant and the structure of departments firmly in place. A few teachers and administrators envision more permeable boundaries between departments, more meaningful ties across subject areas, and more sensible relations between school and work. Among the academic teachers, however, there are few examples of cross-subject curriculum planning. Initiatives that could properly be judged interdisciplinary are simply not present in these schools on any meaningful scale. Among the vocational teachers, the assault on subject boundaries takes the form of campaigns to win academic credit for vocational courses. Cross-department staffing between vocational departments and academic departments (such as when industrial arts teachers are assigned to teach basic math) tends to be seen as an accommodation to existing course demands rather than as pursuit of a policy that favors cross-disciplinary work or that seeks a more robust integration of academic and vocational perspectives. The kinds of fully integrative models proposed by Grubb, Davis, Lum, Plihal, & Morgaine (1991) are not in evidence here.

Those who would venture seriously to alter the character of secondary schooling in the manner undertaken by Sizer's (1992) fictional Franklin High School must contend not only with long-standing assumptions or stereotypes about students and learning, but also with long-standing features of teaching as an occupational and organizational community. Collegial exchange is both more frequent and more varied than outsiders might imagine and less concentrated and less consequential than teachers would require to reinvent their work and their workplace. The departmentalization and subject affiliations that remain powerful facts of life in secondary schools are sustained not only by the dispositions of individuals but also by a range of internal practices and by powerful externalities. Ironically, the very resources that give some departments their strength may operate as obstacles to efforts to create more open boundaries among subject disciplines. For example, a department with a full-time cadre of subject specialists and well-established curricular policies might also be so committed to subject integrity that it would act as a barrier to more broadly conceived secondary curricula. And among the external forces, for example, university admission requirements exercise what Grubb (personal communication) terms a "chilling effect" on innovation in the secondary curriculum. Teachers might be driven to modify their subject orientations and commitments if the university were to require evidence that students had participated in cross-disciplinary coursework or had engaged in projects that required integrating their knowledge from multiple disciplines (a complex problem in urban planning, for example).

Whatever impetus that teachers themselves feel for "redesigning the

American high school," as Sizer (1992) casts it, resides primarily in the shifting composition of the student population, especially in urban districts, and in the escalating cry that schools are failing their students. Another impetus to change, felt less directly by teachers but introduced by the larger community of parents and employers, is the changing nature of the work and workplace that await the young. In the eyes of most reformers, the impetus to change is weakened in part by the conservative force of teachers' subject loyalties and schools' departmentalized structures. That view rings true. At the same time, long-standing divisions between the worlds of the academic and the vocational teacher are fundamentally at odds with the values central to public education. It is in the tensions surrounding such value commitments that the possibilities for change reside. In each of these schools, and perhaps in the many others like them, the multiplicity of perspectives and practices offer more resources for reform than we have so far been able to tap.

REFERENCES

Ball, S. J. (1987). *The micro-politics of the school: Towards a theory of school organization.* London: Methuen.

Ball, S. J., & Lacey, C. (1984). Subject disciplines as the opportunity for group action: A measured critique of subject subcultures. In A. Hargreaves & P. Woods (Eds.), *Classrooms and staffrooms: The sociology of teachers and teaching* (pp. 232–244). Milton Keynes: Open University Press.

Bruckerhoff, C. (1991). *Between classes: Faculty life at Truman High.* New York: Teachers College Press.

Burgess, R. (1983). *Experiencing comprehensive education.* London: Methuen.

Burgess, R. G. (1984). It's not a proper subject: It's just Newsom. In I. Goodson & S. Ball (Eds.), *Defining the curriculum: Histories and ethnographies* (pp. 181–200). London: Falmer Press.

Connell, R. W. (1985). *Teachers' work.* Sydney, Australia: George Allen & Unwin.

Cusick, P. A. (1982). *A study of networks among professional staffs in secondary schools.* East Lansing, MI: Institute for Research on Teaching, Michigan State University.

Elbaz, F. T. (1983). *Teacher thinking: A study of practical knowledge.* London: Croom Helm.

Finley, M. K. V. (1984). Teachers and tracking in a comprehensive high school. *Sociology of Education, 57,* 233–243.

Gehrke, N., & Sheffield, R. (1985). Are core subjects becoming a dumping ground for reassigned high school teachers? *Educational Leadership, 42(8),* 65–69.

Goodson, I. (1988). Beyond the subject monolith: Subject traditions and sub-cultures. In A. Westoby (Ed.), *Culture and power in educational organizations* (pp. 181–197). Milton Keynes: Open University Press.

Goodson, I., & Ball, S. (1984). *Defining the curriculum: Histories and ethnographies.* London: Falmer Press.

Grubb, W. N., Davis, G., Lum, J., Plihal, J., & Morgaine, C. (1991). *"The cunning hand, the cultured mind": Models for integrating vocational and academic education.* Berkeley: National Center for Research in Vocational Education.

Hargreaves, A. (1986). *Two cultures of schooling: The case of middle schools.* London: Falmer Press.

Hargreaves, A. (1988). Teaching quality: A sociological analysis. *Journal of Curriculum Studies, 20,* 211–231.

Johnson, J.M. (1990). The primacy of the department. In M. W. McLaughlin, J. E. Talbert, & N. Bascia (Eds.), *The contexts of teaching in secondary schools: Teachers' realities* (pp. 167–184). New York: Teachers College Press.

Little, J. W. (1992). *Two worlds: Vocational and academic teachers in comprehensive high schools.* Berkeley: National Center for Research on Vocational Education, University of California, Berkeley.

Little, J. W., & Threatt, S. M. (1992). *Work on the margins: The experience of vocational teachers in comprehensive high schools.* Berkeley: National Center for Research on Vocational Education, University of California, Berkeley.

Metz, M. H. (1978). *Classrooms and corridors: The crisis of authority in desegregated secondary schools.* Berkeley: University of California Press.

Neufeld, B. (1984). *Inside organization: High school teachers' efforts to influence their work.* Unpublished Ed.D. dissertation, Graduate School of Education, Harvard University.

Raudenbush, S. W., Rowan, B., & Cheong, Y. F. (1990). *Contextual effects on the self-efficacy of high school teachers.* Stanford, CA: Center for Research on the Context of Secondary Teaching, Stanford University.

Siskin, L. S. (1991). *Realms of knowledge: The academic department in secondary schools.* Unpublished Ph.D. dissertation, Stanford University.

Sizer, T. (1984). *Horace's compromise: The dilemma of the American high school.* Boston: Houghton Mifflin.

Sizer, T. (1992). *Horace's school: Redesigning the American high school.* Boston: Houghton Mifflin.

Talbert, J. (1990). *Teacher tracking: Exacerbating inequalities in the high school.* Stanford, CA: Center for Research on the Context of Secondary Teaching, Stanford University.

Talbert, J. E. (1991). *Quantitative perspectives on boundaries of teachers' professional communities in U.S. high schools.* Stanford, CA: Center for Research on the Context of Secondary Teaching, Stanford University.

Van Maanen, J., & Barley, S. R. (1984). Occupational communities: Culture and control in organizations. *Research in Organizational Behavior, 6,* 287–365.

6

Joan E. Talbert
Stanford University

Constructing a Schoolwide Professional Community: The Negotiated Order of a Performing Arts School

In most high schools, teachers' professional identities are shaped by subject cultures—within which special standards and routines of good practice are defined and between which status and resources are allocated—and teacher communities are forged, more or less, within subject area enclaves (see Chapters 3 and 5). A schoolwide community of secondary teachers is rare indeed (Talbert, 1991; Talbert, Eaton, Ennis, Fletcher, & Tsai, 1990). Against the backdrop of our research in typical high schools, the strong school community that we found at Ibsen, a performing arts magnet school highly successful with its diverse student body, is in striking contrast to the norm.

The school's power to engage its teachers and students is rooted in its special mission and in the leadership of the person who has been principal of the school since its founding in 1978. On the one hand, the school's mission to develop excellence in the performing arts as well as in academics generates strong commitment among the staff and families who share this

Research for this paper was supported by funds from the U.S. Department of Education Office of Educational Research and Improvement (Grant No. G0087C0235) to the Center for Research on the Context of Secondary School Teaching, Stanford University.

vision of education. On the other hand, Beatrice Bronson (our pseudonym for Ibsen's principal) engenders commitment to the school's distinctive community among the academic faculty and the students marginal to its program and culture. Ms. Bronson challenges conventional norms for education and teaching that interfere with the school's program success and its broader mission of supporting the personal growth of each student; at the same time, she works with students and staff to reconstruct relations that engage and empower all members of the school community. In many ways, Ms. Bronson fits the definition of a transformational leader, who "facilitates the redefinition of a people's mission and vision, a renewal of their commitment, and the restructuring of their systems for goal accomplishment" (Roberts, 1985). For most academic teachers at Ibsen, the school context effectively challenges assumptions of teaching practice and of professional relationships that shape teachers' community in traditional school settings. At the same time, it constructs new professional roles and norms that serve the school's mission.

This case study of Ibsen illustrates impediments to a schoolwide professional community of secondary school teachers that are presented by conventional norms of teaching. The chapter describes what Ibsen's mission means for day-to-day relations among students and adults and considers ways in which these patterns depart from traditional professional roles and identities of academic teachers. The tensions between Ibsen's community and the broader culture of high school teaching pose a fundamental challenge for school leadership. The kinds of problems that engage the school staff and recur periodically are rooted in the uncertainties and tensions entailed in displacing sacred norms of practice, such as teacher-controlled pedagogy and grading curves that produce student failures. The case shows that with the dedication and leadership skills of the principal and a nucleus of committed faculty and staff members, a school community can set new parameters for teachers' professional identity and community.

The first section of this chapter describes the school's special mission and policy context, its institutional structure and resources, and indicators of educational success. The next section highlights the professional roles that distinguish Ibsen teachers' work lives from those of their colleagues elsewhere and that appear to be most fundamental to the school's success: student-teacher collaboration, personalization, and collective problem solving.

The third section addresses how each of these distinctive features of Ibsen's community is organized: What is the glue of this schoolwide community? Drawing on interviews with teachers who had recently entered the school and with teacher leaders in the school, the analysis points to conflicts between Ibsen's culture and traditional norms for secondary school teaching and illustrates ways in which the principal mediates these tensions and empowers teachers. Teachers are engaged in constructing and maintaining the school community through ongoing processes of collective problem solving and through the professional transformations entailed in academic teachers' acculturation to the Ibsen community.

The final section highlights the mandates for school leadership presented by conflicts between conventional teaching cultures and school norms essential to Ibsen's success. The new order of Ibsen's professional community goes against strong grains of the multiple, embedded contexts of secondary school teaching and, as such, is vulnerable and needs to be constantly negotiated and enforced.

IBSEN: UNIQUE BUT NOT BOUTIQUE

Until recently, with the expansion of school-choice programs throughout the nation, Ibsen was among a handful of performing arts schools in the country. Unlike most of its counterparts, however, it does not audition students for admission on the basis of performing arts talents; rather, Ibsen applicants are admitted according to a district formula to achieve racial and ethnic balance.

Another unusual feature is the school's 4th to 12th grade structure, a model adopted from an East Coast performing arts magnet to ensure program continuity. This grade structure means that although Ibsen's size of 1,400 is comparable to that of the typical secondary school, its enrollment at the 10th to 12th grade level is only about 400 students.

In its large urban district, Ibsen is 1 of 10 magnet secondary schools. The school draws students from 17 neighborhoods in the city and has a waiting list of about 2,000 minority and majority applicants. Until 1990–1991, Ibsen was located in a predominantly African-American neighborhood, and the school has the second largest African-American student enrollment in the city (with 34 percent African-American students, compared with 9 percent Hispanic, 4 percent Filipino, 2 percent Asian, and 50 percent Caucasian students). The school's relocation to a Southeast Asian community 3 miles from the former school site means that the ethnic composition of Ibsen's waiting list is shifting to include applications from the new neighborhood.

Most distinctive is Ibsen's profile of success—not just among schools for at-risk youngsters, but among affluent schools in the same district. Ibsen has the lowest dropout rate for its high school students in the district, even compared with the most upper-middle-class schools across town. Furthermore, 87 percent of the most recent graduating cohort went on to college, and about two thirds of the graduates went to 4-year colleges. All students perform above the district norms on proficiency tests and at norm on criterion-based tests. Twelfth grade students' performance on the California Assessment Program tests in reading and math place Ibsen well above the district high school average in reading and near the average in math. Ibsen ranked fifth in reading among the 20 district high schools and third among the 10 special high schools. In math, Ibsen ranked 11th among all district schools and 3rd among the 10 magnet high schools.

The school occupies a special niche in the district system, but its success cannot be attributed to special resources. Ibsen's funding level of $3,100 per student (in 1990–1991), which includes magnet funds of $700,000 per year, is below the mean of just over $3,200 for district high schools. Of the 20 district high schools, Ibsen ranks 14th on fiscal resources despite the additional costs incurred in staffing and running the performing arts program. Compared with the other magnet high schools, Ibsen ranks 9th out of 10 on funding level.

Even in recruiting teachers, Ibsen presently has no advantage over other schools in the district. Although the initial faculty was self-selected and thus interested in the school's special mission, new Ibsen teachers are assigned from the district pool. Given large differences in the faculty turnover rates among subjects, there are large subject differences in proportions of teachers who chose the school. Our data indicate that most current math and science teachers at the high school level have been assigned to the school by the district due to substantial staff turnover in these subjects over the years.

TEACHING AT IBSEN: ENABLING STUDENT SUCCESS

The settings in which Ibsen teachers and students interact set contexts for professional roles in the school; they include academic classes, performing arts classes, and out-of-class preparations for performances. Although performing arts classes are officially extracurricular and thus elective, most Ibsen students take at least one performing arts class each day. The performing arts subjects offered at Ibsen include dance, theater, vocal music, instrumental music, and visual arts (the five core performing arts subjects) as well as technical theater and television production. Dance has been the most popular field among students and has the largest faculty. The technical theater area is a program innovation (started some years after the school's founding by an elementary school teacher who was also a contractor and knew how to read blueprints) that enables Ibsen students to take the full range of responsibilities for putting on major productions.

The four major musical productions each year—as well as regularly scheduled theater, dance, and chorus productions put on by classes at the school and in the community—represent important out-of-classroom contexts of students' and many teachers' work lives. Other more typical outside contexts for student-adult relationships are much less inclusive in terms of numbers or time spent: clubs, such as academic decathlon; a tutoring center; peer counseling and support groups, which have emerged in recent years; and the open-door offices of main office staff and administrators (key actors for students include the counseling staff, an attendance officer, and the principal).

The dynamics of adult-student relationships at Ibsen are different in some important ways from those typical in public schools in the same and other districts. This case study highlights those that seem most critical in defining nontraditional roles for teachers that support students' educational success.

COLLABORATION BETWEEN ADULTS AND STUDENTS

Collaboration between Ibsen teachers and students can be seen most dramatically in the performing arts classes. The nature of interactions among teachers and students reveals the collaborative nature of their enterprise: Teacher is coach, guide, and giver of sometimes harsh feedback; student is apprentice; peers are mirrors, props, advisers, and co-workers. They work together at the conceptual level and at the technique or skill level so that everyone understands what they're doing and why and are able to do it. Ibsen students are learning much more than how to dance, sing, or act: They are learning the logic of choreography, harmony, or theater. Further, in the context of performance demands, the apprentice role of student and collaboration among students and teachers is real: All share an interest in the quality of their collective product. The individual work and teamwork extend beyond the classroom to practicing parts and arranging ways to transport themselves and materials to performance sites.

The collaborative roles that one finds in the academic classes are derived largely from contingencies and norms established by the performing arts program. Classroom teaching is quite conventional on the whole, given constraints posed by mandated texts and individual testing programs. However, an important kind of collaboration is established by contractual agreements that students and teachers must make to accommodate pull-outs resulting from rehearsals for major school productions. The large number of high school students who participate in these productions must arrange to master course material that they miss in class. This kind of arrangement shifts conceptions of education away from the idea of teachers transmitting information and toward the idea of students seeking knowledge and skills. It prompts teachers to see students as independent learners and to relax control over the sequence and substance of their educational activities.

Students' experiences in working with teachers in their performing arts classes and on productions also frame relations in academic classes. The students import the collaborative norms and roles into the domain of academic classes, treating both peers and teachers as resources and advisers. Students are much less likely to enact the traditional student role of deferring to the teacher and working diligently alone; thus, academic teachers are cast into more collaborative teaching roles. As a social studies teacher commented, while explaining how academic teachers need to cut back on course demands so that the students don't burn out while trying to balance the arts and academics, "Our school attracts vocal, demonstrative kids who wouldn't do their homework anyway." As this comment illustrates, Ibsen students play a strong role in setting norms for their relations with academic teachers.

Teachers' perceptions of students' special talents and needs also set the stage for collaboration between academic teachers and students in constructing subject knowledge. At Ibsen, teachers aim to connect kids and content. The school culture defines the students as artistic (in spite of the fact that they are not screened on the basis of such talents), and given this view, teachers try hard to adapt instruction to meet students' special talents and interests. Teachers use spatial representations of ideas, incorporate artwork into their curricula, and select supplementary texts and materials that are meaningful to performing artists. An English teacher, for example, selected James Joyce's *Portrait of the Artist as a Young Man* for her seniors last year because it would have special meaning to them; she had them draw and write about the personal meanings of the novel. The widespread efforts to connect subjects to students' interests send them a strong message: "You kids are special, and I will work *with* you to make meaning of this subject matter."

Outside the classroom, the four major school productions each year are a central arena for collaboration among Ibsen students and adults. All students in the school try out for the performing roles in each production, a policy implemented in recent years to guard against overlooking shy, talented students. Most students get one or another role to play: as leads, as supporting actors, as dance or chorus ensemble members, or as part of a vast stage crew that makes props and runs the technical and mechanical operations backstage. Approximately half of the high school students are involved in a major production each year. A large proportion of Ibsen students thus experience the intense collaboration with peers and adults that a major school production entails.

PERSONALIZATION

The school's collaborative teaching and learning roles are central to the special affective relationships that develop between Ibsen students and adults. Classroom life and its spillovers into performances and academic tutoring provide strong evidence to students that their teachers are trustworthy and helpful people. Likewise, teachers at Ibsen express a kind of trust in students—as honorable and capable human beings—that is all too rare among teachers in traditional high schools.

The arena of major productions brings Ibsen students into even closer relationships with their performing arts teachers and with academic teachers who give significant amounts of time to productions on a semivoluntary rotating basis. In this context, the boundaries of course curricula and student-teacher roles break down, and the youth share backstage rapport with adults whom they get to know better as "real people." The daily experiences of working together on a common product allow people to develop *mutual respect and trust*. The major productions play a very special role in creating a *personal* school environment, in which students and teachers alike come to be known in a wide range of roles as whole people. These productions also provide occasions for students and staff to celebrate their common enterprise, to recognize individuals' talents and hard work, and to present the school's self to the outside community. The students see how their personal relations with Ibsen teachers can be translated into something valued outside school boundaries.

However, not all Ibsen students excel in or are interested in the performing arts. These individuals could well become increasingly marginal and fall through the cracks of school life, as so often happens among least-engaged students in traditional high schools. Not so at Ibsen. Both teachers and administrators talk as much or more about the kids who are at risk than they talk about the successes. In itself, this is not unusual because people in all Center for Research on the Context of Secondary School Teaching (CRC) schools worry or complain about the kids they are losing. However, the way in which Ibsen adults talk about these students is different. Rather than being seen and treated as part of a category and ultimately as dropout statistics, the marginal kids are known as individuals with names and families whom teachers and administrators know and work with to define problems and solutions. We have found that high school cultures differ radically in how they deal with the inevitable facts that not all students are integrated easily into school life and that most students will sometimes have personal problems with which they need help. The personal, supportive environment for students at Ibsen is rare among public schools of this size and is maintained by the expansion of professional roles to include caring for individual students.

COLLECTIVE PROBLEM SOLVING

Ibsen's support system truly challenges students to fall between the cracks. The students have learned to take responsibility for each other and to seek adult support in working through problems.

Interviews with Ibsen administrators and staff are filled with stories of how they are helping students to solve problems: forming a support group for drug abuse and exploring community resources, getting rid of a police officer who is about to arrest Ibsen's resident punker for having a knife can opener, helping a student cope with a history of child abuse. The bottom line for successful problem solving between Ibsen adults and students is trust—trust that evolves through collaboration and personal relations between youth and adults in the school.

A success story that Ms. Bronson likes to tell illustrates both what she takes to be important at Ibsen and how problem-solving relationships are socially constructed between students and adults. The story begins with the drug bust of a few Ibsen students early in the school year. It was the students who defined a drug problem in the school for the administration. And it was also the students who were to decide what a first step in dealing with this problem could be and which adults they would like to help them; the students formed a drug support group that included the principal and the attendance officer. The adults offered suggestions on how they might research local resources and made contact with a former alumnus of the school and ex-addict, who volunteered to be a facilitator for the group. Soon after, a few parents approached the administration wanting help to start up their own support group. Both groups are still going strong after 3 years. The latest chapter of the story suggests that strong peer norms have emerged to control drug use among Ibsen students: A group member came to a meeting high on drugs, and his peers asked him to leave, expressing their deep disappointment that he had so little respect for their mutual trust. Recounting the incident, Ms. Bronson commented, smiling, that the adults could never have played that role successfully.

In sum, Ibsen is a special place for students: where adults are collaborators, where each individual counts, and where problems can be made manageable. This is the crux of Ibsen's dramatic success with adolescents, including those who are educationally at risk. Ibsen is also a special, demanding place for teachers, where professional roles well exceed routine classroom teaching, where student failure is not allowed, and where faculty cannot hide problems. A critical role of site leadership and teachers' professional community in the school is enabling teachers to succeed in this demanding school context.

ORGANIZING IBSEN: ENABLING TEACHERS' SUCCESS

When one looks closely at the professional roles and resources that go into constructing the school's special culture, Ibsen's success story becomes a legend of leadership and professional transformation among the academic teachers. The school community could not have evolved within normal definitions of teacher's roles, of school principalship, and of staff support. In fact, almost everyone at Ibsen works well beyond the boundaries of their contractual and normal or typical professional roles. Ms. Bronson and other school leaders whom she has nurtured succeed in transforming the ground of teachers' identities and in engaging and sustaining their commitments to the Ibsen community.

This analysis of Ibsen as an organization highlights the features of school culture and structure that are important to the social construction of student-adult relationships and thus to teachers' special roles and collegial relations. Two issues are addressed:

1. What school norms and structures support collaborative relations, personalization, and collective problem solving among youngsters and adults?
2. How are tensions between Ibsen's school community and broader professional environments of high school teaching managed so that the school can thrive?

The analysis focuses on the academic teachers of secondary-level classes, whose jobs differ substantively from those of their colleagues in traditional high schools. The role demands engendered by the performing arts program and norms for student-teacher relations require experienced or well-socialized new academic teachers to make significant adaptations to fit into the Ibsen school community. The tensions between the Ibsen school culture and traditional teaching culture must be resolved one way or the other by teachers who come to work at the school. Some never adapt to Ibsen's professional community and leave the school, others accommodate and recognize trade-offs between the worlds of school and profession, but most come to define their professional identity and sense of community in relation to the school. The norms and dynamics of the school's professional community and the principal's key role in defining and modeling them are critical in sustaining teachers' commitment to the school and enabling their success.

SUPPORTS FOR COLLABORATION

Demands on academic teachers to collaborate with students in their classes and the arts faculty who pull students out for rehearsals are based on the authority of performing arts in Ibsen and on Ibsen's special professional culture. This situation can be quite threatening to academic teachers. For one, the normal status hierarchy among school subjects is turned on its head; it is the requirements and authority of the performing arts rather than academics that take precedence at Ibsen (see Chapter 5). Also, the traditional latitude that teachers have to pursue their individual priorities is challenged by the need to accommodate demands of the arts program. Furthermore, the expectations of collaborating with students challenge the traditional conception of teacher-student relations as hierarchical.

Teachers new to the school, particularly those in math and science, complain bitterly about the disruptions to normal education caused by the performing arts and the constraints that the performing arts impose on their instructional success. Others, less threatened by school norms, emphasize how important it is that teachers at Ibsen are adaptable. As one teacher commented, "You have to be very flexible, . . . committed, and more prepared. The [school's] purpose is not what it is in other schools." Those who survive and thrive at the school have learned to entrust students with responsibility to master course material and to use school resources, such as the tutoring center.

Subject matter or disciplinary norms appear to play a strong role in how far academic teachers go in adapting to the collaboration norm. Math teachers and, to a lesser extent, science teachers feel compelled to control the sequence and pace of instruction so as to cover in orderly fashion the district curriculum. As a math/science teacher commented, "In math, there are definite skills you want to get across. [In] science, too, but not so much. There are abstract concepts . . . you want them to keep up." Teachers throughout the school community acknowledge the special plight of math teachers in the school. An English teacher explained to us, "Math and language teachers have a hard time, so we lose a lot. They build upon concepts. For them, it's very difficult to maintain continuity of learning [given the need to accommodate students' participation in major productions]."

Another institutionalized rule that collides with Ibsen's norm of collaborating with students is the conception of teachers' relationships with students as hierarchical. In the traditional framework, teachers' sense of professionalism requires that they exercise authority in their relations with students, that students defer to them and their requests, and that administrators enforce this norm of relations. A number of teachers new to Ibsen complained to us that they didn't feel the principal backed up their authority with students.

In general, the academic teachers at Ibsen are working against strong professional currents; they can easily feel that they are falling short of standards and that their own values and worth are undermined by school conditions and norms. An Ibsen math/science teacher once commented that being at Ibsen helped her to understand what the arts teachers felt like at a regular high school. She said she felt like "a one-eyed stepchild," only tolerated in the school. A big problem for academic teachers at Ibsen is the loss of professional worth that they experience—a loss due to the flipping or reversal of their usual status in the hierarchy of high school subjects and also due to the low esteem that they are accorded by their subject colleagues who regard Ibsen's program as inferior. For example, in interviews with teachers and principals in other district high schools, we have heard comments such as "there *are* no science teachers at Ibsen." Ibsen math and science teachers, in particular, pay a significant professional price for teaching in the school.

In a number of ways, the school has organized to support academic teachers' adaptation to the collaboration norm. For one, a myth has diffused within the Ibsen community to acknowledge and pardon problems experienced by math and science teachers and problems created by the high turnover of faculty in these subjects. The right-brain/left-brain myth was repeated by nearly every teacher we interviewed in our first year in Ibsen. The theory is that mathematics and science teachers are left-brained people and therefore have trouble in the school because the students are right-brained artistic types and because left-brained people are less flexible than right-brained people. The myth effectively excuses teachers for their misfit with school policies and helps to heal wounds of rift within the faculty. In some ways, it lessens normative demands of the school community on teachers who pay the largest professional price for teaching in Ibsen; however, it also defines them as marginal, allowing them to feel like "one-eyed stepchildren."

More significantly, Ms. Bronson actively supports the academic teachers' change and growth. She sees professional development as an ongoing and often ad hoc process and works personally with a teacher when she perceives that he or she needs help. For example, Ms. Bronson often works with individual teachers to make an active plan with parents in order to build collaboration between teachers, students, and parents. She also arranges for teachers to share with colleagues what they find to be successful in the classroom. For example, at faculty meetings, she arranges for teachers to share techniques that they have found to be successful in working with Ibsen students. In doing so, she empowers teachers to try new approaches to teaching and to offer help to colleagues.

Beatrice Bronson stirs the schoolwide pot of collegiality at Ibsen. Unlike their peers in typical schools who relate mainly within departments, the teachers regard collegiality as a whole-school phenomenon. The special school mission and the shared demands of the performing arts support a sense of camaraderie that most teachers comment on and value. As one teacher noted, "There's more teaming here. It's the program." Teachers seem to feel that they are working together, although they differ in their views on how professionally and personally rewarding or costly are their contributions to the school's success.

Through her roll-up-sleeves approach to site administration, Beatrice communicates strong commitment to the school's collaborative enterprise over prerogatives of authority. She unambiguously models a flat hierarchy for relations between adults in the school and between adults and students. No role in the school is beneath the principal, and she devotes extraordinary time and energy to making sure that everyone is engaged in the collective enterprise. Her style and activities actively challenge a view of professional authority as a matter of hierarchy.

The transformational quality of Ms. Bronson's leadership and the power of the school community to support teachers' professional growth and commitment to the school are illustrated most dramatically by the case of Rita Enrow (pseudonym). Three years ago, we interviewed Ms. Enrow during her first year as a math teacher at Ibsen. She was so angry and frustrated about the teaching conditions in the school that she apologized to us for becoming agitated when she talked about her job. Among other comments about the school as a workplace, she said:

> They [district] just put me here. Frankly, it's hard to get teachers to come here. . . . It's very kid oriented and arts oriented. It's hard on the arts teachers, too. There's a lot more frustration built into this school than [is] typical.

Regarding the norm of collaboration and her perception that the principal doesn't back up teachers' authority with students, she said, "I want to close my door and have the administration deal with problems!" Three years later, Ms. Enrow pulled us aside to describe how much her feelings about the school had changed. By then she was an active member in the school community and a close, collaborative colleague of the English teacher in the adjacent room. Her comments to us about her transformation explicitly recognized the professional cost of her acclimation to Ibsen. As Rita put it:

> I now appreciate what we do for students here that doesn't happen in a regular school. I now see what the trade-offs are between having a regular math department and this. The personal values and support are worth it.

In 3 years, Rita's resistance to the school culture, particularly the collaboration norm, had transformed into advocacy and a sense of professional well-being.

SUPPORTS FOR PERSONALIZATION

The norm of personalization is embedded in a broader set of norms, which together with school structures and routines enforce and support teachers' commitment to this feature of Ibsen's community. The personalization norm is anchored by the principle that "everyone counts, everyone is different and special." Diversity among students is celebrated, and peer pressures to conform are discouraged by the schoolwide culture. Ms. Bronson likes to tell of Ibsen's resident punker, who is apparently a source of pride in a school that prides itself for individuality and diversity. She recently told the story of students rushing into her office one day to get her to stop two local police officers from arresting the kid for possession of a knife that he used to open a can for lunch; without insulting the boy's sense of dignity in costume, she convinced the officers that he was harmless and a good school citizen.

Norms that govern teachers' relations with students in their classes both express and enforce the personalization norm. For example, teachers' individualized handling of a student who is failing or misbehaving in a class is one personalization mandate. A teacher is not supported if he or she wishes to kick a student out of class or fail a student without a series of efforts, including parent phone calls and conferences with student and parent, referrals to the tutoring center, and consultation with other teachers of the student. Indeed, Ms. Bronson takes an active role in facilitating this norm, which she regards as a core personal value:

> You don't realize your values and what you can't go against until you have to [do something like] run a school. One of mine is personalization. I tell teachers to try anything, even if bizarre. Be an advocate for the kids . . . if they fail a test, you're the advocate. My job is to motivate the adults.

The personalization norm extends well beyond supporting each student's academic success to actively caring for kids—taking time to get to know them as whole persons. This norm is modeled by the principal and visible administrators and is supported by the Adopt-a-Student program for kids most at risk in the school. The principal has a number of adopted children of her own and works closely with six or seven Ibsen students. Increasing numbers of teachers have taken on one or more students since the program was officially initiated in 1990; however, as Ms. Bronson says, many more do this regularly on an informal basis. The formal structure ensures that the caring adult gets a regular and timely flow of information on the student.

The school's wide grade span and the practice of assigning counselors to students by alphabet ensure continuity in the students' contact with adults in the school and thus represent other structural supports for personalization in Ibsen. Responsible and caring adults get to know the students very well, over often the 6 or even 9 years that they spend at the school. As the head counselor told us, "This isn't a typical school. There's a humanness. It's the size." In fact, the school's enrollment of 1,400 is comparable to that of typical high schools, and it is substantially larger than other personalized CRC schools (McLaughlin, Talbert, Kahne, & Powell, 1990). However, the smaller scale at particular grade levels and the continuity of relationships among Ibsen students and adults create important structural conditions for personalization. As many teachers have told us in describing Ibsen as a place to teach, "It's like a family." They often add that students have a very difficult time leaving when they graduate. Compared with other CRC public schools, Ibsen scores substantially higher on a survey measure of personalization and, in this respect, is similar to the private schools in our sample.

As with the norm for teacher-student collaboration, the personalization norm challenges teachers' claim to professional authority in the sense of exercising prerogatives. As a math teacher new to the school commented, "If there is ever a question of what's a priority, it's what the kids want, not the teachers—what's best for the students." Complaining that the principal sided with kids against teachers, she said, "Sometimes support isn't where it should be. I've been in places where I thought the principal would stand on your side."

The principle that everyone counts at Ibsen extends to students and teachers alike unless their interests are seen as conflicting, such as when a teacher fails a student. This is not okay and is strongly sanctioned by Ms. Bronson. In this context, what enables student success is experienced by some teachers as constraining or punishing. To support teachers' success with Ibsen's personalization norm, Ms. Bronson has established mechanisms for students, parents, and teachers to work together to define an academic problem and to decide how to solve it. For example, she invented "failure-free" letters for teachers to use in communicating their concerns about a student's performance. She also provides "parent effectiveness training" with the faculty to promote active listening skills and motivate teachers to keep parents well informed. Teachers are to develop an action plan with parents that defines them as one third responsible for their child's improvement.

Ms. Bronson personally invests considerable energy in working with parents to make sure that they don't feel like bad parents when their son or daughter has a problem—to enable them to be a support for their kid in working through a problem. She helps parents connect with their children even when a problem is upsetting; she says, "Home is where the emotional support can happen; your kid's gonna need a hug before you deal with this problem." Parents clearly see Ms. Bronson as a valuable resource and have asked her to come into their community to help them solve problems.

Finally, the extended roles required for personalization demand enormous time and energy of the faculty. A full-time chorus teacher once remarked that she was driven to take a sabbatical that year—by which she meant limiting her job to a normal teaching load. She talked about never seeing her family the year before and getting to a point of burnout. Ms. Bronson supported her proposal for a sabbatical and later helped a burning-out theater production teacher to develop a sabbatical plan. The teacher said that without the sabbatical, he would have been forced to leave the school for the sake of sheer survival.

The performing arts teachers have, on average, much greater demands on their time and energy in the school, given the need to manage the performing side of the school as well as classroom teaching. Many of these teachers also maintain professional lives outside the school community—ties with the local performing arts community that are valuable to the school for reasons of reputation, support, and student placement. Personal and family lives of the performing arts faculty are jeopardized by the inordinate demands of their teaching jobs at Ibsen. Ironically, the faculty best positioned in the school to enjoy the intrinsic rewards of teaching at Ibsen appear to expend much greater effort and time than do the academic faculty.

Teachers' willingness to take on extended roles outside the classroom and contract boundaries is supported by their individual commitment to students, to Ibsen, and to the success of the performing arts program. A number of academic teachers and staff spoke of "falling in love" with the school after being assigned there. Ms. Bronson's leadership in the school and the celebrations of school mission and values go a long way toward engendering this kind of affection for the school and its students.

SUPPORTS FOR COLLECTIVE PROBLEM SOLVING

In many ways, the problem-solving dynamic of student-adult relations at Ibsen is an outgrowth of the collaboration norms and personalization norms more central to the school's mission. The mandate to solve problems collectively is also key to Ms. Bronson's leadership role. She applies the principle in earnest to all relationships in the school: those among the faculty, between faculty and staff/administration, and between students and teachers. One can observe this norm in faculty meetings, where conflicts are aired in the interests of reaching a hard decision. Problems are defined and tackled, not avoided. Much of the energy one can observe and hear at Ibsen is generated by the belief that "if we work together, we can solve whatever problems we have."

An Ibsen English teacher provides testimony of the principal's leadership in modeling and supporting the problem-solving norm:

> Bea has done so much to help. She's wonderful. In fact, I owe her my whole career. [In supporting faculty,] she will say, "Go with it!" If it's good for the students, she'll support it. She'll say, "We'll find a way." That attitude and support have had a tremendous influence on me. I'm kind of like that now. I'm a better teacher and a better parent. I do the same with my students. Let's work on things together. If there's a problem, let's work on it.

This theme of the principal's support for working through professional and personal problems comes through in many of our interviews with Ibsen teachers. In contrast to most high schools, in which teachers struggle privately to manage the challenges of teaching today's students, Ibsen is a problem-solving community for teachers and students alike. Among the 12 public high schools in the CRC sample, Ibsen scores highest on survey measures of innovativeness and teachers' perceived support for professional growth. The school's collaborative culture creates a supportive learning environment for adults as well as students.

The structures that have evolved to address the needs of at-risk Ibsen students are an important complement to the problem-solving norm. Whereas teachers in the typical high school are left alone to solve problems of students' absences, academic failure, and personal stresses in their classrooms, Ibsen teachers have a range of supports. Other adults and groups in their environment are committed to working with them and a problem student: the tutoring center, perhaps a teacher who has adopted the student, a student support group, a counselor who knows the student well, the attendance officer, and always the principal.

Norms for defining and solving faculty problems are also strong. In the context of Ms. Bronson's leadership, teachers cannot hide problems but can expect support in solving them. The faculty also take responsibility for enforcing school norms and supporting colleagues' efforts to change. In fact, under a district mandate that all schools restructure themselves, the faculty voted to establish a committee of teachers whose job it is to enforce school norms and sanction colleagues who deviate from those norms. In traditional school settings, such a structure would be avoided or defined as a radical new organizational form. At Ibsen, this structural innovation expresses, on one hand, the faculty's commitment to school norms and, on the other, their recognition that tensions between Ibsen and teachers' broader professional culture represent risks to the school community. The innovation satisfied the district's restructuring mandate by formalizing collegial control norms and problem-solving norms already in operation. The organizational structures that emerge and survive at Ibsen are those whose functions embody and serve the school's core values and norms.

LEADING IBSEN: TRANSFORMING TEACHERS' PROFESSIONAL CULTURE

Core principles of Ibsen's special schoolwide community underlie the norms and features of school organization discussed in this paper. Chief among them are:

- Educational success is a collective undertaking.
- Every individual counts.
- Problems are to be solved, not hidden.

To understand Ibsen's professional community is to see how teachers' work lives serve these core principles. To understand the challenge for leadership in the school is to see more than how Ms. Bronson celebrates Ibsen's principles and models its special professional norms. Important among the leadership strategies that have allowed the school community to thrive are confrontations with traditional teaching culture. Some of the sacred norms of teaching conflict with Ibsen's core principles and constitute a continual threat to the school's integrity. Indeed, residues of dominant teaching culture are sources of tensions in the school—the weeds that keep cropping up—and need to be displaced regularly by Ms. Bronson and other leaders in the Ibsen community.

Our research in typical high schools and research of others before us isolate traditional norms for high school teaching that run counter to the imperatives of Ibsen's community. They include the norm of ranking and tracking students on the basis of their academic performance (Oakes, 1985); the norm of privacy that enforces teachers' autonomy (Little, 1987, 1990; Rosenholtz, 1989); the primacy of academic over nonacademic subjects (see Chapter 5); and norms that define teachers' professional authority and responsibility in terms of their possession and transmission of subject knowledge (Powell, Farrar, & Cohen, 1985; Sizer, 1984; Talbert, McLaughlin, & Rowan, 1992). The ways in which Ibsen departs from these dominant norms—especially its inversion of subjects' hierarchy and limited development of high-status academic courses—prompt secondary teachers in typical district schools to regard the school as somehow illegitimate and the faculty as therefore inferior. The academic teachers pay a price for Ibsen's deviance from norms of real school and real high school teachers.

As a strategy to neutralize the power of traditional norms and of outside sanctions against Ibsen teachers for their professional deviance, Ms. Bronson has developed formal policy and control mechanisms that challenge conventions of teaching. The policies officially void the authority of professional norms operating outside Ibsen and make explicit the nature of teachers' professional deviance mandated by the school community. The controls help to motivate and support teachers' struggles to reconstruct their practice, as most Ibsen teachers learned and assimilated traditional teaching culture through their experiences as students, as student teachers, and as teachers in other schools.

One example of counternormative school policy is the rule that prohibits student tracking practices that reproduce social inequalities. The policy allows teachers to track courses (for example, to offer honors and advanced placement classes), but the classes must reflect the student composition of the school. This policy mandates equality of opportunity for minority students but—as in the performing arts world, where not everyone can become a star—not equality of outcomes. Ms. Bronson enforces this policy by examining the student composition of all teachers' classes. It is up to teachers to work out entrance requirements for advanced courses and the logistics of course scheduling that will achieve an equitable student mix. The counselors responsible for putting together master schedules work with teachers and the administration to implement this policy.

The principal's regular review of class data for individual teachers provides a strong challenge to the norm of privacy, which enforces the autonomy of teachers' judgments in most teaching settings. Thus, teachers who have not bought into the school culture or have not yet translated its norms into teaching practice become visible and are counseled and supported to adopt teaching practices consistent with core school values. As it happens, class records are quite useful as windows through which to detect a teacher's adherence to traditional teaching norms that compete with school norms. Ms. Bronson scrutinizes grade records to detect the practice of curve grading, which defines some students as failing, as well as to monitor the race and ethnic composition of advanced academic classes.

A further example of policy that challenges dominant professional norms concerns the definition of students' academic success as receipt of knowledge transmitted instead of as a collective responsibility. The fail-free form that Ms. Bronson developed and the policy that requires teachers to communicate with parents about any defined student problem insist that the teacher neither take nor pass along to the student the blame for learning difficulties in the classroom. This policy and its earnest enforcement by the administration and faculty challenge the powerful tendency in the broader educational culture to view education as fundamentally a matter of individual student performance rather than as a transactional and collaborative enterprise. For Ibsen's norm of collaboration between adults and students to operate, the dominant norms need to be debilitated.

In fundamental ways, then, the mandate for leadership in the Ibsen community is as much about challenging powerful institutional forces that could undermine the school's success as about enacting and enabling the school's special mission and core values. On one hand, Ms. Bronson invests policy and administrative controls in dismantling beliefs and practices that could undermine the school's success. On the other hand, she works hard and well to tip the balance of academic teachers' professional identity and loyalty in the direction of the school community. She does this by consistently expressing the mission and core values of the school to support students' growth, by providing teachers with opportunities to develop skills essential in reaching this goal, and by modeling her commitment to collaborative culture.

This case study illustrates the challenges to leadership that establishing a schoolwide community among high school teachers entails. Regardless of how much and which particular school values conflict with dominant professional norms, the inevitable entropy toward disciplinary communities and dominant educational standards is likely to thwart the intentions of all but leaders prepared and able to help *transform* teachers' professional identities, commitments, and practice. The many educational reform proposals that target the school as a locus for change clearly underestimate the challenges posed in creating a schoolwide community.

Understanding the leadership strategies effective in the Ibsen school community allows us to see that although "policy cannot mandate what matters" (McLaughlin, 1987), policy *can* mandate against constraints on what matters. Put differently, policy can challenge dominant standards for teaching that inhibit teachers' professional growth toward preferred educational values. Transformational leadership enlists formal policy to challenge constraints on teachers' professional lives while orchestrating conditions that enable individuals to learn and succeed in a new vision.

ACKNOWLEDGMENTS

I wish to thank the Ibsen school staff for letting us scrutinize their professional lives over the past 3 years and for helping us to understand the school community from within. Thanks also to Milbrey McLaughlin, Steven Fletcher, Dan Perlstein, Choya Wilson, and Judith Powell at Stanford University; Judith Little, Susan Sather, and Susan Threatt at the University of California, Berkeley, for help in conducting interviews and compiling field data for the paper; and Marian Eaton and Shu-er Tsai for help in analyzing survey data for Ibsen and other CRC schools.

REFERENCES

Leithwood, K. A. (1992). The move toward transformational leadership. *Educational Leadership, 36,* 8–12.

Little, J. W. (1987). Teachers as colleagues. In V. Richardson-Koehler (Ed.), *Educators' handbook: A research perspective* (pp. 491–518). New York: Longman.

Little, J. W. (1990). The persistence of privacy: Autonomy and initiative in teachers' professional relations. *Teachers' College Record, 91,* 509–536.

McLaughlin, M. W. (1987). Learning from experience: Lessons from policy implementation. *Educational Evaluation and Policy Analysis, 9,* 171–178.

McLaughlin, M. W., Talbert, J. E., Kahne, J., & Powell, J. (1990). Constructing a personalized school environment. *Phi Delta Kappan, 72,* 230–235.

Oakes, J. (1985). *Keeping track: How schools structure inequality.* New Haven: Yale University Press.

Powell, A., Farrar, E., & Cohen, D. K. (1985). *The shopping mall high school.* Boston: Houghton Mifflin.

Roberts, N. (1985). Transforming leadership: A process of collective action. *Human Relations, 38,* 8–12.

Rosenholtz, S. J. (1989). *Teachers' workplace: The social organization of schools.* New York: Longman.

Sizer, T. R. (1984). *Horace's compromise: The dilemma of the American high school.* Boston: Houghton Mifflin.

Talbert, J. E. (1991). *Boundaries of teachers' professional communities in U.S. high schools.* Paper presented at the annual meeting of the American Education Research Association, Chicago, Illinois.

Talbert, J. E., Eaton, M., Ennis, M., Fletcher, S., & Tsai, S. (1990). *Brief report on goal divergence among U.S. high schools: Trade-offs with academic excellence* (Grant No. R90-2). Stanford, CA: Center for Research on the Context of Secondary School Teaching, Stanford University.

Talbert, J. E., McLaughlin, M. W., & Rowan, B. (1992). *Understanding context effects on secondary school teaching.* Stanford, CA: Center for Research on the Context of Secondary School Teaching, Stanford University.

Judith Warren Little
University of California, Berkeley

Milbrey Wallin McLaughlin
Stanford University

Conclusion

The six chapters assembled here pursue the cultures and contexts of teaching by delving into the dynamic, complex, and often subtle interpretations that teachers construct of their work. In so doing, the chapters supplant monolithic and context-independent conceptions of individualism and community in teachers' worlds. The chapters contest theoretical models that fail to account for the interplay of individual and institution and for the ways in which the multiple contexts of teaching—students, subjects, fellow teachers, school, and community—form compatible or contradictory grounds for teachers' work. Finally, the chapters challenge reform initiatives that rely on structural change defined at some distance from local communities of practice.

The book's title is comprehensive and inclusive; it promises an agenda for inquiry and action that is both broader and deeper than we have expressed in these few chapters. Indeed, these chapters form part of a larger and rapidly unfolding conversation. We devote this conclusion to scanning the horizon, sketching some of the domains that we believe are central to this line of inquiry but remain relatively underdeveloped or opaque in these chapters. We then ponder the ways in which taking cultures and contexts seriously requires a shift in the prevailing stance toward policy and reform.

BOUNDARIES OF COMMUNITY

The six chapters examine teachers' professional community largely within the organizational frame of the school. Within that frame, we have been able to show the ways in which the school is home to multiple and sometimes competing or conflicting environments for teachers' work. Smaller microclimates replace the school as the most meaningful unit of analysis or arena for change, especially in secondary schools. By concentrating on teachers' intersubjective interpretations, we avoid reifying structural units such as departments and instead capture the multiplicity and fluidity of teachers' affiliations. Neighboring departments, for example, are often fundamentally different realities for teachers. Further, these different realities are enacted and sustained in daily interactions and interpretations that center on teachers' relations with students and with one another.

Teachers' professional and personal worlds extend beyond the school, although the meanings attached to "being a teacher" in those domains generally remain opaque in these chapters. Huberman's concept of the "independent artisan," connected in principle to a broad community of artisans together with isolated references to teacher networks, signals the presence and potential salience of more elaborated relations that extend well beyond the school walls; such relations reinforce or attenuate teachers' school loyalties and reveal a complex interplay of professional and personal interests (Lieberman & McLaughlin, 1992; Little & McLaughlin, 1991; Wagner, 1991). In these portraits, we reveal little about how men and women, elementary and secondary teachers, and urban and rural teachers manage the interplay of personal and professional obligations or the tensions between individual and institutional prerogatives (Acker, 1989; Biklen, 1993). In all, the web of contexts and interpretations promises to be still more intricate.

Such inquiries will benefit from a more systematic attention to individual cases and a biographical perspective. We have made relatively little use of biography and of the way in which teachers' individual and collective "whole stories" offer insight into organizational and occupational cultures. Yet all of us have heard the threads of such stories in teachers' accounts. They are in part tales of work history: paths into teaching, good or difficult classes, career prospects enhanced or thwarted, and unexpected turns in professional or personal fortunes. Teachers' biographies also suggest how teachers' own class, racial, ethnic, and gender identities dispose them in particular ways toward being teachers and toward their colleagues, students, and workplaces. Such accounts add to the challenge of sorting out the relationship between institution and individual or of gauging the likely effects of policy on practice.

THE ORDINARY AND THE SPECIAL

On the whole, the strength of these chapters lies in their analyses of life in "ordinary" schools. With rare exception, as in Talbert's investigation of

Ibsen High School for the Performing Arts, the chapters portray schools modeled on conventional lines. At a time when many analyses center on processes of change in schools found to be innovative, these analyses center on the ways in which teachers get through the day and through the year in circumstances less special: ordinary schools with ordinary resources and the ordinary mix of today's students.

Dwelling amid the ordinary makes culture hard to see, even while it strengthens our claims to theoretical rigor and relevance. During periods of crisis or reform and in schools launched on some innovative course, teachers and others may more readily display aspects of culture that are most salient, compelling commitment or sparking resistance. To exploit the relative advantages of ordinary and special contexts thus requires some variations on our methodological choices. In these chapters, only in passing do we examine the organizational biography of groups or schools and the ways in which features of culture and context are made visible during periods of transition and turmoil. To locate our studies in schools undergoing profound change or to remain in ordinary schools over long periods of time would be to illuminate with greater sensitivity and confidence the contours of culture and context. Through such studies, for example, we could begin to uncover the dynamics that account for the remarkable stability and resilience of subject affiliations in secondary schools over time (as in Siskin, 1991).

TEACHERS' WORK AND THE
MULTIPLE PURPOSES OF SCHOOLING

Finally and perhaps most crucial to the larger agenda are questions about the purposes and consequences of schooling. To some extent, Huberman's model of the independent artisan accounts well for teachers' enduring commitment to and engagement in their classroom endeavors but begs the question surrounding benefit to students. Hargreaves acknowledges that the risk of individualism lies in its potential for compromising the social good, and he posits a form of social responsibility that is satisfied largely in the "ethic of care" and "ethic of responsibility" expressed by individual teachers. Yet on the basis of Metz's analysis, we would have to argue that teachers' situated constructions of "care" and "responsibility" sometimes prove difficult to defend on the basis of student benefit. This is a prospect that underlies research initiated by Cochran-Smith and Lytle (1992) jointly with Philadelphia-area teachers (for example, Fecho, 1992) to render visible and problematic teachers' responses to student diversity. Their work, together with the analyses in these chapters, suggests that problems of professional development and school leadership revolve less around instructing teachers in new knowledge and skills than around generating interpretations supportive of students' learning.

POLICY PERSPECTIVES

These chapters deliver a message about policy and practice that is clear, consistent, promising, and troublesome. Over and over, we discover that context matters and locally shared interpretations of practice, for good or ill, triumph over categorical and abstract principles. We discover that institutional perspectives and priorities are mediated by structural conditions of teacher isolation and independence and by the complex web of communities within schools. This is a substantial advance beyond analyses premised on notions that the school is the most useful unit of analysis (and change) and that school-level indicators are adequate to assess conditions of teaching and learning. It is also an advance beyond single-issue, single-variable analyses that promise theoretical parsimony but remain blind to the multiplicity of practical considerations.

Policy, then, must come meaningfully to terms with the common-sense disclaimer that "it all depends on the context" and with the possibilities that reside in a creative tension between individuality and community. The greater the appreciation for context specificity, the less that categorical statements appear to be a sound basis for policy.

This "context imperative" suggests policy possibilities that are simultaneously promising and troublesome. The promise lies in our ability to make the nature and dynamics of context less mysterious and to create a persuasive link between policy initiatives and student benefit. There are, indeed, policy and leadership strategies to pursue. The troublesome features take two forms. First, in showing and emphasizing the complexity of within-school contexts, we risk leaving the impression that complexity is chaos and thus feeding the impetus toward control and regulation. We emphasize, in response, that complexity is patterned rather than chaotic and that it is inevitable. Second, the context imperative places demands on administrators and policymakers to act in a manner that is unfamiliar and unpracticed.

It is not news that state and local policies are filtered through the screen of individual circumstance and shared context. However, these analyses take us some distance beyond the discovery of "local context" and "mutual adaptation." They suggest that meaningful policy responses are irretrievably local and that policymakers serve less to regulate than to inform and connect local actors.

Our discoveries call into question prevailing policy frames that center on the formal, structural, and material aspects of the school workplace; they cast doubt on rule-making systems, standardized incentives, accountability systems, and reorganized governance structures as routes to better schools. More promising, we argue, are policy frames and strategies consistent with a metaphor of the school as community. Such frames require attention to the situated norms and beliefs of practice (for example, what counts as a good teacher and a good colleague?), to the priorities expressed by teachers and their students, and to the problems of mutual support and mutual obligation.

To embrace the metaphor of community as a guide to policy and leadership is to transform the work of local administrators or teachers in leadership positions. The task of leadership is complicated by the fact that there is no categorical inventory of effective practices that one might recommend. The same practice in different contexts may have different consequences. The metaphor of community shapes a set of questions and perspectives on which local leaders might consistently act. Central are questions that begin with students' experience and do so in ways more revealing than standardized test scores, discipline referrals, or dropout rates. What are administrators' and teachers' routine opportunities to discover what students are learning or if, where, and how students feel supported by their teachers and families? To what extent are administrators attuned to the ways in which teachers' confidence and commitment have been affected by specific teaching assignments? To what extent are administrators adept at learning how teachers think about students and subjects instead of tallying observable behaviors in classrooms? What is the range of opportunities for teachers to engage in open discussion and debate or to express dissent on matters of practice? What messages about teachers and teaching are conveyed by prevailing practices of teacher evaluation or professional development at the school level and the district level? In what ways do districts recruit and reward administrators for engendering healthy culture and context, not just managing efficient organizations?

The common points of departure here are not structural or programmatic conceptions of the good school, but students' experiences of their schooling and teachers' orientations to their students and their subjects. It is only in the close attention to teachers' and students' perspectives that the local meaning of specific strategies can be assessed: One teacher's opportunity is another teacher's coercion. One cannot manage or command but can only cultivate and support the values and norms compatible with truly successful school environments.

Informed by the context imperative, our ventures into research and reform bring us closer to being able to link conditions of teaching to consequences of schooling. What are the demonstrable links between these elements of individualism and community in teachers' cultures and between the individual learning, interpersonal relations, and social justice that students witness? Ultimately, we must contend with the way in which the social organization of teachers' work bears on and is intertwined with students' experience of schooling and with the relations among schools, their communities, and the larger social order.

REFERENCES

Acker, S. (1989). *Teachers, gender, and careers.* London: Falmer Press.

Biklen, S. K. (1993). *Communication unbound: How facilitated communication is challenging taditional views of autism and ability/disability.* New York: Teachers College Press.

Cochran-Smith, M., & Lytle, S. L. (1992). *Interrogating cultural diversity: Inquiry and action.* Paper presented at annual meeting of the American Educational Research Association, San Francisco.

Fecho, B. (1992). *Language inquiry and critical pedagogy: Co-investigating power in the classroom.* Paper presented at annual meeting of the American Educational Research Association, San Francisco.

Lieberman, A., & McLaughlin, M. W. (1992). Networks for educational change: Powerful and problematic. *Phi Delta Kappan, 73,* 673–677.

Little, J. W., & McLaughlin, M. W. (1991). *Urban math collaboratives: As the teachers tell it.* Stanford, CA: Center for Research on the Context of Secondary School Teaching, Stanford University.

Siskin, L. S. (1991). *Realms of knowledge: The academic department in secondary schools.* Unpublished Ph.D. dissertation, Stanford University.

Wagner, J. (1991). Teacher professionalism and school improvement in an occupational community of teachers of English. Paper presented at the Ethnography and Education Forum, University of Pennsylvania, Philadelphia.

Index

Absenteeism, 82
Abuse, 30; child, 171; drug, 82, 126, 171
Accountability: expectations for, 63; pressures for, 63; systems of, 58, 189
Acker, S., 186
Activity: collaborative, 25; formats of, 20; instructional, 38, 45; planning, 20; self-governed, 38; teacher-valued, 43
Administration: benevolent authoritarianism in, 38; decision making in, 79; district, 11; justification for collaboration, 64; leadership in, 37, 39; noninvolving style in, 62; power plays in, 36; pressures from, 35; punishment-reward system in, 39; reinforcement of practice in, 36; school-level, 11; supports in, 35
Affiliations, 6
Anomie, 31
Anxiety, 54; competence, 55; presence of, 57
Ashton, P., 41, 51, 56, 104
Authority: analysis of, 109; decision making, 65; legitimate, 105; prerogatives of, 175; professional, 181; teachers', 110; traditional, 132; and vulnerability, 108–113
Autonomy, 24, 62, 97, 181; classroom, 19, 29–30; collective, ix, 1; functional, 13; guarding of, 54; individual, ix, 1, 155; professional, 19, 37, 44, 71; threats to, 71

Bacharach, S., 80
Ball, D., 79
Ball, S., 6, 138, 139, 144, 150
Barker, R., 25
Barley, S., 137
Barnard, C., 109
Bauer, S., 80
Behavior: automatic, 17, 21, 22; classroom patterns of, 20; conforming, 105; control of, 26; difficulty in

explaining, 17; disruptive, 42; helping, 55; infantile, 31; patterns of, 24; rules for, 124; student, 26
Bellah, R., 3
Bereiter, C., 22
Berman, P., 24
Berry, B., 80
Biklen, S., 186
Bishop, J., 29
Boundaries: classroom, 18, 66; community, 185–186; curriculum, 170–171; departmental, 154–157; permeability of, 155, 161
Boyd, W., 38
Boyer, E., 112
Brainstorming, 72
Bruckerhoff, C., 5, 154
Burgess, R., 139

Campbell, R., 59
Cao, H., 88
Career ladders, 80
Celotti,, 24
Center for Research on the Context of Secondary School Teaching's, 80
Cheong, Y., 81, 146
Churchman, C., 16
Clark, C., 20, 22
Classroom: aesthetic aspects of, 18; affective aspects of, 18; autonomy in, 19, 29–30; behavior patterns in, 20; boundaries of, 18, 66; change in, 32, 37, 87, 88; construction of, ix; ecology of, 20, 25; effectiveness in, 80; ideological aspects of, 18; immediacy in, 25–29; independence in, 9; locus of action in, 18; practices, 9, 80, 81, 83, 92, 98; privacy in, 158; situational constraints in, 25; specificity of life in, 25–29; structural independence in, 23–25; technical aspects of, 18
Clune, W., 80
Cochran-Smith, M., 187
Coercion, 111

191

Social: atomization, 69; class, 106; cohesiveness, 41, 155; conditions, 134;
construction of heresy, 51–74; definition, 98; development, 144; inequalities, 181; interaction, 34; mandates,
41, 42; norms, 31; organization, 2,
12, 23, 55, 56, 139, 190; relationships, 94; responsibility, 187; unity, 9,
69
Socialization, 28; mandate for, 32; professional, 63
Socioeconomic status, 37, 106–108,
113, 121, 122–129
Solitude, 72–73; enforced, 73
Southworth, G., 4, 6, 31, 54
Space, scarcity, 62
Spillane, J., 79
Staff development, 51, 53
Standards: academic, 123; behavioral,
123; credentialing, 80; district-level,
ix, 24; maintenance of, 85, 94, 128;
national, ix; professional, 4; state, ix;
student, 80; traditional, 85, 94, 124
Status: alternative claims to, 139; in assistance situations, 35; hierarchies of,
141, 142–144; subject, 138–149,
160–163
Stern, P., 20
Stoll, L., 51
Storr, A., 73
Student(s): absenteeism, 82; achievement
of, 41, 42, 51; alienation in, 127;
behavior of, 26; characteristics of,
81–83; cooperation in, 105, 106, 109,
112; cultural diversity of, 82, 88, 187;
development of, 13; disengagement of,
86; disruptive, 42; distance from
school, 124, 125, 129, 131; enabling
success in, 167–172; gangs, 82, 126;
high-achieving, 40; immigrant, 82, 83,
88, 95; independence of, 105; interpretation of school role, 106; minority,
37, 83, 90, 111, 132; mobility of, 82;
motivation of, 82; nontraditional, 85,
87, 89, 94, 95; performance of, 13,
26, 121; placement policies for, 147;
self-esteem in, 82; social class of, 106,
121–129; special education, 65; stress
on, 82, 179; and subject status,
142–144; teachers' dependence on,
104–134; teachers responses to,

89–97; tracking of, 84, 112, 181
Subject areas, x; hierarchies in, 139, 181;
networks in, 4; segmentation of, 158;
specialties in, 138–149; and status,
138–149, 160–163
Substance abuse, 82, 126, 171
Sullivan, W., 3
Supervision: loose, 13; of teachers, 37,
38, 39
Swidler, A., 3
Szaz, T., 52, 69

Talbert, J., 81, 87, 97, 99, 142,
164–183, 186–187
Task(s): attention to, 108; centered
lessons, 21; centered planning, 33;
engagement, 37; environment, 16, 17,
21; focused interactions, 41; political,
38; proficiency in, 16; rationalization
in, 45; redundancy in, 21; responses
in, 17; sequence of, 19; time on, 112
Teacher(s): and control expectations,
105, 110; authority, 110; automatic
behavior, 17, 21, 22; classroom-centered, 63; collaboration among, 2;
competition for students, 121, 159,
160; confidence of, 113–119; and
control, 108–113; and control of
rewards, 105; cooperation with principals, 38; credentialing of, 80; culture,
1–7, 33, 51–74; in curriculum development, 58; cynicism in, 85, 116, 121,
131, 132; demands on, 26; dependence on students, 104–134; desire for
isolation, 31; disengagement of, 86;
expertise, 6, 19, 22, 25; grade-level
shifts and, 26; head, 32; improvisation
in, 15–16; incentives for, 41, 80; as
independent artisans, 9, 11–47; individualism in, 53; insensitivity in, 88;
interaction among, 5–6; interdependence in, 2; isolation of, x, 2, 9, 53;
judgment of one another, 6; leadership
in, 105; legal constraints on, 112; middle-class, 128, 134; minority, 132,
134; mobility in, 34; motivation of,
80; negotiation with students, 112;
novice, 27–28, 29; observation of, 37,
57; personal beliefs of, 91; planning,
19, 20; possessiveness in, 65; practice

About the Contributors

Andy Hargreaves is Professor in Educational Administration and the Centre for Leadership Development at the Ontario Institute for Studies in Education. Before moving to Canada from England in 1987, he taught primary school and later lectured at the universities of Oxford and Warwick. His research entails close ethnographic attention to the conditions and character of teachers' work, and attention to the policy environments affecting teaching. Hargreaves also has been widely involved in research and improvement activities with teacher federations, universities, school boards, education ministries, and charitable foundations on both sides of the Atlantic. Among his recent publications are *What's Worth Fighting for: Working for Your School,* with Michael Fullan (Ontario Public School Teachers Association, Canada and North East Education Lab, USA, 1991), *Changing Teachers* (Teachers' College Press, New York, and Cassell, London, forthcoming), *Curriculum and Assessment Reform* (Toronto, OISE Press and Milton Keynes, Open University Press, 1989), and *Rights of Passage* (with Lorna Earl, Toronto, Queens Printer, 1990).

Michael Huberman is Visiting Professor at the Harvard Graduate School of Education and Senior Research Associate at the Northeast Laboratory for School Improvement. He continues to commute to Switzerland, where he has worked for close to 20 years at the University of Geneva. His areas of interest include teacher cognition and development, qualitative research methodologies, and knowledge dissemination and use. His most recent books are *The Lives of Teachers* (Cassell, in press, translation from the French), *Putting Research into Practice* (P. Lang, 1991), and *Qualitative Data Analysis* (Sage, forthcoming, second edition, co-authored with Matthew Miles). In addition to day-to-day work in schools, he has also been involved in creating experimental schools, research centers, and training facilities.

Judith Warren Little is Associate Professor of Education at the University of California, Berkeley. Her research interests have centered on the school as a professional environment, with special attention to teachers' relationships as colleagues, teachers' careers, and the policies and practices surrounding teachers' professional development. She has authored numerous articles and chapters on these topics, and is currently writing a book on aspects of collegiality in secondary schools.

Milbrey Wallin McLaughlin is Professor of Education and Public Policy and Director of the Center for Research on the Context of Secondary School Teaching at Stanford University. Her research interests include the organizational contexts of teaching, policy implementation, educational settings of nontraditional students, and neighborhood-based organizations for youth. She has written, co-authored, and edited numerous books on these topics including *Teaching for Understanding: Challenges for Practice, Research and Policy* (Jossey-Bass, forthcoming, with David K. Cohen and Joan E. Talbert); *Possible Selves: Achievement, Ethnicity and Gender for Inner-City Youth* (Teachers College Press, forthcoming, with Shirley Brice Heath); *The Contexts of Teaching in Secondary Schools* (Teachers College Press, 1990, with Joan Talbert and Nina Bascia); *Teacher Evaluation: Improvement, Accountability, and Effective Learning* (Teachers College Press, 1988, with R. Scott Pfiefer); and *Steady Work* (The RAND Corporation, 1988; with Richard E. Elmore).

Mary Haywood Metz is Professor and Chair of the Department of Educational Policy Studies at the University of Wisconsin-Madison. She holds a doctorate in sociology from the University of California at Berkeley, and is the author of *Classrooms and Corridors* (University of California Press, 1978) and *Different by Design* (Routledge, 1986). Working as an ethnographer, she has studied authority, links between levels of school and school district organization, school culture, and social relations in desegregated schools, in addition to the study of teachers' working lives from which the chapter in this volume is derived.

Joan E. Talbert is Senior Research Scholar and Associate Director of the Center for Research on the Context of Secondary School Teaching at Stanford University. Her research concerns the ways in which social and organizational contexts of teaching affect individuals' professional practice and careers. She has published articles on teachers' careers, school organization, and professional communities among secondary school teachers. She has edited two books concerning the collegial, organizational, and policy contexts of teaching: *Teaching for Understanding: Challenges for Practice, Research, and Policy* (Jossey-Bass, forthcoming, with David K. Cohen and Milbrey W. McLaughlin) and *The Contexts of Teaching in Secondary Schools* (Teachers College Press, 1990, with Milbrey W. McLaughlin and Nina Bascia).